AF368245

The Sufi Path of Light

The Sufi Path of Light

By the Sufi Master and Knower of God
Mohamed Faouzi al-Karkari
May God sanctify his secret

Translated by
Khalid Williams & Yousef Casewit

L·7 LES 7 LECTURES

The Sufi Path of Light is published by the nonprofit
organization Anwar and its publishing house **Les 7 Lectures**

44, Fernand Brunfaut Street
1080 Brussels, Belgium

Cover art: Dr. Khaled Salem
© Les 7 Lectures, 2023
All rights reserved

ISBN: 978-2-930978-82-6
Deposit number: D/2023/14.291/03 (Belgium)
Legal Deposit: September 2023

All rights reserved. No part of this publication may be reproduced,
distributed, or transmitted in any form or by any means, including
photocopying, recording, or other electronic or mechanical
methods, without the prior written permission of the publisher,
except in the case of brief quotations embodied in critical
reviews and certain other non commercial uses permitted by
copyright law. For permission requests, write to the publisher.

Table of Contents

أعوذ بالله من الشيطان الرجيم

بسم الله الرحمن الرحيم

بسم الله الرحمن الرحيم

بسم الله الرحمن الرحيم

بسم الله

بسم الله

بسم الله

الله

الله

الله

ولا حول ولا قوة إلا بالله العلي العظيم

I seek refuge in the Light of the Path and the Breath
of the All-Merciful from every darkness and devil

In the Name of God, the All-Merciful, the Ever-Merciful
In the Name of God, the All-Merciful, the Ever-Merciful
In the Name of God, the All-Merciful, the Ever-Merciful

In the Name of God
In the Name of God
In the Name of God

Allāh Allāh Allāh

There is no power nor strength but in God,
the Sublime, the Magnificent

Blessings and greetings of peace be upon the noblest Messenger,
our master Muḥammad, and upon His family, companions,
and those who follow them virtuously
until the Day of Requital

Introduction

Praise be to God, Who manifests through the magnificence of the Essence, and discloses Himself through the Light of the attributes. He is the First in His beginninglessness and the Last in His endlessness. He has made Light the means of witnessing Him, and the Path the way of knowing Him. I bear witness with certainty that there is no god but God, and I bear witness that Muḥammad is His servant and Messenger, the delight of the holy spirits, the quarry of the innate disposition of human souls. May peace and blessings be upon him and upon his family, companions, and all who follow his guidance. Let us begin.

Light: Light is that which is hidden by the intensity of its own manifestation. It brings things forth into manifestation from the concealment of nonexistence to the outpouring of existence, as our master the Messenger of God ﷺ said, "God Almighty created mankind in darkness, then took some of His Light and cast it upon them. Some of them it touched, and some of them it missed, each according to His will; and He knew those it would touch from those it would miss. Whomever the light touched would be guided, and whomever it missed would go astray." ʿAbd Allāh ibn ʿAmr said after relating this, "This is why I say that the pen has dried."[1]

Knowledge of Lights is a knowledge rooted in the experiential taste of the saints. The noble folk who bathe in the glow of the divine Presence have spoken about it, and composed volumes of poetry to sing of their love and passion for it. The time has come for me to throw in my lot with them, and to pull back the veil from the subtle effusions of a pearl named *al-Maḥajja al-Bayḍāʾ*, the Radiant Path,[2] so that you may drink of an exquisite wine sealed with the subtleties of yearning, and feel the holy breezes of nearness blow over you, and so that your spirit may roam through the meadows and gardens of ecstasy and divine proximity, exulting in the Light of the Beloved.

In all of this, I oscillate between concealing and divulging, and I incline more towards concealing it, because the science of our spiritual Tribe is first and foremost a matter of heart-to-heart transmission:

I conceal the jewels of my knowledge,
Lest the ignorant should see them and be tempted.

---

1   Ibn Ḥibbān, *Ṣaḥīḥ*, 6170.
2   The original Arabic title of this work is *Kitāb al-Maḥajja al-bayḍāʾ* (lit. The Radiant Path). It was first published in 2014 by Maṭbaʿat ṣināʿat al-kitāb, Casablanca. The following English translation was made possible through the generous support of Abdullah Elkammar.

Thus I follow in the way of the Father of Ḥasan,
Who passed it on to Ḥasan and Ḥusayn.[1]

Therefore I shall reveal to you the pure meaning of Light in the imaginal world, and the forms it assumes in the disclosure-site of the eye. This will allow you to take the first step upon the Path. I shall ignite the lamp of experiential taste and presence in your heart, that your saintly aspiration might flow forth with desire to walk the Sufi way. You must know that the Radiant Path is a lived reality by way of unveiling, not merely a phrase that you read in the noble ḥadīth and pass by with respectful indifference while invoking a blessing upon the Best of Mankind ﷺ. Your heart will then become illuminated by the Lights of the Path, and you will learn how its night is as bright as its day, and how to stray from it is to pursue self-destruction.

I will take you back to the realms of **Yea, we bear witness** in order to help you understand what this means. For when the spirits were compounded in the bodies, and the atoms in the accidental qualities the scales became unbalanced, hearts hardened, souls changed, and tastes were crushed between the hammer of the sensory realm and the anvil of pure meaning.

Our Lord is Light; our Prophet ﷺ is Light; our unswerving Islam is Light; our Holy Qur'ān is Light; and our prayer is Light.

---

1   Lines attributed to al-Ḥallāj.

Why then do you wish to live in darkness? Why do you aloofly imagine, with your delimited and narrow mind, that the Light is merely an abstract concept that cannot be seen?

The self-disclosure of Lights is the beginning of witnessing, and witnessing is the beginning of verifying the truth of the proclamation of divine Oneness. You know Islam with your bodily idol, yet your spirit does not recognize it, for you are absent from witnessing the Lights of the Real and the Lights of the Real's Messenger ﷺ.

You say, "I bear witness", yet your insight is blotted out, your heart blind, and your inner heart rusted over. Your testimony is mere speech, not witnessing.

Come with me, then, upon a voyage into the depths of pure meaning. Let us travel from one verse to another, until you come to know that the road has been one from the Messenger of God ﷺ until today—the road named the Radiant Path, whose night is as bright as its day, from which none stray but those bound for ruin.

I write these words in the early hours of the year 2014 after the birth of Christ, may blessings and peace be upon him and upon our Prophet. I hope that the Almighty will make it a year of joy and delight, as well as divine assistance as we bring it into the open, by the glory of the Light of the Radiant Path.

Chapter I

The Centrality of Light in the Qur'ān and Hadith

Verses of Light in the Qur'ān

Our Lord says in His glorious Book—after I seek refuge in God from Satan the accursed, in the Name of God, the All-Merciful, the Ever-Merciful:

— Their parable is that of one who kindled a fire, and when it lit up what was around him, God took away their Light, and left them in darkness, unseeing.[1]

— God is the Protector of those who believe. He brings them out of the darkness into the Light. As for those who disbelieve, their protectors are the idols, bringing them out of the Light into the darkness. They are the inhabitants of the Fire, abiding therein.[2]

— O mankind! Verily there has come unto you a proof from your Lord. And We have sent down unto you a clear Light.[3]

— O People of the Book! Our Messenger has come unto you, making clear to you much of what you once hid of the Book, and pardoning much. There has come unto you, from God, a Light and a clear Book, whereby God guides whosoever seeks

1   Q Baqara 2:17.
2   Q Baqara 2:257.
3   Q Nisā' 4:174.

His Contentment unto the ways of peace, and brings them out of darkness into Light, by His Leave, and guides them unto a straight path.[1]

— Truly We sent down the Torah, wherein is a guidance and a Light, by which the prophets who submitted [unto God] judged those who are Jews, as did the sages and the rabbis, in accordance with such of God's Book as they were bidden to preserve and to which they were witnesses. So fear not mankind, but fear Me! And sell not My signs for a paltry price. Whosoever judges not by that which God has sent down—it is they who are disbelievers.[2]

— And in their footsteps, We sent Jesus son of Mary, confirming the Torah that had come before him, and We gave him the Gospel, wherein is a guidance and a Light, confirming the Torah that had come before him, as a guidance and an exhortation to the reverent.[3]

— Praise be to God, Who created the heavens and the earth, and made darkness and Light. Yet those who do not believe ascribe equals to their Lord![4]

— They did not measure God with His true measure when they said, "God has not sent down aught to any human being." Say, "Who sent down the Book that Moses brought as a Light and a guidance for mankind, which you make into parchments

1   Q Māʾida 5:15-16.
2   Q Māʾida 5:44.
3   Q Māʾida 5:47.
4   Q Anʿām 6:1.

that you display, while hiding much? And you were taught that which you knew not, neither you nor your fathers." Say, "Allāh," then leave them to play at their vain discourse.[1]

— Is he who was dead, and to whom We give life, making for him a Light by which to walk among mankind, like unto one who is in darkness from which he does not emerge? Thus for the disbelievers, what they used to do was made to seem fair unto them.[2]

— Those who follow the Messenger, the unlettered Prophet, whom they find inscribed in the Torah and the Gospel that is with them, who enjoins upon them what is right, and forbids them what is wrong, and makes good things lawful for them, and forbids them bad things, and relieves them of their burden and the shackles that were upon them. Thus those who believe in him, honor him, help him, and follow the Light that has been sent down with him; it is they who shall prosper."[3]

— They desire to extinguish the Light of God with their mouths. But God refuses to do aught but complete His Light, though the disbelievers be averse.[4]

1   Q An'ām 6:91.
2   Q An'ām 6:122.
3   Q A'rāf 7:157.
4   Q Tawba 9:32.

— He it is Who made the sun a radiance, and the moon a Light, and determined for it stations, that you might know the number of years and the reckoning [of time]. God did not create these, save in truth. He expounds the signs for a people who know.[1]

— Say, "Who is the Lord of the heavens and the earth?" Say, "God." Say, "Then have you taken, apart from Him, protectors who have no power over what benefit or harm may come to themselves?" Say, "Are the blind and the seer equal, or are darkness and Light equal?" Or have they ascribed unto God partners who have created the like of His creation, such that that creation seems alike to them? Say, "God is the Creator of all things, and He is the One, the Paramount."[2]

— Alif. Lām. Rā. [This is] a Book that We have sent down unto thee, that thou mightest bring forth mankind out of darkness into Light, by the leave of their Lord, unto the path of the Mighty, the Praised.[3]

— We indeed sent Moses with Our signs, "Bring thy people out of darkness into Light, and remind them of the Days of God. Truly in that are signs for all who are patient, thankful."[4]

— God is the Light of the heavens and the earth. The likeness of His Light is as a niche, wherein is a lamp. The lamp is in a glass. The glass is as a shining planet kindled from a blessed

1   Q Yūnus 10:5.
2   Q Ra'd 13:16.
3   Q Ibrāhīm 14:1
4   Q Ibrāhīm 14:5.

olive tree, neither of the East nor of the West. Its oil would well-nigh shine forth, even if no fire had touched it. Light upon Light. God guides unto His Light whomsoever He will, and God sets forth parables for mankind, and God is Knower of all things.[1]

— Or like the darkness of a fathomless sea, covered by waves with waves above them and clouds above them—darknesses, one above the other. When one puts out one's hand, one can hardly see it. He for whom God has not appointed any Light has no Light.[2]

— He it is Who blesses you, as do His angels, that He may bring you out of darkness into Light. And He is Merciful unto the believers.[3]

— Not equal are the blind and the seeing, nor the darkness and the Light, nor the shade and the scorching heat. Not equal are the living and the dead. Truly God causes whomsoever He will to hear, but thou canst not cause those in graves to hear.[4]

— What of one whose breast God has expanded for submission, such that he follows a Light from his Lord? Woe unto those whose hearts are hardened to the remembrance of God! They are in manifest error.[5]

1   Q Nūr 24:35.
2   Q Nūr 24:40.
3   Q Aḥzāb 33:43.
4   Q Fāṭir 35:19-22.
5   Q Zumar 39:22.

— The earth will shine with the Light of its Lord, the Book will be set down, and the prophets and the witnesses will be brought forth. Judgment will be made between them in truth, and they shall not be wronged.[1]

— Thus have We revealed unto thee a Spirit from Our Command. Thou knewest not what scripture was, nor faith. But We made it a Light whereby We guide whomsoever We will among Our servants. Truly thou dost guide unto a straight path.[2]

— He it is Who sends down clear signs upon His servant to bring you out of darkness into Light, and truly God is Kind and Merciful unto you.[3]

— On the Day when you see the believing men and the believing women with their Light spreading before them and on their right, "Glad tidings unto you this Day: Gardens with rivers running below, therein to abide. That is the great triumph." On the Day when the hypocrites, men and women, will say to those who believe, "Wait for us that we may borrow from your Light," it will be said, "Turn back and seek a Light!" Thereupon a wall with a gate will be set down between them, the inner side of which contains mercy, and on the outer side of which lies punishment.[4]

— And those who believe in God and His messengers—it is they who are truthful and are witnesses before their Lord. They

1   Q Zumar 39:69.
2   Q Shūrā 42:52.
3   Q Ḥadīd 57:9.
4   Q Ḥadīd 57:12-13.

have their reward and their Light. And those who disbelieve and deny Our signs, they are the inhabitants of Hellfire.[1]

— O you who believe! Reverence God and believe in His Messenger; He will give you a twofold portion of His Mercy, make a Light for you by which you may walk, and forgive you— and God is Forgiving, Merciful.[2]

— They desire to extinguish the Light of God with their mouths, but God completes His Light, though the disbelievers be averse.[3]

— So believe in God and His Messenger and the Light We have sent down. God is Aware of whatsoever you do.[4]

— …A Messenger reciting unto you the clear signs of God to bring those who believe and perform righteous deeds out of darkness into Light. And whosoever believes in God and works righteousness, He causes him to enter Gardens with rivers running below, to abide therein forever. God has indeed prepared for him a beautiful provision.[5]

— O you who believe! Repent unto God with sincere repentance. It may be that your Lord will absolve you of your evil deeds and cause you to enter Gardens with rivers running below—the Day when God will not disgrace the Prophet and those who believe with him, with their Light spreading before

1   Q Ḥadīd 57:19.
2   Q Ḥadīd 57:28.
3   Q Ṣaff 61:8.
4   Q Taghābun 64:8.
5   Q Ṭalāq 65:11.

them and on their right, while they say, "Our Lord, complete our Light for us and forgive us. Truly Thou art Powerful over all things."[1]

1   Q Taḥrīm 66:8.

Ḥadīths of Light

'Abd Allāh ibn Mas'ūd said, "Your Lord is not subject to night or day. **The light of the heavens and the earth is from the Light of His Face.** The duration of each day for you is twelve hours. Your deeds of yesterday are presented to Him at the beginning of each day; He examines them for three hours, and anything displeasing to Him therein incurs His wrath. The first to learn of His wrath are the Throne-carriers who praise Him, for they feel their burden grow heavy. So the Throne-carriers, attendants, the angels-brought-nigh, and all the other angels glorify Him. Then Gabriel ﷺ blows the horn, and everything hears it. They glorify the All-Merciful for three hours until He is filled with mercy. That is six hours. Then the wombs are brought before Him and He examines them for three hours. Thus He says in His Book, **He it is Who forms you in the wombs however He will.**[1] **He creates whatsoever He will, bestowing females upon whomsoever He will, and bestowing males upon whomsoever He will, or He couples males and females, and causes whomsoever He will to be barren. barren. Truly He is Knowing, Powerful.**[2] That is nine hours. Then pro-

---

1   Q Āl 'Imrān 3:6.
2   Q Shūrā 42:49-50.

visions are brought before Him, and He examines them for three hours. Thus He says in His Book, **Truly thy Lord outspreads and measures provision for whomsoever He will.**[1] **Every day He is upon some affair.**[2] That is your affair, and the affair of your Lord."[3]

***

Abū Hurayra related that the Messenger of God ﷺ said, "There are servants of God who are not prophets, yet the prophets and martyrs envy them." Someone said, "Tell us who they are, that we might show them love." He replied, "**They are those who love one another through the Light of God**, not through family ties or lineage. Their faces are Light, upon pulpits of Light. They do not fear when others fear, nor grieve when others grieve." Then he recited, **Behold! Truly the friends of God, no fear shall come upon them, nor shall they grieve.**[4]

***

Abū Hurayra related that the Messenger of God ﷺ said, "When God created Adam, He patted his back, and from it fell all the people He would create from his progeny until the Day of Resurrection. Between the eyes of each of them, **He placed a mark of Light.** Then he presented them to Adam, who said, 'Lord, who are they?' He replied, 'They are your progeny.' He saw a man among them and was impressed by the mark

1   Q Isrā' 17:30.
2   Q Raḥmān 55:29.
3   Ṭabarānī, *Kabīr*, on the authority of 'Abd Allāh ibn Mas'ūd, 8886.
4   Q Yūnus 10:62. Ibn Ḥibbān, *Ṣaḥīḥ*, 578.

between his eyes. He asked, 'Lord, who is that?' He replied, 'A man from one of the latter communities of your progeny, named David.' He said, 'How long will You make him live?' He replied, 'Sixty years.' He said, 'Lord, give him forty years from my life.' Then when Adam's life was over, the Angel of Death went to him. He said, 'Do I not have forty years left?' The angels replied, 'Did you not give them to your son David?' Thus Adam contended, and his progeny contended; and Adam forgot, and his progeny forgot; and Adam erred, and his progeny erred."

Abū ʿĪsā [Tirmidhī] said, "This ḥadīth is sound and authentic."[1]

***

Anas ibn Mālik said, "I went out with the Prophet ﷺ from the house to the mosque, where there were some people raising their hands in supplication. He said, 'Do you see in their hands what I see?' I asked, 'What is it?' He replied, **'There is Light is their hands.'** I said, 'Pray to God to show it to me.' He did, and God showed it to me. Then he hurried in, and we raised our hands."[2]

The version in Ṭabarānī's *Kitāb al-Duʿāʾ* has, "He prayed, and I saw it. Then he said, 'Anas, quick, let us join them.' I hurried in with the Prophet of God ﷺ, and we raised our hands."[3]

***

Anas ﷺ related that two men left the Prophet ﷺ one dark night, **and a Light was before them until they parted, where-**

---

1   Tirmidhī, *Jāmiʿ*, 3021.
2   Bukhārī, *Tārīkh*, 649.
3   Ṭabarānī, *Duʿāʾ*, 191.

upon the Light divided between them. Ma'mar related on the authority of Thābit that Anas identified the men as Usayd ibn Ḥuḍayr and a man of the Helpers, while Ḥammād's narration from Thābit states that the men were Usayd ibn Ḥuḍayr and 'Abbād ibn Bishr.[1]

***

Abū Zubayr related that he heard someone ask Jābir ibn 'Abd Allāh about the passage through Hell at the Resurrection. He said during his answer, "The communities will call upon their idols and the things they worshipped, one by one. Then afterwards our Lord will come and say, 'Whom are you awaiting?' They will reply, 'We are awaiting our Lord.' He will say, 'I am your Lord.' They will say, 'Let us see You first.' So He will disclose Himself to them, laughing."

He then related that he had heard the Prophet ﷺ say, "He will lead them off, and they will follow Him. **He will give each person, whether hypocrite or believer, a Light.** Then they will follow Him across the Bridge over Hell, where hooks and thorns will grab whomever God wills. **Then the light of the hypocrites will be extinguished, and the believers will be saved. The first to be saved will be a throng whose faces are like full moons, seventy thousand of them, who will not be reckoned. Then those who follow them will be like the brightest stars in the sky; and so on.** Then intercession will be allowed, and all those who said, 'there is no god but God' and

---

1   Bukhārī, *Ṣaḥīḥ*, 3805.

had a hair's weight of goodness in their hearts will come out of Hell, and be placed in the courtyard of the people of Paradise, who will sprinkle water upon them until they begin to sprout like plants on a riverbank. Then he will ask until the entire world has been given to him, and again ten times over."[1]

***

Muslim's narration on the authority of Abū Saʿīd al-Khudrī has, "During the time of the Messenger of God ﷺ, some people asked, 'Messenger of God, will we see our Lord on the Day of Resurrection?' The Messenger of God ﷺ replied, 'Yes. Do you struggle to see the sun at noon on a cloudless day? Do you struggle to see the full moon on a cloudless night?' They replied, 'No, Messenger of God.' He said, 'You will not struggle to see God Almighty on the Day of Judgment any more than you struggle to see those. When that Day comes, a herald will call every community to follow what they worshipped. All those who worshipped idols and statues instead of God will fall into Hell, until there remain only those who worshipped God, whether they were righteous or sinful, and the People of the Book. The Jews will be called forward and asked, "Whom did you worship?" They will reply, "We worshipped ʿUzayr the son of God." They will be told, "You lie. God took neither consort nor son. What do you desire?" They will reply, "We are thirsty, Lord. Give us water!" But they will be directed to return not, and gathered into the Fire as it churns like a mirage, and they will fall into it.

1   Aḥmad, *Musnad*, 14818.

35

"'Then the Christians will be called forward and asked, "Whom did you worship?" They will reply, "We worshipped Christ the son of God." They will be told, "You lie. God took neither consort nor son. What do you desire?" They will reply, "We are thirsty, Lord. Give us water!" But they will be directed to return not, and gathered into the Fire as it churns like a mirage, and they will fall into it.

"'Finally there will remain only those who worshipped God, whether they were righteous or sinful. The Lord of the Worlds will go to them in the least form in which they could have imagined Him, and say, "What are you waiting for? Every community has followed what it worshipped." They will say, "Lord, we separated from the people in the world and did not keep their company, despite our dire need for them." He will say, "I am your Lord." They will cry, "We seek refuge in God from you! We associate no partners with God!" This will repeat two or three times, until some of them are close to turning. Then He will say, "Is there a sign between you and Him by which you may recognize Him?" They will reply, "Yes." **Then He will reveal a shin,** and all of those who ever prostrated to God of their own volition will be permitted to prostrate to Him. As for those who prostrated out of fear of other people or ostentation, God will fix their backs straight as though they had but a single backbone, and when they try to prostrate they will fall flat.

"'**Then they will raise their heads, and He will have transformed into the form in which they saw Him the first time.** He will say, "I am your Lord." They will reply, "You are our Lord."

Then the Bridge over Hell will be let down, and intercession will be allowed. They will say, "Dear God, grant peace, grant peace!"'

"Someone said, 'Messenger of God, what is the Bridge?' He replied, 'A slippery surface baited with hooks, spikes, and thorns like those of the Saʿdān plant in Najd. The believers will pass over in the blink of an eye, like lightning, like wind, like birds, and like swift horses. Some will be unscathed, others will get scratched but make it across, and others will tumble in the Fire of Hell. Once the believers are safe from Hell, by the One in Whose hands is my soul, they will call upon God on behalf of their brethren in Hell more passionately than anyone has ever called upon God to redress a right. They will say, "Lord, they used to fast with us, and pray, and make pilgrimage!" They will be told, "Take out all whom you recognize," for the Fire will be prevented from disfiguring them. They will take out a great many, the Fire having reached their ankles, or halfway up their shins, or their knees. Then they will say, "Lord, there are none left in it of those whom You told us to take out." He will say, "Go back and take out anyone in whose heart you find a dinar's weight of goodness." They will take out a great many, then say, "Lord, we have taken out all those whom You told us to." He will say, "Go back and take out anyone in whose heart you find a mote's weight of goodness." They will take out a great many, then say, "Lord, we have taken out all those whom You told us to."'"

(Abū Saʿīd al-Khudrī used to say, "If you do not believe me about this ḥadīth, then recite: **Truly God commits not so much**

as a mote's weight of wrong: if there is a good deed, He will multiply it and grant from His Presence a great reward.[1]")

"'Then God Almighty will say, "The angels have interceded, and the prophets have interceded, and the believers have interceded. None remains but the Most Merciful of the Merciful." He will take a handful from the Fire, and bring out those who never did any good at all. They will have been reduced to charcoal. He will cast them into a river on the edge of Paradise called the River of Life, and they will emerge like seeds carried by water—do you see how they are borne to rocks or trees, and those that grow in the sun are yellow and green, while those that grow in the shade are white?' The people said, 'Messenger of God, you must have spent time herding in the desert!'

"He continued: 'They will come out like pearls, with rings about their necks. The people of Paradise will recognize them as God's freed ones, whom He admitted into Paradise though they performed no works and did no good. Then He will say, 'Enter Paradise. All that you see is yours.' They will say, 'Lord, You have given us something You have never given to anyone in the worlds.' He will reply, 'With Me you shall have something even better.' They will say, 'Lord, what could be better than this?' He will reply, 'My boundless approval, for I shall never be angry with you again.'"[2]

✳✳✳

---

1   Q Nisā' 4:40.
2   Muslim, Ṣaḥīḥ, 274.

'Abd Allāh ibn 'Amr said, "I heard the Messenger of God ﷺ say, 'God Almighty created His creation in darkness, **then cast some of His Light upon them**. Those whom the Light touched were guided, and those whom it missed went astray.' That is why I say that the pen has dried." Tirmidhī declared this ḥadīth to be sound.[1]

***

Abū Hurayra said, "The Messenger of God ﷺ took me by the hand and said, 'God Almighty created the land on Saturday, and created the mountains in it on Sunday, and created the trees on Monday. On Tuesday He created the objects of labor. **On Wednesday He created the Light**. On Thursday he scattered the animals throughout it. He created Adam ﷇ on Friday evening, at the end of creation in the final hour of Friday, between afternoon and night.'"[2]

***

Abū Saʿīd related that the Messenger of God ﷺ said, "There are four hearts: a heart laid bare that shines like a lamp, a sealed heart with a knot tied about it, an inverted heart, and a heart turned on its side. **The heart laid bare is the heart of the believer, his lamp shining with Light**. The sealed heart is the heart of the unbeliever. The inverted heart is the heart of the hypocrite, who recognizes and then denies. The heart turned on its side is the one that harbors both faith and hypocrisy; the

---

1   *Jāmiʿ*, 2585.
2   Muslim, *Ṣaḥīḥ*, 5002.

faith in it is like a plant replenished with clean water, while the hypocrisy in it is like a boil replenished with pus and blood. The fate of this heart depends on which source of replenishment wins out."[1]

***

'Ikrima related that Ibn 'Abbās said, "Muḥammad saw his Lord." 'Ikrima said, "But doesn't God say, **Sight perceives Him not, but He perceives all sight?**"[2] He replied, "Woe betide you! **That is when He discloses with His Light, which is His Own Light.** But Muḥammad saw his Lord twice." Tirmidhī declared this hadith to be sound and singular through his chain of transmission.[3] Ṭabarānī narrated it in his *Kabīr* from Ibn 'Abbās as, "Muḥammad ﷺ saw his Lord twice—once with his eyes, and once with his heart."[4]

***

Anas ibn Mālik related that the Messenger of God ﷺ went out one day and was approached by a youth of the Helpers named Ḥāritha ibn al-Nu'mān. He said, "How are you this morning, Ḥāritha?" He replied, "This morning I am a true believer." The Messenger of God ﷺ said, "Watch what you say, for each truth has its reality. What is the reality of your faith?" He replied, "I have withdrawn myself from the world, and gone without sleep by night and without drink by day. **It is as though**

1   Aḥmad, *Musnad*, 10917.
2   Q Anʿām 6:103.
3   *Jāmiʿ*, 3220.
4   12406.

40

I can see the Throne of my Lord before me, and as though I can see the denizens of Paradise visiting one another therein, and as though I can see the denizens of Hell warring with one another therein."

The Prophet ﷺ said to him twice, "You have seen, so persevere." Then he ﷺ said, **"Here is a servant in whose heart God has illuminated faith."**

One day a call went up to battle, "Riders of God, mount up!" Ḥāritha was first in the saddle, and first to be martyred. His mother went to the Prophet ﷺ and said, "Messenger of God, tell me—where is Ḥāritha, my son? If he is in the Garden, I will not weep or grieve. If he is in Hell, I will weep as long as I live." The Messenger of God ﷺ said to her, "Umm Ḥāritha, there is not only one Garden, but many. Ḥāritha is in the Highest Paradise." She went away laughing and saying, "Ah Ḥāritha, rejoice!"[1]

***

Ḥudhayfa ﷺ related that the Messenger of God ﷺ said, "Gabriel ﷺ came to me holding something like a mirror with a black spot in its center. I said, 'Gabriel, what is this?' He replied, 'It is the world and its purity and beauty.' I said, 'What is that black spot?' He replied, 'It is Friday.' I said, 'What is Friday?' He replied, 'A tremendous day among the days of your Lord.' He described its nobility and virtue, and its name in the hereafter. When God sends the people of Paradise to Paradise and the people of Hell to Hell, there will no longer be night or

---

1   Bayhaqī, *Shuʿab al-Īmān*, 9884.

day, yet God will know the measure of those hours. When the time of Friday comes, at the moment when those who kept it used to head out to their prayer, a herald will call, 'People of Paradise! Come out to the Abode of Increase!' They will go out to a dune of musk, whiter than flour. When they have sat down in their places, God will send a gust of wind that stirs up the white musk and carries it through their clothing and out of their sleeves. The wind will know how to apply that perfume more expertly than any of your wives can manage with the perfumes of this world.

"Then God will say, 'Where are My servants who obeyed Me in secret, and believed My messengers without seeing Me? Ask of Me now, for this is the Day of Increase.' They will all utter together, as if one man, 'We are content, so be content with us!' The reply will come from Him, 'People of Paradise, if I were not content with you, I would not have brought you to dwell in My Paradise. Yet this is the Day of Increase, so ask of Me!' They will all utter together, as if one man, 'Show us Your Face, that we may look upon it.' Then God Almighty will pull back the veils and show Himself to them, and **His light will envelop them** so powerfully that had God not decreed that they would never die, they would burn up. Then He will say to them, 'Return to your homes.' They will return, unable to see their spouses and their spouses unable to see them, **so enveloped by His Light they are.** The Light will continue to dominate until at last they return to normal, or to their dwellings as they were. Their spouses will say to them, 'You look different now to how you did when you left.' They will reply, 'Our Lord showed Himself to us, and what we saw made us hidden from you.' They will bathe in the musk and bliss of Paradise on every seventh day, the Day of Increase."[1]

***

Ibn 'Abbās related that the Prophet of God ﷺ said, "God has a Preserved Tablet of white pearl, with pages of red ruby. **Its pen is Light, and its writing is Light.** God looks upon it three hundred and sixty times every day, creating and providing, giving life and dealing death, exalting and abasing, doing as He will."[2]

***

Ibn 'Abbās said, "On the Day of Resurrection, people will sit with God to the right of the Throne—and both God's hands are right hands. **They will sit upon pulpits of Light, with faces of Light.** They are not prophets, martyrs, or folk of truest faith. Someone said, 'Messenger of God, who are they?' He replied, 'Those who love one another in God's Majesty.'"[3]

***

Ibn 'Abbās ﷦ said, "When the Prophet ﷺ got up at night to pray the *tahajjud*, he would say, 'Dear God, praise be to You! You are the Upholder of the heavens and the earth and all that they contain. Praise be to You! Yours is the dominion of the heavens and the earth and all that they contain. Praise be to You! **You are the Light of the heavens and the earth.** Praise be to You! You are the Truth; Your promise is true, Your meeting is

---

1   Bazzār, *Musnad,* 2526.
2   Abū Nu'aym, *Ḥilya,* 5887.
3   Ṭabarānī, *Kabīr,* 12524.

43

true, Your word is true, Paradise is true, Hell is true, the prophets are true, Muḥammad is true, and the Hour is true. Dear God, to You I submit, and in You I believe, and on You I rely, and to You I turn, and for You I fight, and to You I defer. Forgive me my deeds, past and future, open and secret. It is You Who send forth, and You Who hold back. There is no god but You.'"[1]

***

Abū Mālik al-Ashʿarī related that the Prophet ﷺ said, "Purity is half of faith. 'Praise be to God' (*al-ḥamdu lillāh*) fills the scale. 'Glory be to God and praise be to God' (*subḥān Allāh walḥamdu lillāh*) fills everything between heaven and earth. **Prayer is light**. Charity is proof. Patience is illumination. The Qurʾān is a proof, whether for you or against you. All those who live to see another day sell their souls—into freedom, or into ruin."[2]

***

Abū Dharr asked the Prophet ﷺ, "Did you see your Lord?" He replied, "**I saw light** – how could I see Him?"[3]

***

Abū Hurayra related that a Jewish man came to the Prophet ﷺ and asked, "Abū al-Qāsim, did God veil Himself from His creation with something other than the heavens and the earth?" He answered, "Yes. Between Him and the angels around the Throne, there are seventy veils of fire, **seventy veils of Light**, seventy veils of darkness, seventy veils of sparkling

---

1   Bukhārī, *Ṣaḥīḥ*, 1059.
2   Muslim, *Ṣaḥīḥ*, 333.
3   Muslim, *Ṣaḥīḥ*, 266.

brocade, seventy veils of radiant silk, seventy veils of white pearls, seventy veils of red pearls, seventy veils of yellow pearls, seventy veils of green pearls, seventy veils of glow from the fire and the light, seventy veils of ice, seventy veils of water, seventy veils of cloud, seventy veils of cold, and seventy veils of divine majesty that cannot be described." The man asked, "Tell me about the angel of God that follows." The Prophet said, "Do you believe what I have just told you?" He answered, "Yes, I do." The Prophet ﷺ said, "The next angel is Isrāfīl, then comes Gabriel, then Michael, then the Angel of Death, may God bless them all."[1]

***

Sahl ibn Sa'd related that the Messenger of God ﷺ said, "God Almighty is behind seventy thousand **veils of Light** and darkness. Any soul that sensed the tiniest sound from those veils would die on the spot."[2]

***

Anas ibn Mālik related that the Prophet ﷺ said, "I asked Gabriel ﷺ, 'Do you see your Lord?' He replied, 'There are seventy **veils of Light** between me and Him. If I saw even the closest of them, I would burn up.'"[3]

***

The Messenger of God ﷺ spoke of prayer one day and said, "When someone is mindful of the prayer, it will becomes a

---

1   Ṭabarānī, *Awsaṭ*, 9175.
2   Ṭabarānī, *Kabīr*, 5664.
3   Ṭabarānī, *Awsaṭ*, 6580.

45

Light, a proof, and salvation for him on the Day of Resurrection. But if he is not mindful of it, he will have no proof, no light, and no salvation, and on that Day he will find himself in the company of Qārūn, Hāmān, Pharaoh, and Ubayy ibn Khalaf."[1]

***

Abū Dharr ﷺ related, "I said, 'Messenger of God, counsel me.' He replied, 'I counsel you to have reverence for God, for that is the summit of your entire affair.' I said, 'Messenger of God, give me more.' He said, 'Recite the Qur'ān and invoke God, **for that will be a Light for you in the heavens, and a Light in the earth.'** I said, "Messenger of God, give me more.' He said, 'Do not laugh too much, for it kills the heart and removes **the Light of the face.'** I said, 'Messenger of God, give me more.' He said, 'Engage in struggle, for it is the monasticism of my Community.' I said, 'Messenger of God, give me more.' He said, 'Be silent unless you have something good to say, for it will keep Satan from you and help you with your religion.' I said, 'Messenger of God, give me more.' He said, 'Look to those below you, not those above you, so that you do not overlook God's favors upon you.' I said, 'Messenger of God, give me more.' He said, 'As long as you are on God's side, do not fear reproach from anyone.' I said, 'Messenger of God, give me more.' He said, 'Love for others what you love for yourself.' Then he patted me on the chest and said, 'Abū Dharr, there is nothing more intelligent than thinking ahead, and nothing

---

1   Ibn Ḥibbān, *Ṣaḥīḥ*, 1497.

46

more pious than abstinence, and nothing more noble than beautiful character.'"[1]

***

'Abd Allāh ☙ related that the Messenger of God ☙ said, "Anyone who suffers anxiety or sorrow should say, 'Dear God, I am Your servant, the son of Your servant, and the son of Your maidservant. My forelock is in Your hand, Your decree upon me is binding, Your rule over me is just. I ask You with every name of Yours with which You have named Yourself, or taught to any of Your creatures, or revealed in Your book, or kept hidden in the unseen knowledge that is with You, to make the Qur'ān the spring of my heart, **and the Light of my breast**, and the remedy for my sorrow, and the cure for my woes.' Anyone who says this will find that God dispels his woes and sorrows, and replaces them with joy." Someone said, "Messenger of God, should we learn this?" He replied, "Yes, everyone who hears it ought to learn it."[2]

Abū Mālik al-Ash'arī reported that the Messenger of God ☙ said: "Purity is half of faith. 'Praise be to God' (*al-ḥamdu li-Llāh*) fills the scale. 'Glory be to God and praise be to God' (*subḥāna Llāhi wa'l-ḥamdu li-Llāh*) fills everything between heaven and earth. Prayer is light. Charity is proof. Patience is illumination. The Qur'ān is an argument either for you or against you. All those who live to see another day sell their souls—either into freedom or into ruin."[3]

---

1 Ṭabarānī, *Kabīr*, 1627.
2 Aḥmad, *Musnad*, musnad 'Abd Allāh ibn Mas'ūd, 3583.
3 Muslim, *Ṣaḥīḥ*, 333.

***

'Irbāḍ ibn Sāriya ﷺ related that the Messenger of God ﷺ said, "I was the servant of God and the Seal of Prophets when my father was still being molded in his clay. Let me tell you how: I am the answer to the prayer of my father Abraham, the good tiding of Jesus, the dream that my mother Āmina saw, just as all the mothers of the prophets have dreams." As she was giving birth to him, the Prophet's ﷺ mother saw **Light emanating from him that illuminated the palaces of Syria to her.** Then he recited, **O Prophet! Truly We have sent thee as a witness, as a bearer of glad tidings, and as a warner, as one who calls unto God by His Leave, and as a luminous lamp.**[1] Ḥākim declared this authentic.[2]

***

Abū Saʿīd al-Khudrī ﷺ related that the Prophet ﷺ said, "The one who recites Sūrat al-Kahf on Friday will be given **Light to illuminate him** until the next Friday." Ḥākim declared this authentic.[3]

***

Abū Mūsā ﷺ related that the Messenger of God ﷺ said, "God Almighty does not sleep, and it would not behoove Him to sleep. He lowers the Scales and raises them. The deeds of night are lifted to Him before the deeds of day. **His veil is Light,** and if He were to lift it, the rays of His Face would burn

---

1   Q Aḥzāb 33:45-46.
2   *Mustadrak*, 3496.
3   *Mustadrak*, 3318.

everything of His creation, as far as His gaze reaches." Abū Bakr's narration has, "His veil is fire."[1]

***

Anas ibn Mālik ﷺ related that the Messenger of God ﷺ said, "As I was sitting, Gabriel ﷺ came to me and nudged me between my shoulders. I went to a tree that had something like two bird's nests in it. He sat in one, and I sat in the other, and it grew and rose up until it filled the horizons. Had I desired to, I could have reached out and touched the sky. I looked at Gabriel, and he appeared like a transparent cloth. I realized that his knowledge of God was greater than mine. But then one of the doors of heaven opened to me, **and I saw the Supreme Light.** A veil studded with pearls and rubies fell before me, and then God revealed to me what He wished to reveal."[2]

***

Abū Mūsā ﷺ related that the Prophet ﷺ said, "The parable of the Muslims, Christians, and Jews is like that of a man who hires some people to work for him for a full day until nightfall for an agreed payment. They work until midday, then say, 'We do not need the pay you promised, and the work we have done was in vain.' He says, 'No, you should finish your work and take your payment in full.' But they refuse, and leave. So he hires some other workers and tells them, 'Work for the rest of the day, and I shall give you the payment I promised those others.' They work

---

1   Muslim, *Ṣaḥīḥ*, 268.
2   Abū Nuʿaym, *Ḥilya*, 2632.

until the time of the afternoon prayer, then say, 'The work we have done was in vain. Keep the pay you promised us.' He says, 'Finish your work, the day is almost over!' But they refuse. So he hires some others to work for the rest of the day, and they work until sunset, and receive all the pay that was offered to the others. That is just like them **and what they received of this Light.**"[1]

***

The Prophet ﷺ said, "Give glad tidings to those who walk to the mosque in the dark, that they shall have **perfect Light** on the Day of Resurrection."[2]

---

1   Bukhārī, *Ṣaḥīḥ*, 2120.
2   Tirmidhī, *Jāmiʿ*, 207.

Ḥadīths on the Path

Jābir ibn ʿAbd Allāh related that ʿUmar ibn al-Khaṭṭāb went to the Prophet ﷺ with a book he had received from one of the People of the Book, and read it to him. The Prophet ﷺ grew angry and said, "Will you fall into confusion too, Ibn al-Khaṭṭāb? By Him in Whose hand is my soul, I have brought it to you **radiant and clean.** Do not ask them about things, lest they tell you something true and you deny it, or something false and you believe it. By Him in Whose hand is my soul, if Moses were alive now, he would have no recourse other than to follow me."[1]

***

ʿIrbāḍ ibn Sāriya said, "The Messenger of God ﷺ gave us a speech that brought tears to our eyes and made our hearts tremble. We said, 'Messenger of God, that seemed like a farewell speech. Give us one last counsel.' He replied, '**I have left you upon the Radiant Path,** whose night is as bright as its day. Anyone who strays from it after me will fall to ruin. Some of you will live long enough to witness much conflict. You must adhere to what you recognize of my Sunna and the Sunna of the righteous rightly-guided vicegerents. You must obey, even if the ruler be an Abyssinian slave. Bite down on it with your

---

1   Aḥmad, *Musnad*, 15156.

51

teeth; for the believer is like a camel with a nose ring; wherever it is led, it goes.'"[1]

***

Ḥudhayfa related that the Messenger of God ﷺ said, "If you appoint Abū Bakr caliph, you will find that he is strong in God's command but weak in his body. If you appoint 'Umar, you will find that he is strong in God's command and strong in his body. If you appoint 'Alī—which I do not think you will do—you will find that he is a guided guide **who carries you upon the Radiant Path.**"[2]

***

Ḥudhayfa ﷺ related that the people said, "Messenger of God, what if you were to appoint a caliph for us?" He replied, "If I were to appoint a caliph for you, and you disobeyed him, you would be punished." They said, "What if you appointed Abū Bakr?" He replied, "If I made him your caliph, you would find him to be strong in God's command but weak in his body." They said, "What about 'Umar?" He replied, "If I made him your caliph, you would find him to be strong, trustworthy, and beyond reproach in God's cause." They said, "What about 'Alī?" He replied, "You would not do it; but if you did, you would find him to be a guided guide who leads you along **the Straight Path.**"[3]

***

<hr>

1   Aḥmad, *Musnad*, 17142.
2   Shajarī, *al-Amālī al-Khamīsiyya*, 507.
3   Ḥākim, *Mustadrak*, 4372.

Abū Dardā' ﷺ related that the Messenger of God ﷺ said, "I have left you upon **the Radiant Path**, whose night is as bright as its day. Anyone who strays from it after me will fall to ruin."[1]

---

1   Aḥmad 4/126; Ibn Mājah, *Sunan*, 1/4.

Light in the Terminology of the Karkarī Order

In the Karkarī Order, Light (*nūr*) means that which unveils all that is concealed, and reveals all that is hidden. It is hallowed beyond quantity, modality, direction, color, and location.

It is the supreme spirit, the effacer of shadows, and the manifestor of things to the eye. It is manifest in itself and causes other things to be manifest. It is the simple substance that is known through self-evidence, and it is that which truly exists. It is the celestial mount that carries the gnostics to the Lord of the Worlds.

It is the imprint of the spirit, the shade of the secret, the core of pure meaning, and the eye of certainty. It is the beginningless attribute of the Real, subsisting through His Essence, manifesting in the world of possibility by the principle of existence and perception, and disclosing itself in the forms of the possibilities.

According to those who have verified the truth, it is the first incorporeal creation; the ink of the Pen; the liminal intermediary between the temporal and the eternal. It is the wine of union, which assists the realities of the secret of Necessity in becoming expressed through perspectives and determinations.

According to the folk of the Path, it is an attribute that subsists through the Essence, and is neither identical with It nor other than It.

The Path in the Terminology of the Karkarī Order

The Radiant Path (*al-maḥajja al-bayḍāʾ*) is the first instance of discontinuity from the center of the Cloud (*al-ʿamāʾ*), disclosed by the concealing blackness of the unseen realm. It is the manifestation-site of opposites, the disclosure-site of existence from nonexistence, the Sunna of the Best of Creation, and the title that brings together the Book of his normative words, deeds, approvals, and attributes. Through it, the servant passes away from his own attributes and then his own essence, thereby subsisting through God, sustained by Him in all of his states, returning to Him through all of his deeds, becoming firmly established by Him, in Him, and for Him.

The *Maḥajja* is the path of deliverance from idolatry, whether subtle or obvious. Through it one realizes sincerity and the *tawḥīd* of the spiritual elect. It is the disclosure-site of love and direct witnessing upon the field of divine protection and providential care. It is the very source of of the spirit of faith; to drink from it is to imbibe the qualities of eternity from the cup of yearning. It is the plain path and the straight way for all those destined for providential care, those who turn away from other-than-God and cling to the Protector. It is the sword of Dhul-Faqār, brandished against the false gods of passion, lower self, and ego. It is God's straight path.

God says, **There has come unto you, from God, a Light and a clear Book, whereby God guides whosoever seeks His Contentment unto the ways of peace, and brings them out of darkness into Light, by His Leave, and guides them unto a straight path.**[1]

The Path is the way of unveiling, spanning from the soul to the spirit over the chasm of the hellish tendencies of base human nature. It is the road from the world of forms and images to the world of pure meanings. It is the road to union with the Holy Presence, manifest in the herebelow as the Light of faith, and in the hereafter as the bridge of salvation. Everyone will cross it in the measure of the Light of their faith; for that which is pure meaning in this world will become tangible in the hereafter.

The Prophet ﷺ says in a noble ḥadīth concerning the Day of Resurrection, that the people **"will be given their Light in the measure of their deeds.** Some will be presented with mountain of Light before them, others with even more Light. Others will be presented with Light like a palm tree in their right hands, others with less than that. Others will be presented with Light upon their big toes, which sometimes shines and sometimes falls dark. When it shines, they will proceed forward; when it falls dark, they will stop. They will all pass over the Bridge, which is as narrow as a sword's edge, slippery and perilous. They will be told, 'Proceed in the measure of your Light.' Some will pass over like shooting stars, some like the wind, some like

1   Q Māʾida 5:15-16.

the blink of an eye, some like galloping horses. They will pass one after another in the measure of their deeds, until those whose Light is on their toes will pass, their hands slipping then grasping, their feet stumbling then holding, their sides touching the fire, yet getting safely across. Once they are across they will say, 'Praise be to God, Who has saved us from you after showing you to us! God has given us something no one has even been given.'"

Bayhaqī's *Shu'ab* contains a narration of Anas, who related that the Prophet ﷺ said, "There is a bridge over Hell as narrow as a sword's blade, leading up to Paradise. It is slippery and perilous, with hellish hooks and thorns at its sides. God will subject to it whomever of His servants He wishes, and many will be the men and women who stumble upon it that day. The angels will be by its sides calling, 'Dear God, make it safe! Dear God, make it safe!' Those who come with the truth will pass across. **On that day they will be given Light in the measure of their faith and their deeds.** Some will pass over like lightning, others like the wind, others like swift horses. Some will walk across it, others will run. Some will be given Light at their feet. Some will go crawling across, the fire exacting retribution from them for the sins they committed. It will burn whomever of them God wills in the measure of their sins, until they make it safely across. The first across will be a group of seventy thousand who will not be reckoned at all, nor punished. Their faces will shine like full moons. Those who come after them will shine like stars in the sky, until they arrive in Paradise by the mercy of God."[1]

The Radiant Path is the firmest handhold, for it is the flow of connecting Light between the noneternal and the eternal, between the possible and the necessary. It is the door to spiritual excellence. God says, **And whosoever submits his face to God and is virtuous has indeed grasped the firmest handhold; and unto God is the end of all affairs.**[2]

The Radiant Path is the secret of the illusory division between the one called servant and the one called Lord. It is manifested in the Seven Oft-Repeated Verses through God's proclamation upon the tongue of the Prophet ﷺ, the Interpreter of presence of ultimate union, who said, "God Almighty says, 'I have divided prayer into two halves between Me and My servant, and My servant shall have what he requests.' When he says, *Praise be to God, Lord of the worlds*, God says, 'My servant has praised Me.' When he says, *the Compassionate, the Merciful*, God says, 'My servant has lauded Me.' When he says, *Master of the Day of Judgment*, God says, 'My servant has glorified Me and entrusted his affair to Me.' When he says, *Thee we worship and from Thee we seek help*, God says, 'This is between Me and My servant, and My servant shall have what he requests.' When he says, *Guide us upon the straight path, the path of those whom*

---

1 Bayhaqī, *Shuʿab al-Īmān*, 346.
2 Q Luqmān 31:22.

Thou hast blessed, not of those who incur wrath, nor of those who are astray, God says, 'This is for My servant, and My servant shall have what he requests.'"[1]

It is God's sturdy rope, for it is the covenant of connective Light which we pledged in the realm of the seed; for it is that Light which was cast upon the darkness of nonexistence.

'Abd Allāh ibn 'Amr related that he heard the Messenger of God ﷺ say, "God Almighty created His creation in darkness, then cast some of His Light upon them. Whomever the light touched that day would be guided, and whomever it missed would go astray." 'Abd Allāh ibn 'Amr said after relating this, "This is why I say that the pen has dried according to the knowledge of God."[2]

1   Muslim, *Ṣaḥīḥ*, 603.
2   *Majmaʿ al-Zawāʾid*, 11812.

Outward Vision and Inward Vision

In the terminology of the Karkarī Order, **outward vision** (*baṣar*) is what perceives sensory, delimited, and witnessed objects in the world of wisdom. Through it the forms of things are observed, and gross and noneternal entities are distinguished, for it is a mirror upon which the human world (*nāsūt*) is reflected.

In the Karkarī Order, **inward vision** (*baṣīra*) is the eye of the heart illuminated by the Light of eternity, which itself comes from the treasuries of the unseen and extends from the world of divinity (*lāhūt*), through the eye of the needle of divine power, to the human world.

Outward vision is the eye of the sensory realm, and inward vision is the eye of outward vision, or the eye of the eye. For it perceives things as they actually are, since it is free from pupils and eyelids. It is hallowed beyond the imprint of forms and created beings. The object of outward vision is delimited, while the object of inward vision is nondelimited.

Physical sight is stained by all manner of blemishes, which our master Abū Ḥāmid al-Ghazālī ﷺ discussed in "The Niche of Lights," (*Mishkāt al-Anwār*), saying:

Know that the light of eyesight sees other things, but not itself. It cannot see what is too far from it, nor what is too close to it, nor what is veiled from it. It sees the outside of things, not their inside. It sees only part of what exists, not all of it. It sees finite things, not infinite things. Its vision often errs: it takes large things to be small, distant things to be close, stationary things to be in motion, or things in motion to be stationary. These then are seven defects from which the outward eye cannot be free. If there should happen to exist any eye that is free of them all, I would say that it deserves the name of "light" most of all. You should know, then, that there is an eye in the human heart too which is endowed with this very perfection. This eye is what is called the intellect, the spirit, or the human soul.

Yet pay no heed to these expressions, for a person lacking in insight might mistake a multitude of expressions to denote a multitude of meanings. What we mean is the thing that distinguishes the intellect from the mind of an infant, a dumb beast, or a madman. We call it the intellect (*'aql*) because that is the term that is given to it in common parlance. Yet the intellect is more worthy of being called a Light than the outward eye, for it is above the aforementioned seven defects. Let us examine them in turn:

The **first** defect is that the eye cannot see itself. The intellect, however, perceives other than itself and perceives its own attributes as well. It perceives that it is endowed with knowledge and potential, and perceives that it knows this, and that it knows that it knows this, and so on *ad infinitum*. Such is inconceivable for that which is perceived by the physical senses; and beyond this lies a secret that would be long to explain.

The **second** defect is that the eye cannot see what is too far from it nor what is too close to it. Yet proximity and distance make no difference to the intellect, which may soars to the highest heights and plummets to the lowest lows in an instant. In truth, the intellect in its holiness is not bound by the concepts of proximity and distance at all, for the latter refer to physical bodies, whereas the intellect is a similitude of the Light of God; and every similitude is an emulation of the original, though not its equal. This may inspire you to contemplate the secret of the Prophet's ﷺ words, "God created Adam in His own image," though I shall not delve into it now.

The **third** defect is that the eye cannot perceive what is veiled from it. The intellect, however, may roam freely about the Throne, the Pedestal, and what lies beyond the veils of the heavens. It may move within the Supreme Assembly and the higher spiritual realm just as freely as it moves in its own domain, by which I mean the body. No realities whatsoever are veiled from the intellect, unless the intellect veils itself by means of attributes that are akin to the way the eye is veiled when the eyelids are closed.

The **fourth** defect is that the eye perceives only the outward surface aspect of things, not the inner. It sees their receptacles and forms, not their true realities. The intellect, however, penetrates into the inner dimensions and secrets of things, perceiving their realities and spirits, gleaning their causes, reasons, purposes, and wisdoms.

The **fifth** defect is that the eye only sees some existent things, for all intelligible concepts and many sense objects are beyond it. It cannot perceive sounds, smells, tastes, temperatures, nor the faculties of perception, by which I mean the senses of hearing, sight, smell, taste, nor the inner attributes of the soul such as delight, happiness, discontent, sorrow, pain, pleasure, passion, desire, power, will, knowledge, and countless other existents. Its scope is thus exceedingly narrow. It cannot go beyond colors and shapes, which are the most basic things in existence; for corporeal bodies are the most basic category of existents, and color and shape are their most basic accidental qualities. Yet the scope of the intellect covers all things in existence, for it perceives all of the things we enumerated above, as well as those we did not, which constitute the major part. It may roam freely among all of them, and pass judgments upon them that are certain and truthful. Inward secrets are manifest to it, and hidden meanings are plain to it. How could the outward eye compete with it for the title of Light? It simply could not. The outward eye may be a light relative to other things, but it is darkness relative to the intellect. Outward vision is merely one of the intellect's spies, charged with watching over the lowliest of its treasuries, that of color and shape, and reporting back to it. The intellect then passes judgment on these reports according to the dictates of its piercing insight and powerful judgment. The five senses are its spies, and it has inward spies too: imagination, sense-intuition, reflective thought, recollection, memory, beyond which lie servants and hosts subjected to its will, each in its specific realm. It sets them to work and exercises control over them as a king does his subjects, and with greater control still. To explain this thoroughly here would take too long...

The **sixth** defect is that the eye cannot see what is infinite, for it sees only the attributes of corporeal bodies, which can only be conceived as finite. Yet the intellect perceives concepts, and concepts cannot be conceived as finite. It is true that a given bit of information attained by the intellect in the present moment must be finite, but it has the potential to conceive of the infinite. For example, consider arithmetic. The intellect can conceive of an infinite series of numbers, or indeed the infinite multiplication of a given number. It can conceive of relationships between the numbers that can only be infinite. Indeed, it can apprehend its knowledge of something, and its knowledge of this knowledge, and its knowledge of this knowledge of this knowledge, and so on.

The **seventh** defect is that the eye can err, such as by viewing a large object as small. It sees the sun the size of a bowl, and the stars like coins scattered upon a blue carpet. The intellect knows that the sun and the stars are many times larger than the earth. Likewise, the eye sees the stars as stationary, and even the shadow before it as stationary. The eye sees a child and deems it to be of constant size, while the intellect knows that it is constantly growing, and that the shadows are in motion, and that the stars move many miles in every blink of the eye. The Prophet ﷺ said to Gabriel, "Has the sun moved?" He replied, "No—yes." The Prophet ﷺ asked, "How so?" Gabriel replied, "From when I said no to when I said yes, it moved a distance equal to a journey of five hundred years." The errors of the eyesight are many, but the intellect—i.e., inner vision—transcends them all.[1]

Yet despite all the defects of outward vision, when the illumination of inward vision becomes strengthened and shines forth, it whelms the former and cleanses it of the vision of created things. Outward vision then frees itself of the outward manifestations of contingency. When the cover of delusion is lifted from the eyesight and it becomes piercing, it beholds divine power in the heart of wisdom with the aid of inward vision. To this effect, God says: **You were indeed heedless of this. Now We have removed from you your cover; so today your sight is piercing.**[2] Nothing but death can pull back this cover. Death has two forms: the compulsory death that all must endure, and the voluntary death, of which the tradition says, "Reckon yourselves before you are reckoned." This death occurs through spiritual struggle and intense striving, and is granted by the share grace of Almighty God.

1   *Mishkāt al-Anwār*, pp. 121-127.
2   Q Qāf 50:22.

Know too that inward vision has three levels: knowledge, the eye, and truth. The first level, knowledge of inner vision (*ʿilm al-baṣīra*), is the ray of divine success and the thunderbolts of guidance. Through it you witness the magnificence of God's nearness and encompassment, thereby knowing that He is nearer to you than your jugular vein, and that He encompasses you in a manner that astounds the mind. God says, **And [remember] when We said unto thee, "Surely thy Lord encompasses mankind."**[1]

The middle level, the eye of inner vision (*ʿayn al-baṣīra*), allows you to witness your own nonexistence and His existence, so that you do not set up your ego as a partner to Him. It is then that the cosmos burns away and all things in existence vanish. That is the meaning of, "God was, and there was nothing with Him."

Finally comes the truth of inner vision (*ḥaqq al-baṣīra*), through which you witness His existence, not your nonexistence or your existence. This is the meaning of, "He is now as He was." Sidi Ibn ʿAjība says:

It is called the truth of inner vision because when the inner vision perceives the truth at its root and becomes absent from the Light of the branches by the Light of the roots, it is called the truth of inner vision on account of how it perceives the truth and is blind to creation. This is the station of the truth of certainty (*ḥaqq al-yaqīn*). The ray of inner vision is the Light of

---

1   Q Isrāʾ 17:62.

faith for the folk of watchfulness (*murāqaba*); the eye of inner vision is the Light of spiritual excellence for the folk of witnessing (*mushāhada*); the truth of inner vision is the Light of stability and mastery for the folk of intimate converse (*mukālama*).

Or one could say that the ray of inner vision is the Light of the knowledge of certainty; the eye of inner vision is the Light of the eye of certainty; and the truth of inner vision is the Light of the truth of certainty. The knowledge of certainty is for the folk of proof and argument; the eye of certainty is for the folk of unveiling and elucidation; and the truth of certainty is for the folk of witnessing and beholding.

For instance, a person who has heard of Mecca but never seen it possesses the knowledge of certainty. If he views the city from afar without entering it, he has the eye of certainty. But when he actually enters the city and finds himself within it, he has the truth of certainty. The same applies to the seeker of God. As long as he is behind the veil, annihilated in pious works, he has the knowledge of certainty. When he approaches annihilation in the Essence but does not master it, he has the eye of certainty. When he attains mastery and stability in annihilation, he has the truth of certainty.

Or one could say that the ray of inner vision is for the people of the physical realm (*mulk*), the eye of inner vision is for the people of the spiritual realm (*malakūt*), and the truth of inner vision is for the people of the realm of invincibility (*jabarūt*). Or one could say that the ray of inner vision is for those who are annihilated in works, the eye of inner vision is for those who are annihilated in the Essence, and the truth of inner vision is for those who are annihilated in annihilation.

The ray of inner vision shows you how near God is to you; that is, it makes you witness how near the Light of God is to you. God says, **We did indeed create man, and We know what his soul whispers to him; and We are nearer to him than his jugular vein;**[1] and He says, **He is with you wheresoever you are.**[2]

The eye of inner vision shows you your nonexistence; it makes you recognize the illusory nature of your existence beside His existence, for it is impossible to witness Him while witnessing anything besides Him. When your illusion fades and you become annihilated to your own existence, you witness your Lord through your Lord. This is the sign that the inner vision is opened and the innermost heart is cured, as the master of our masters Sidi 'Abd al-Raḥmān al-Majdhūb said:

If you see the Being-Giver through the realm of being,
Your inner vision is still sealed;

When you see the realm of being through the Being-Giver,
Your innermost heart will be healed.

The truth of inner vision shows you the existence of God alone, not your own existence since you are entirely absent, nor

---

1   Q Qāf 50:16.
2   Q Ḥadīd 57:4.

even your nonexistence since there is no question of nonexistence for something that never had any existence to begin with. There was never anything besides God; "God was, and there was nothing with Him, and He is now as He was." Those last words [and He is now as He ever was] are not actually part of the ḥadīth, but their meaning is true, for it is impossible for God to undergo change. Muḥyī al-Dīn Ibn al-ʿArabī ﷺ said, "Successful is the one who sees creatures as motionless; advanced is the one who sees them as lifeless; arrived is the one who sees them as pure nothingness." I would add that the one who sees them with the eye of nonexistence had attained mastery in his arrival. A poet said:

Behold creation as a mirage,
And ascend beyond the veil of disparity,

To an existence that you behold as a stitched mass,
Without distance, dialogue, or duality.[1]

1   *Īqāẓ al-himam,* pp. 103-104.

Knowledge

Sidi Ibn ʿĀshir says in his didactic poem, "The first duty of the legally responsible person is to know God and the Messengers." When a person reaches the age of religious accountability (*taklīf*), his first duty is to know God and to know His Messenger ﷺ. This means attaining knowledge and realization of the meaning of the Testimony of Faith. The Testimony of Faith is the door that leads into the religion of God and out of the herebelow.

Knowledge, according to those who know pure meaning, is the true root of godfearing, which is the vehicle of self-disclosure and witnessing. God says, **Only those among His servants who know, fear God. Truly God is Mighty, Forgiving.**[1] Observe, may God have mercy on you, how He links knowledge with fear because of how the two stations are inseperable. The more one knows God, the more one fears Him. It is authentically reported that the Master of Existence ﷺ said, "By God, I know God better than any of you, and I fear Him the most." Fear begins with viewing others with reverence because one witnesses the flow of the Real within them, and belittling one's own self, keeping always within the bounds of the Law, and maintaining a constant attitude of awe before God. This is the

---

1   Q Fāṭir 35:28.

attribute of the perfected gnostics, for it is the celestial mount of gnosis that transports them from the station of imaginal conceptualization to gnostic self-disclosure.

From *al-Baḥr al-Madīd*:

Rabī' ibn Anas said, "The one who does not fear God has no knowledge." Ibn 'Abbās said, commenting on this verse, "Renunciation is knowledge enough." Ibn Mas'ūd said, "God-fearing is knowledge enough, and excuse-making is ignorance enough." One of al-Iskandarī's aphorisms reads, "The best knowledge is that which is accompanied by fear."

Al-Iskandarī's "Book of Illumination" (*al-Tanwīr*) reads, "Whenever the Qur'ān and Sunna speak of knowledge, they mean beneficial knowledge which is accompanied by fear and shrouded in reverence. God says, **Only those among His servants who know, fear God**, which shows that fear must accompany knowledge. This means that the people of knowledge are those who have fear."

Shaykh Ibn 'Abbād ﷺ said, "Beneficial knowledge is and has always been recognized as the knowledge that leads the one who attains it to fear and pious reverence, and inspires in him humility, lowliness, and the other qualities of faith. This causes him to disdain the world and abstain from it, and to prefer the hereafter to it, and to maintain proper courtesy with God, and other such sublime attributes."

Al-Iskandarī says in his "Subtle Graces" (*Laṭā'if al-Minan*), "The true knowledge that God desires is evidenced by fear, and fear is evidenced by conformity to the divine command. If knowledge is accompanied by desire for the world, ingratiating oneself to worldly people, aspiration for wealth, pride, covetousness, ambition, and neglect of the hereafter, then someone characterized by such qualities is as far removed as possible from being an heir of the Prophets. Can an inheritance pass to an heir in any other attribute than the one in which it was held by the one who bequeaths it? A scholar with attributes such as these is like a candle, which provides light to others even as it burns itself. God makes such a person's knowledge a proof against him, and a cause of manifold punishment."

The literal phrasing of the Qur'ānic verse [**God, among His servants, is only feared by those who know**] mentions God's name first, and mentions those who know (*al-'ulamā'*) last, indicates that only the godfearing servants can be called "knowers." Had He said it other way around, with "Those who know only fear God," it would mean that they fear nothing but Him.

The Prophet ﷺ reportedly said, "God will say to the knowers on the Day of Resurrection when He sits upon His pedestal to judge His servants, 'I placed My knowledge and My forbearance within you only so that I might forgive you on account of it, and I care not!'" Al-Mundhirī said, "Consider His words 'My knowledge and My forbearance,' and you will see that by attributing it to Himself, He did not mean most of the knowledge that people today possess, which is bereft of praxis and sincerity." Another narration has, "I placed My wisdom within you only because I intended good for you. Enter Paradise on account of what is within you!"

The Prophet ﷺ also said, "On the Day of Resurrection, the ink of the learned and the blood of the martyrs will be weighed, and the ink will outweigh the blood."

Spiritual allusion of the verse: there are two kinds of knowers: those who know the laws of God, and those who know God. Those who know His laws fear His wrath and punishment, while those who know God fear to be veiled and distanced from Him. Those who know His laws strive to avoid sin, while those who know Him strive to avoid discourtesy in His Presence. The fear of those who know God is subtler and deeper. They take their knowledge from God, while those who know His laws take their knowledge from the dead.

Shaykh Abū Yazīd ﷺ said of the narrators, "Poor things! They receive their knowledge from one dead man after another, while we receive ours from the Living One who never dies."

Regarding the terms *khawf*, *rahba*, and *khashya* [all of which broadly mean "fear", with *khashya* being the term used in the verse under discussion], *khawf* means fear of punishment, *rahba* fear of censure, and *khashya* fear of distance. Qushayrī said, "The difference between *khashya* and *rahba* is that *rahba* is fear that makes a person flee and get away from what he fears, while *khashya* is fear that makes a person freeze in terror, so that he remains with God. Thus *khashya* is superior to *rahba*. *Khawf* pertains to faith, hence God says, **Fear Me [khāfūnī], if you are believers.**[1] *Khashya* pertains to knowledge and awe.

---

1   Q Āl 'Imrān 3:175.

The learned man has *khawf* of being remiss before his Lord; the gnostic has *khashya* of falling short of proper courtesy and respect with Him, such as by being expansive at the wrong time, uttering a word at the wrong time, or failing to do what is absolutely best."

Al-Wartajbī [Rūzbihān Baqlī] said, "*Khawf* is general, while *khashya* is specific. The Almighty links *khashya* to knowledge, meaning knowledge of God and His majesty, power, and lordship, and one's servitude to Him. True *khashya* is the presence of awe for God in the hearts of the gnostics, combined with reverence and recognition of His grandeur and might. None can attain this but one who has witnessed beginninglessness, endlessness, eternity, and subsistence. As knowledge of God increases, so does fear of Him. Thus the Prophet ﷺ said, 'I know God better than any of you, and fear Him the most.'"

The Messenger of God ﷺ was asked which deed is best and replied, "Knowledge." They said, "What knowledge?" He replied, "Knowledge of God Almighty."[1]

Al-Iskandarī states in one of his aphorisms, "Beneficial knowledge is that whose rays expand within the chest, and which lifts the veil from the heart." Thus, knowledge is a gnostic ray of Light which, when it expands within the heart, lifts the veil of otherness and duality. The darkness of creation comes to nought, and the attributes of the Creator are made

---

1   *Baḥr al-Madīd,* pp. 120-121.

manifest as His Lights spread through the heart. This is what beneficial knowledge means: to witness the Light of God and His Messenger.

God describes Himself as Light when He says, **God is the Light of the heavens and the earth. The parable of His Light is a niche, wherein is a lamp. The lamp is in a glass. The glass is as a shining planet kindled from a blessed olive tree, neither of the East nor of the West. Its oil would well-nigh shine forth, even if no fire had touched it. Light upon Light. God guides unto His Light whomsoever He will, and God sets forth parables for mankind, and God is Knower of all things.**[1]

He also describes His Prophet as a lamp when He says, **O Prophet! Truly We have sent thee as a witness, as a bearer of glad tidings, and as a warner, as one who calls unto God by His Leave, and as a luminous lamp.**[2]

The true nature of knowledge, then, is to adorn oneself with the Light of the lordly presence sent down by the Lamp of knowledge in the Glass of our master the Messenger of God ﷺ, manifest by the Niche of revelation, hidden in the Planet of union in the night of concealment, kindled from the Tree of the secret beyond the traces of spatiality.

May God reward Imam Shāfiʿī who said:

---

1   Q Nūr 24:35.
2   Q Aḥzāb 33:45-46.

When I complained to Wakī' of my poor memory,
He advised me to give up my sinful ways;

*For knowledge, he told me, is a **Light**,*
And God's Light is not granted to a sinner.

Knowledge, then, is Light, not lines upon a page. It is a Light by which God's intent is apprehended with every breath; it is holy water sent down from the heavens of the unseen to the earth of the believer's heart.

The Prophet ﷺ reportedly said, "The guidance and knowledge with which God has sent me is like rain that falls upon land. The fertile land absorbs the water and brings forth much grass and herbs. The solid land retains the water, and God benefits people with it so that they may drink, water their animals, and irrigate. The rest falls into an abyss, which neither retains the water nor produces plants. Such is the likeness of the one who understands the religion of God and benefits from that with which God has sent me, learning and teaching others. Then there is the one who neither raises his head to it, nor accepts God's guidance with which I have been sent."[1]

Observe, may God have mercy on you, how the Prophet ﷺ, who never spoke out of caprice, described the levels of people with regard to knowledge in this parable. First there are the people of Light, the true folk of knowledge; then there are those

---

1   Muslim, *Ṣaḥīḥ*, 2282.

who have only the semblance of knowledge; then finally there are those who have neither true knowledge nor the semblance of it.

The first are those who are receptive of the water of prophetic knowledge in the land of their virtuous souls, which burst into outward verdure by the meanings of the divine names, then produce the fruits of knowledge. The Beloved ﷺ likened them to fertile land that produces much grass and herbs, because of how they receive the water of revelation in the good land of their hearts, and recognize the descents of the names in the attributes, and the attributes in the acts, and the acts in the laws. They speak to people in the measure of their understanding, and manifest at all times what is most beneficial for their hereafters. A poet said of such people:

With the water of the unseen make your ablution,
If you have the secret; and if not, with earth or stone.

Send forth an imam whom you once placed behind you,
And offer the dawn prayer when the afternoon comes.

This is the prayer of those who know their Lord;
If you are one of them, sprinkle the ocean upon the land.

The second group are those who retain the water and give it to others. This is the way of the outward scholars, particularly in our times, who memorize things and then recite what they have memorized. The Beloved ﷺ described how they benefit other people by retaining the water of the unseen, though they do not benefit from it themselves except in the form of the payment they receive for retaining it. They will be rewarded, but the first group will benefit from their retention of the water of the unseen by drinking, watering their animals, and irrigating.

Then there is the third group, the abyss that neither retains the water nor produces plants; they neither receive reward for outard memorization, nor possess the secret of preserving the inward Lights. God spare us!

Knowledge, then, is not merely a matter of memorizing then reciting what you have memorized. This makes you no better than an audiorecording. True knowledge is to learn the verse, then act upon it, then reap the fruit of your action in the form of Lights by which you understand God's intent. It is then that you may give each thing its rightful due with courtesy, spiritual state, and experiential taste.

Al-ʿAyn: The Eye/Entity-in-Itself

In the terminology of the Karkarī Order, the ʿayn[1] as an "entity-in-itself" is the secret of the trace and the holy essence of a thing. It is the disclosure-site of the universal will from which the manifestations of relative and perspectival traces spring forth. It is the root of the branch, the seed of the tree, the law of existence that demarcates the contours of separative entities. It is the subtlety that can only be perceived in the illusory realm of the senses. Wherever the trace is, there is the entity-in-itself; the locus is one, but the perspective differs.

Concerning the ʿayn as eye, Al-Ghazālī ﷺ says:

There are two eyes (sing. ʿayn): one outward, another inward. The outward eye is of the sensory and visible world ; the inward eye is of another world, the spiritual realm (malakūt). Each eye has a sun and a Light which makes it able to see properly. One of these suns is outward, the other inward. The outward sun is of the visible world, i.e. the physical sun. The inward sun is of the spiritual realm; it is the Qurʾān and God's revealed Scriptures. When this is fully unveiled to you, the first door to the

---

1   The Arabic word ʿayn means "eye; spring; source; identity; entity," all of which meanings are relevant here.

spiritual realm will be opened to you. This realm contains wonders that make the visible world seem trifling.

The one who does not travel to this world, but is held back by his shortcomings in the lowlands of the visible world, is still a beast and is deprived of the distinguishing characteristic of man. Indeed he is even lower than a beast, for the beasts do not have the potential to ascend to this world. Thus God says, **Such as these are like cattle. Nay, they are even further astray.**[1] The visible world in relation to the spiritual world is as the husk to the kernel, like the body to the spirit, like darkness to Light, like below to above. This is why the spiritual world is called the higher world, the world of the spirit, the world of light, as opposed to the lower world of corporeality and darkness.[2]

God says, **Did We not make for him two eyes?**[3] This alludes to the eye of Lights and secrets, and the eye of the senses and alterity. The possessor of the luminous eye of the heart sees existence as Lights overflowing from the magnificent oceans of the Essence, descending to the meadows of the spiritual world, then to the receptacles of the physical kingdom. He sees nothing but the Lights of the Real, and beholds creation as a mirror for the Creator's self-disclosures, moons upon whose essences the sun of existence shines. The oneness of uncreated reality does not veil him from beholding the multiplicity of creation, for although these entities are immutable in God's pre-eternal

1   Q An'ām 7:179.
2   *Mishkāt al-anwār*, p. 10.
3   Q Balad 90:8.

knowledge, they are nonexistent in the realm of illusory existence. They are affirmed but have no existence; they possess affirmation in the realm of illusion, but have no existence in the imagal or imaginary realm. They do not catch a whiff of existence whatsoever, even though they are witnessed by the pre-eternal eye, and distinguished within it in their nonexistence and in their composition, without being separate from the realm of possibility.

In contrast, the sensory eye discerns delimited things and spatial directions that are harbored in the realm of illusion. The one who beholds delimited things is unable to look upwards to behold pure meaning. Such a person seeks proof for the Real in illusory things, and for necessity in possibility, and for the Creator in creation, and for subsistence in annihilation. How strange! Can there be proof for Him in that which is attributed to Him? This eye is sensory and can see only what is sensory; it is delimited by its lids and lashes, conquered by the bow of the eyebrow above it; delimited by the lids, veiled by the brow.

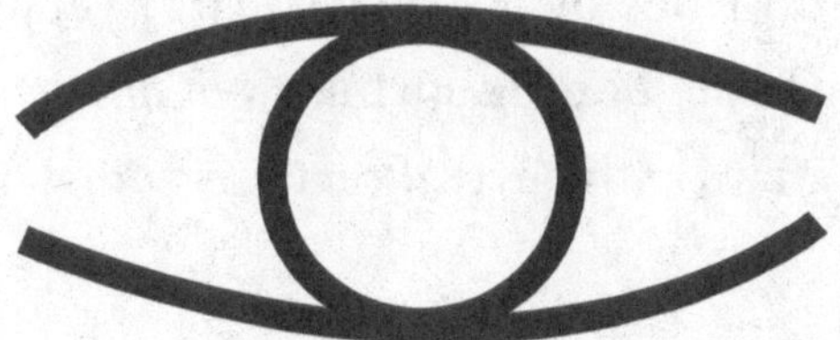

It its material composition, the eye is the locus of opposites, for it combines the opposing colors of white and black. This is why the eyes of the Universal Man ﷺ are described as having very black pupils and very white whites; for he ﷺ truly brought together opposites. The shape of the eye also brings together opposing arcs, which delimit the eye both horizontally and vertically. This is why it is the gate to the body and the spirit. The eye is thus the prophetic allusion and the Muḥammadan tiding for those who possess lordly gnostic sciences, disclosures of the All-Merciful, and holy secrets, as he ﷺ said, "I am the City of Knowledge, and ʿAlī is its gate. He who would enter the city must go through the gate."[1]

The word *ʿayn* is also used in the terminology of those who are worthy of the Presence to mean the Perfect Man, the source (*ʿayn*) of sources. For he is the very source of existence, having realized the nature of the supreme isthmus. He is the locus of the Gaze, the eye-witnessed reality transcendent beyond alterity and otherness, the demonstrative proof of direct witnessing without conjunction or disjunction of his All-Merciful breaths, the ultimate root of delimitation and nondelimitation, and the essence of all things. Every *ʿayn* draws from his *ʿayn*, whether it knows it or not. Indeed he is every *ʿayn*, for he proceeds from every soul and rules over every spirit. Every kind of *ʿayn* belongs to him: the **boiling spring** (*ʿayn āniya*),[2] the **flowing spring** (*ʿayn jāriya*),[3] the **eye of certainty** (*ʿayn al-yaqīn*),[4] the

1   *Mustadrak*, 4574.
2   Q Ghāshiya 88:5.
3   Q Ghāshiya 88:12.
4   Q Takāthur 102:7

murky spring *('ayn ḥami'a),*[1] the **fount of molten copper** *('ayn al-qiṭr),*[2] the **coolness of the eye** *(qurrat 'ayn),*[3] and so on.

The folk of presence say that there are seventy 'ayns, as per the number of the veils between God and creation. Therefore the eye has seventy veils and seventy languages. The vastness of the cosmos and the sum of all sensory things are engraved within it. When it is decorated with the kohl of eternity by the hand of a lordly Mediator, and its Light shines forth, the eye of inner vision gains master over it and it becomes the door to the spirit.

The Prophet ﷺ said, "Beware the believer's perspicacity, for he sees by the Light of God." Then he recited, **Truly in that are signs for those who discern.**[4] The luminous eye has the power to read the language of the eyes, plunge into their depths, and discern the veils through the colors of the lens.

The great principle behind this is the blessed prophetic ḥadīth narrated by Abū Razīn al-'Aqīlī, who said, 'I asked the Messenger of God ﷺ, "Where was our Lord before He created the heavens and the earth?" He replied, "In a Cloud with no air above it and no air below it."'[5] The secret of perspicacity lies in the word *'amā'* (cloud), which is the code for deciphering the languages of the eyes, by the Light of God.

---

1   Q Kahf 18:86.
2   Q Saba' 34:12.
3   Q. Sajda 32:17, et al.
4   Q Ḥijr 15:75. Tirmidhī, *Jāmi'*, 3071.
5   Ibn Ḥibbān, *Ṣaḥīḥ* 6275.

'Amā' is composed of the letters *'Ayn, Mīm, Alif,* and *Hamza.* The secret thus begins with the letter *'Ayn,* whose numerical value is seventy, corresponding to the number of veils between God and creation. Then comes the Muḥammadan Mīm, which expresses a circle of annihilation that changes from one name to the next; for the name is the designation of the individual's existence. Then comes the subtle flow of the Singular *Alif,* qualified by the *Hamza* in motion.

Therefore our master the Messenger of God ﷺ is the true Universal Man, the first one to fully comprehend the true meaning of his name. When the first letter of his name, the Mīm whose value is forty, was complete, he went into seclusion in the Cave of Ḥirā' and plunged into it with his entire being, which was the sensory Mīm. God then transformed this Mīm into an essential Alif, and so he is Muḥammad on earth and Aḥmad in Heaven.

Ask the people of remembrance, if you know not

God Almighty says, **We sent no messengers before thee, save men unto whom We revealed—ask the people of remembrance, if you know not.**[1] The remembrance of God is the door to the divine Presence, the prism of the beatific vision, the secret of disclosures, the gate of spiritual openings, the water of ablution from the impurities of engendered being and sensoriality. Through it the glory of the herebelow and the nobility of the hereafter are attained. The Prophet ﷺ said, urging us to engage in remembrance and praising those who do, "Go forth! There is Mount Jumdān. The *mufarridūn*[2] have gone ahead." His Companions said, "Who are the *mufarridūn*, Messenger of God?" He replied, "They are the men and women who remember God much."[3]

---

1   Q Naḥl 16:43.

2   Translator's note: A *mufarrid* can mean someone who is single-minded or singled out. Moreover, while *tawḥīd* means to declare God's oneness, *tafrīd* means to proclaim God's exclusive singularity. Hence, the *mufarridūn* in Sufi texts can mean those who realize the highest level of *tawḥīd* and abandon themselves in God.

3   Muslim, *Ṣaḥīḥ*, 4840.

'Abd Allāh ibn Bishr ⬥ related that a man said, "Messenger of God, the laws of Islam are too much for me. Tell me something I can hold onto." He ⬥ replied, "Keep your tongue moist with the remembrance of God."[1]

Abū Mūsā ⬥ related that the Messenger of God ⬥ said, "The one who remembers his Lord and the one who does not are like the living and the dead."[2]

Abū al-Dardā' related that the Prophet ⬥ said, "Shall I not inform you of the best of your deeds, and the purest in the sight of your Master, which raises you to the highest degrees, and is better for you than spending gold and silver in charity, and better than confronting and fighting against your enemy, striking one another's necks?" The Companions answered, "What is it, Messenger of God?" He replied, "The remembrance of God."[3]

Those who remember God are the first to reach the pavilions of glory. They are a mercy for the inhabitants of earth. Whoever keeps their company will not be disappointed; whoever stays by their side will not be wronged. The least of them are great in God's sight, and the lowliest of them are glorious in His measure. Togetherness with God has illuminated their inner beings. They have swept all that is other-than-God from their hearts, so that they can embrace His magnificence. Their remembrance is a luminous connection, unbroken by heedlessness. Neither buying nor selling distract them from the

1   Tirmidhī, *Jāmiʿ*, 3322.
2   Bukhārī, *Ṣaḥīḥ*, 5955.
3   Ibn Mājah, *Sunan*, 3788.

remembrance of God. The Almighty says, **Make thy soul patient with those who call upon their Lord morning and evening, desiring His Face. Turn not thine eyes away from them, desiring the adornment of the life of this world, nor obeying one whose heart We have made heedless of the remembrance of Us and who follows his caprice and whose affair exceeds the bounds.**[1]

He also says, proclaiming the virtue of the people of remembrance in the stations of divine proximity: **For submitting men and submitting women, believing men and believing women, devout men and devout women, truthful men and truthful women, patient men and patient women, humble men and humble women, charitable men and charitable women, men and women who fast, men and women who guard their private parts, men and women who remember God often, God has prepared forgiveness and a great reward.**[2] This verse contains ten stations, of which remembrance is the highest.

Behold, may the Lord guide you, how God commands us to ask the people of remembrance, and how He singled them out from among all the people of knowledge. This is because they are truly knowledgeable, for they act on what they know, and are aware of the machinations and devices of the soul. They behold divine power from behind the veil of wisdom, and are plunged in the ocean of lordly knowledge.

1   Q Kahf 18:28.
2   Q Aḥzāb 33:35.

So if you would ask, you must seek out the people of Light, for they possess the cure to reach the presence of the Real. To be near them is mercy, and to enter their presence is to be chosen by God.

Ask those who have a permanent connection to the divine Presence, and whose knowledge subsists through God's knowledge. Ask those who read, in the Name of their Lord, the true nature of their souls; and when they came to know themselves, they knew every soul, and no ailment was hidden from them. They treat these ailments with the Lights of nearness, a balm for the darkness of separation and distance.

May God reward Sidi al-Būzīdī (d. 1909) who said:

Every jurist knows what is required and recommended,
As for me, my knowledge is tremendous and unlimited.

I am the cupbearer, serving my own dear wine;
I am the veil-lifter, and the Presence is mine.

Many an unschooled man has come to join my Way,
And transformed into a wise one, a master of his day.

Take off thy sandals, disappear, if you would approach me;
I am the wellspring of life, if you would know me.

I am the eye of certitude, if you seek to behold,
I am the Path; in my grasp the cosmos I hold.

The world is a mirage, as the Holy Book describes;
Nothing but dust in the wind, for those who realize.

My dot emerged from the oceans of invincibility,
Colored by dominion, clothed in humanity.

Joseph's Shirt

God says, [Jacob said,] "Take this shirt of mine and cast it upon my father's face; he will come to see. And bring me your family, all together."[1]

In "The Spirit of Elucidation," (*Rūḥ al-Bayān*), the Qur'ān exegete al-Būrsawī cites God's Messenger ﷺ on the authority of Anas ibn Mālik as saying: "When the tyrant Nimrod threw Abraham into the fire, God sent down Gabriel with a shirt and rug from Paradise. He placed the shirt upon him and the rug beneath him, and sat there conversing with him. Abraham passed this shirt on to Isaac, and he to Jacob, and he to Joseph."[2]

The shirt is at once a formal symbol of the sensory human realm, and a supra-formal reality of sheer union when it manifests in the station of **Yea, we bear witness**. In the beautiful story of Joseph, it not only symbolizes illness—for God says, **And they brought forth his shirt with false blood. He said, "Nay, your souls have seduced you in this matter. Beautiful patience! And God is the One Whose help is sought against that which you describe"**[3]—but also healing. It is thus a disclosure-site of the secret of opposites.

1   Q Yūsuf 12:93.
2   Ḥaqqī, *Rūḥ al-Bayān*, 4/314.
3   Q Yūsuf 12:18.

The Perfect Man is the essence of existence and the secret of being, for he is the comprehensive sum of the meanings of the cosmic book. This is why he is blessed; and wherever he goes, the divine Lights go. Everything his essence touches is decorated with the talisman of guidance and providential care. This is how Khiḍr got his name; for everywhere he went, the ground would burst into greenery (*khuḍar*) because of his blessing. God's folk, annihilated in the Muḥammadan Light, have themselves become Light, for they are totally cleansed of the impurities of sensoriality and divested of human delimitations. Whatever they touch, be it a rosary, a staff, or a garment, a brand of their Light is transferred—without separation or division—onto that thing. The Light affects it and changes its properties. This is why the righteous seek blessings from one another's garments. It is related that Imam Aḥmad ibn Ḥanbal sought blessing by drinking the water in which the shirt of Imam Shāfiʿī had been washed, may God be pleased with them all.

Al-Baqlī said:

The wisdom of [Joseph] sending the shirt [to Jacob] was that he knew that Jacob would not be able to bear a full reunion all at once. He therefore arranged for the reunion to take place in stages, so that he would not die of joy as soon as they met. Therefore he sent the shirt so that its scent would give him strength and consolation.

Also, Jacob's eyes had turned white, but he was not completely blind; it was only that their light had faded somewhat. So Joseph sent the shirt to heal his eyes before he looked upon his son once more, the shock of which would have burned away the rest of their light.

What is more, the shirt had been made in Paradise, and Joseph was aware of His Lord's jealousy, and so he sent it to his father so that he would begin by scenting the fragrance of divine nearness. Finally, the shirt was a sign between Joseph and his father.

The same spirit is present in the custom of the Shaykh giving his disciple the patched garment (*muraqqa'a* or *khirqa*), so that blessings are instilled in his essence, and his inward vision is cured of the vision of sensory objects, and so that the Lights of divine domination descend through the levels of the colors dominion and become subtle; for the disciple's spirit could not withstand for the Lights of Beauty to be unveiled to him all at once, just as the delimited sensory eye could not stand to behold the sun of supra-sensory meaning all at once. Ibn 'Ajība says in his commentary "The Vast Ocean," (*Al-Baḥr al-Madīd*):

God has given humanity two sensory eyes with which to perceive sensory objects, and has give the heart two supra-sensory eyes to perceive supra-sensory meanings. The first is called outward vision, the second inward vision. One of the heart's eyes sees the Lights of the Law, and the other sees the secrets of Reality. The heart can become enveloped by the darkness of unbelief, covering both these eyes. This is blindness of inner vision. Or it can be covered by the darkness of sin, selfish interests, and caprice, so that the eye of Reality becomes blinded while the eye of Law remains protected, and the heart can still see something. The company of a gnostic Shaykh is required to provide this shirt and say, "Take this shirt of mine and cast it upon the face of your inner vision, and it will be able to know as well as to see. When this shirt approaches it, the breeze of arrival blows upon it and it becomes ecstatic."[1]

The shirt, then, is a spiritual allusion which the Inheritor Shaykh casts upon the eye of the heart of the disciple who seeks to know God. From it he catches the scent of spiritual opening and intimate union, and through it the meanings of Josephian beauty and Muḥammadan perfection are disclosed to him.

This, moreover, is a mercy that the Shaykhs extend to their disciples. For the awesome assault of divine Beauty overwhelms the sensory human realm, annihilates it, and sweeps away its illusory existence. The heart of the disciple cannot bear this in the beginning, and indeed it could draw him into a state of total divine attraction, rendering him a madman who is imprisoned in his station and neither benefits others nor is able to tread the path. Therefore the wisdom of the shirt is to provide consolation, to evoke the awesome power of the divine Presence, and to teach proper courtesy.

1   *Al-Baḥr al-Madīd,* p. 306.

Hast Thou not Seen?

A distinct Qur'ānic expression with which the Almighty addresses His noble Prophet ﷺ over thirty times in the Qur'ān is, **Has thou not seen?** This teaches his Community that direct witnessing (*mushāhada*) is a foundational Qur'ānic principle for gnosis and unveiling, and a path for reaching the truth of certainty. God says:

Hast thou not seen that unto God prostrates whosoever is in the heavens and whosoever is on the earth, the sun, the moon, the stars, the mountains, the trees, and the beasts, and many among mankind? But for many the punishment has come due. Whomsoever God disgraces, none can ennoble. Truly God does whatsoever He will.[1]

Hast thou not seen how God sets forth a parable? A good word is as a good tree: its roots firm and its branches in the sky.[2]

Hast thou not seen thy Lord, how He spreads out the shade—and had He willed, He could have made it still—and then We make the sun an indicator of it.[3]

---

1   Q Ḥajj 22:18.
2   Q Ibrāhīm 14:24.
3   Q Furqān 25:45.

Hast thou not seen that God makes the night pass into the day and makes the day pass into the night, and that He made the sun and the moon subservient, each running for a term appointed, and that God is Aware of whatsoever you do?[1]

Hast thou not seen that God sends down water from the sky, wherewith We bring forth fruits of diverse colors? And in the mountains are streaks of white and red, of diverse hues, and others pitch-black.[2]

Have you not seen how God created the seven heavens one upon another?[3]

Hast thou not seen how thy Lord dealt with the masters of the elephant?[4]

In every verse containing the words **Hast thou not seen**, there is a teaching for the Messenger ﷺ that pertains to witnessing the disclosure-sites of God in the levels of being, whether it be the secrets of the oceans, earths, mountains, and plants, the glorifications of all created things, or the conditions of the communities of old.

For the seeker, **Hast thou not seen** is the station of the separation of union (*farq al-jamʿ*), which is a voyage (*siyāḥa*) through the forms of the spiritual realm to obtain knowledge, then to return with it to the station of union. This return from separation to union is manifested in God's words, **Read in the**

1   Q Luqmān 31:29.
2   Q Fāṭir 35:27.
3   Q Nūḥ 71:15.
4   Q Fīl 105:1.

Name of thy Lord Who created,[1] for any knowledge that does not take you back to the presence of divine Oneness is a step by step journey to deception, not a spiritual opening.

Direct knowledge of God, then, is not authenticated through a veridical dream alone. The true dream is certainly part of gnosis, for it is the first stage of unveiling; authentic narrations state that revelation for the Messenger of God ﷺ began with true dreams that he saw as plainly as the dawn. The true dream is one forty-sixth of prophethood, for these dreams visited him ﷺ for six months, while the total period of the revelation spanned twenty-three years.

Sainthood, for its part, is the shadow of prophethood, for the Prophet receives revelation of law, while the saint receives revelation of inspiration. God says of the mother of Moses, **So We revealed to the mother of Moses, "Nurse him. But if you fear for him, then cast him into the river, and fear not, nor grieve. Surely We shall bring him back to you and make him one of the messengers."**[2] The Prophet ﷺ reportedly used to say, "In the communities before you, there were people who were spoken to (*muḥaddathūn*); if there were one such in my Community, it would be 'Umar ibn al-Khaṭṭāb."[3]

Unveiling and sainthood, then, are not matters of sensoriality, sleep, and feelings; they are matters of explicit unveiling unaccompanied by even an atom's weight of doubt, enduring

---

1   Q 'Alaq 96:1.
2   Q Qaṣaṣ 28:7.
3   Muslim, *Ṣaḥīḥ*, 2398.

constantly without interruption. It was from this station that the great masters spoke when they made such utterances as Abū al-'Abbās al-Mursī, may God sanctify his secret: "If the Messenger of God ﷺ were to be absent from me for even the blink of an eye, I would no longer number myself among the Muslims."

The one who is asleep is dead. How can he wake another when he himself needs someone to wake him? The one who lacks something cannot give it. This is in no way meant to detract from the status of the true dream, but only to explain things to anyone who wishes to enter the Presence of the All-Knowing King.

Direct witnessing in the waking world is built upon certain foundations and principles which must be adhered to; for to slip in this matter is to fall into great peril. God establish them in the verse, **God is the Light of the heavens and the earth**: they are the Niche, the Lamp, the Glass, and the Resplendent Planet. Every disclosure must be brought back to these principles; for as the saying goes, "virtue lies in returning to one's roots." All of these levels or roots must be kindled from the Blessed Tree, which is the perfected Shaykh who constitutes an isthmus between worlds, and beholds the higher realms while proclaiming the oneness of worlds and dimensions.

Anyone who travels the path without a guide will stumble, even if he believes himself to have arrived. The climb is steep, and the maladies of the soul are subtle and difficult to see. Therefore the guide is the genuine disciple's mirror, displaying to him all his hidden blemishes and cracks, showing him the truth of his soul, wresting from him all the instruments of his self-adoration, pretension, and hypocrisy. This mirror lifts the veil of human nature from him, and takes him on a voyage through the cosmos of his existence.

Direct witnessing in the waking world is thus an indispensable pillar of the journey to God. There can be no gnosis without direct witnessing. The station of spiritual excellence in reality is nothing other than realization of direct witnessing; that is, to worship God as if you see Him (*ka-annaka tarāh*); to worship Him through the Kāf of imaginal similitude.

Chapter II

Āyat al-Nūr: The Verse of Spiritual Opening

The Verse of Spiritual Opening

God is the Light of the heavens and the earth. The likeness of His Light is as a niche, wherein is a lamp. The lamp is in a glass. The glass is as a resplendent planet kindled from a blessed olive tree, neither of the East nor of the West. Its oil would well-nigh shine forth, even if no fire had touched it. Light upon light! God guides unto His Light whomsoever He will, and God sets forth likenesses for mankind, and God is Knower of all things. In houses that God has permitted to be raised and wherein His Name is remembered, He is therein glorified morning and evening, by men whom neither trade nor buying and selling distract from the remembrance of God, the performance of prayer, and the giving of alms, fearing a day when eyes and hearts will be turned about, that God may reward them for the best of that which they have done, and increase them from His Bounty. And God provides for whomsoever He will without reckoning.[1]

We call this verse the verse of spiritual opening (*āyat al-fatḥ*) because it encapsulates the levels of direct witnessing and spiritual opening, beyond the disclosures of images and forms. God Almighty begins the verse with an expression of the pure

---

1   Q Nūr 24:35-38.

oneness of the attributes, declaring, **God is the Light.** He brings together all the attributes in the attribute of Light, and describes Himself as the Light of all Lights. All things are kindled from His Light, and He is their reality; and the cosmos is His descent in the illusory realm. He alone is truly Light, and shares this with no other. Without Light, there can be no perception. Ghazālī ﷺ says:

To explain this, one must consider the meaning of Light according to the first sense used by the common believer, then the second sense used by the elite, then the third sense used by the elite of the elite. Then one must consider the realities of the levels of Lights as described by the elite of the elite, in order to recognize that God is the Highest Most Sublime Light, and that He alone is the true Light, and has no partner in this...[1]

Indeed, I do not hesitate to say that when the name Light is used to mean anything other than the First Light, which is God Almighty, it can only be in a figurative sense; for all that is not Him possesses no Light whatsoever in and of itself, but borrows its Light from another. Its Light is sustained not by itself, but by another, and it is only figuratively that a borrowed thing can be attributed to the one who borrows it. If a man borrows a horse and riding apparel, and rides it when and as the lender allows, can we call it "his" in anything but a figurative sense? Is it the lender who owns it, or the borrower? Without doubt, the borrower is as poor as can be, and the lender is the rich one, for

---

1   Ghazālī, *Mishkāt al-anwār,* p. 4.

it is he who lends and owns, and it is he who will take his possessions back in the end.

True Light, then, is He in Whose hand is the creation and the command, and from Whom comes illumination first and perpetual bestowal second. None can share the true meaning of this name with Him or lay claim to it, except in the sense that He Himself extends it to them and graces them with the name, in the manner of a master who gives something to his slave and then calls him its owner. If the truth is revealed to the slave, he will realize that both he and his possessions belong to his master alone, and that he has no share in them whatsoever.

Now that you understand that Light goes back to God's self-manifestation, His bringing into manifestation, and the levels of manifestation, know also that there is no darkness darker than the concealment of nonexistence. A thing is called "dark" because there is no way for the faculty of sight to reach it. The eyesight cannot arrive at it even though in itself it does exist. But if a thing does not exist at all, neither to others nor to itself, does it not deserve to be called the darkest thing of all, opposed to existence, which is Light? For if the very essence of a thing does not manifest in itself, then it cannot manifest to others.

Existence may be divided into what a thing possesses intrinsically, and what it possesses extrinsically. If a thing's existence is from outside itself, then its existence is borrowed and it cannot sustain itself. Considered in and of itself, it is pure nonexistence, and exists only in relation to other than itself. That is not real existence, as we saw above in the example of the borrower and the lender. The true existent is God, just as the true Light is God.

From here, the knowers of God ascend from the depths of metaphors to the heights of realities. They complete their ascension and behold with eye-witnessing that there is nothing in existence but God, and that **All things are perishing, save His Face.**[1]

This verse does not mean that **things** will perish at some particular moment, but that they have always been perishing and always will be. It cannot be otherwise, for everything but Him is simply nonexistent when viewed in and of itself, and is only existent when viewed in respect of the existence that flows to it from God, the Prime Reality. Things are not existent in themselves, but solely in respect of their Existentiator. The only existent is the Face of God Almighty.

Everything therefore has two "faces," one toward itself and the other toward its Lord. And since nothing truly exists but God and His Face, **All things** have always been, and will always be, **perishing, save His Face.** The knowers of God do not need to wait until the Day of Resurrection to hear the Creator's call, **Whose is the sovereignty this Day? It is God's, the One, the All-Subjugating;**[2] for they are hearing this call at all times. They

1   Q. Qaṣaṣ 28:88.
2   Q. Ghāfir 40:16.

do not take the expression "God is Greater" (*Allāhu akbar*) to mean that He is greater than other things—far be it, for nothing exists alongside Him such that He would be greater than it. Nothing is at the level of being alongside Him, or even subordinate to Him; nothing but Him exists at all, except in respect of its facing Him. What exists is His Face alone, and it could not be said that He is greater than His own Face. What the expression means is that He is greater than any suggestion of comparison or analogy, greater than any notion of His greatness being apprehended by another, even a Prophet or an angel. No one but God can truly know God; and it would not befit the Majesty and Grandeur of God to be reduced to an object of knowledge within the gnostic's grasp.[1]

God then provides a parable of the levels of disclosure of His Light and its descent into the hearts of His beloved ones. The fact that He represents the levels of His Light is proof that the beatific vision is possible in this world; for if it were impossible, He would not have likened His Light to anything. He can therefore be seen in this world by one whose spirit-eye has been opened by a mentoring Shaykh. Ibn Mas'ūd read the verse as, **The likeness of His Light in the believer's heart is as a niche,** and Ubayy ibn Ka'b read it as, **The likeness of the light of the heart of the one who believes.**[2] If the vision were impossible, then Moses the Confidant of God ﷺ would not have requested

---

1   *Mishkāt al-anwār*, p. 14-16.
2   *Mishkāt al-anwār*, p. 24.

it by saying, **My Lord, show me, that I might look upon Thee.**[1] The Prophets know the Law better than anyone, and they would never ask God for something that contravenes it.

The secret of the parable described in this verse is that it represents a method, rooted in divine immanence, for bringing down supra-sensory meanings into tangible forms. There is a correspondence and parallelism between the sensory and supra-sensory realms, and every atom in the illusory world of the senses is an expression of a meaning that exists in the spiritual worlds. This is akin to how the meanings of dreams may be brought down and explained in terms of sensory phenomena. To this effect, Ghazālī, may God sanctify his secret, says:

The science of dream interpretation illustrates how parables are made, for dreams are one fortieth of prophethood. Consider how in dreams, the sun represents the sultan because of the spiritual meaning they have in common, namely dominance and influence over all. The moon represents the minister, for the sun shines its light upon the world through the mediation of the moon when it is absent, just as the sultan shines his lights through the minister upon those who are not in the sultan's presence. If a man dreams that he has upon his hand a signet ring with which he seals the mouths and loins of men and women, this symbolizes that he will be a muezzin who calls for the prayer before dawn in Ramaḍān. If a man dreams that he is

1   Q Aʻrāf 7:143.

pouring oil into an olive, this means that his concubine is his own mother, unbeknownst to him.

I could give endless other examples to convince you of this, but what I will say is that just as some higher spiritual beings may be symbolized by the sun, moon, and stars, others may be symbolized by other things when you consider characteristics other than luminosity. For example, if a higher spiritual being is immutable and never changes, great and never diminishes; and if waters of esoteric sciences flow from it into the valleys of human hearts, carrying precious minerals of unveiling, then it is symbolized by the Mountain. If the beings that receive those precious minerals are of diverse quality, some superior to others, then they are symbolized by the Valley. If after those precious minerals connect with human hearts, they flow from one heart to another, then those hearts are also valleys. The head of the valley represents the hearts of the Prophets, then the sages, then those who follow them. If these valleys are lower than the first and receive their water from it, the first must surely be the **right bank of the blessed valley,**[1] on account of its righteousness and exalted status...

But if **the spirit of the Prophet is a luminous lamp,**[2] and this lamp is kindled by the mediation of Revelation, as God says, **We revealed unto thee a spirit from Our Command,**[3] then the symbol of the source of that kindling is fire. Those who receive

<hr>

1   Q Qaṣaṣ 28:30.
2   Q Aḥzāb 33:45-46.
3   Q Shūrā 42:52.

from the Prophets are divided into those who merely emulate what they hear, and those who have a portion of inner vision. The symbol of the one who merely emulates is the report, while the symbol of the one graced with inner vision is a fire-brand, torch, or meteor. The one who has experiential taste shares in some of the Prophet's states, which is symbolized by warming: to be warmed by a fire, one must be near it, not merely hear a report of it.

If the first station of the Prophets is the ascent to the realm hallowed beyond the turbidity of sense and fantasy, that station is symbolized by the **Holy Valley**. One cannot tread upon that **valley** without first doffing the two worlds, the herebelow and the hereafter, and turning toward the One Real. The herebelow and the hereafter are adjacent counterpart states in which the luminous human substance dwells, and therefore they may be doffed and donned at will. The symbol of their doffing is the **removal of the sandals**[1] for entrance into the consecrated state, when one turns toward the Ka'ba of Holiness.

Indeed let us ascend to the Presence of Lordship once more, and say that if there is anything in that Presence by which knowledge in all its diversity is engraved upon the substances that receive it, it is symbolized by the **Pen**. The element in those

---

1   Hast thou heard tell of Moses, when he saw a fire and said unto his
     family, "Stay here. Verily I perceive a fire. Perhaps I shall bring you a
     brand therefrom, or find guidance at the fire"? Then when he came to
     it, he was called, "O Moses! Verily I am thy Lord. Take off thy sandals.
     Truly thou art in the holy valley of Ṭuwā. Q Ṭā Hā 20:9-12.

receiving substances that first receives is symbolized by the **Preserved Tablet**, while the element that transmits to others is symbolized by the **Outspread Parchment**. If there is something above the inscribing Pen that controls it, its symbol is the **Hand**. If there is something that embodies and orders the combined presence of **Hand, Tablet, Pen, Book,**[1] then its symbol is the Image. If the human image has its own order in the same likeness, then it bears the Image of the All-Merciful. There is a difference between saying "the image of the All-Merciful" and "the image of God", for the divine Mercy is what caused the divine Presence to have this image. Then God graced Adam and gave to him His own Image, which comprised and embraced every genus in the world, as if he himself were the world entire, or a comprehensive copy of it. This Image—the Image of Adam— was inscribed in God's own Script, the divine Script that is neither character nor letter, for His Script transcends both, just as His Speech transcends voice and syllable, His Pen transcends wood and reed, and His Hand transcends flesh and bone. If not for this mercy, the human being would be unable to know his Lord, for one cannot know one's Lord unless one knows oneself.[2]

Therefore we shall explain the verse to you by beginning from, and returning to, your own self. Our proof for this is found in God's own words: **Whosoever is rightly guided is**

1   The Qur'ānic images cited in this passage can be found in Q Qalam 68:1; Burūj 85:22; Ṭūr 52:3; Fatḥ 48:10.
2   *Mishkāt al-anwār*, pp. 24-26.

only rightly guided to his own soul, and whosoever is astray is only astray from it;[1] that is, the one who is guided is only guided to knowledge of his soul and its secrets and levels, and the one who is astray is only astray from its secret, which is hidden between the refuse of human nature and the blood of the world.

---

1   Q Isrā' 17:15.

The Niche

In the terminology of the Karkarī Order, the Niche (*mish-kāt*) is the breast consoled by the company of God, prepared to respond to the summons of **read**[1] from the presence of union until it expands to accommodate the lordly meaning.

The Niche is the purified hidden cave, the heart of every lover chosen by eternity for the tidings of the Light of divine nurture, his inner eye decorated with the kohl of preeternal glory, his heart caressed by the purity of love, its courtyard honored to receive it as a guest, by the authority of **He loves them, and they love Him.**[2] Reflect on this, may God have mercy on you, and think deeply about these eternal words. **He loves them** first, though He is independent of them and has no need for their worship or remembrance, and then **they love Him.** When they draw nearer to Him by a hand's span, He draws nearer to them by an arm's length. When they go to Him walking, He goes to them running.

God says in a Holy Saying, "I, mankind, and the jinn are wrapped up in a tremendous tiding. I create, yet others are worshipped; I provide, yet others are thanked. My good descends

1   Q ʿAlaq 96:1.
2   Q Māʾida 5:54.

upon My servants, while their evil ascends to Me. I show them love through blessings though I have no need of them, and they show Me hatred through sin, though they are as needy of Me as can be. Those who remember Me are those who keep My company; whosoever would keep My company, let him remember Me. Those who obey Me are My beloved ones, yet I do not make those who disobey Me despair of My mercy. If they repent to Me, then I am their beloved. If they refuse, then I am their physician; I try them with misfortunes to cleanse them of faults. Should any of them approach Me to repent, I will go to meet him from afar. Should any of them turn away from Me, I will call to him from nearby, saying, 'Where are you going? Do you have any lord besides Me?' I reward good deeds tenfold, and punish evil deeds only once, or else pardon them. By My glory and majesty, if they were only to ask My forgiveness, I would forgive them."[1]

The Niche is the alcove in the wall of human nature. It is the heart vast enough to accommodate the self-disclosures of God's Identity. It is the Ḥirā' of meaning if you would understand it; the abode of mercy, the fortress of guidance. God says, **Take refuge in the cave. Your Lord will spread forth something of His Mercy for you, and make you incline to ease in your affair.**[2] And in a Ḥadīth Qudsī He says, "Neither My earth nor

---

1   The first part of the hadith is found in Bayhaqī, *Shu'ab*, 4238; the rest is attested to in several other ḥadīths, and the meaning is sound.

2   Q Kahf 18:16.

My heaven can contain Me, but the heart of My believing servant can contain Me."[1]

The Niche is heart upon which the breezes of divine attraction have blown, causing the human shell to pass away, and the "I" to be lifted and melted in the presence of the **Luminous Lamp**, who said, "None of you believes until I am more beloved to him than his child, his father, and all humanity."[2]

The Niche is the first symbol on the Path of Light. Through it, you leave behind human traces and forms, and stand upon the shore of the ocean of spiritual realities, awaiting the arrival of the ship of Lights, raising the sail of aspiration, awaiting the winds of grace to carry you forward, little by little, until it bears you across the waves of the Names and Attributes.

The first stage of the Path is that you make a Niche of your heart that can accommodate the lordly Presence, which loves and reveres all creation, and does not disparage any of God's creatures, for they are all disclosure-sites for the magnificence of the Lord, disclosure-sites for the power of the Real, disclosure-sites for the Names of the Master, who says, **And walk not exultantly upon the earth; surely thou shalt not penetrate the earth, nor reach the mountains in height.**[3] The proper conduct of the servant is that he should be humble and meek before the

---

1   Scholars have said much about this ḥadīth, and some have dismissed it as baseless and claimed that it suggests divine indwelling, but Ghazālī cites it in the *Iḥyā'*, and the Folk of God recognize that its meaning is sound. Muslim, *Ṣaḥīḥ*, 70.

2   Muslim, *Ṣaḥīḥ*, 70.

3   Q Isrā' 17:37.

manifestations of Lordship; that his "I" be erased by the "He." Ibn Kathīr, may God have mercy on him, said in commentary on this verse:

Nor [shall you] reach the mountains in height; that is, with your pride and self-satisfaction. Indeed, the one who attempts to do so may be punished with the opposite, as in the authentic narration, "Once in the days of old a man was walking along wearing two cloaks in which he took great pride, when suddenly the earth swallowed him up. His cries will echo therein until the Day of Resurrection." God related the same of Korah (*Qārūn*), who was strutting before the people in his finery when God caused the earth to engulf him and his home. Another ḥadīth declares, "When someone humbles himself for God, God lifts him up, so that although he disparages himself, other people think highly of him. When someone is proud, God lowers him, so that although he thinks highly of himself, other people disparage him until he becomes more hateful to them than a dog or a swine."[1]

Do not walk around feeling pleased with your lowly evil-enjoining soul, for you will not pass beyond the earth of your passionate nature, nor reach the station of God's Folk. They are the **sturdy mountains** which seem to you to be **fixed** due to your lack of inner vision, when in reality they **move like clouds**[2] with no air above or below them. God Almighty says of the station

---

1   Ibn Kathīr, *Tafsīr*, 5/75-76.
2   Q Naml 27:88.

of humility, **The servants of the Compassionate are those who walk humbly upon the earth, and when the ignorant address them, say, "Peace," and who pass the night before their Lord, prostrating and standing.**[1] Ibn Kathīr comments:

They walk without pride, exultation, arrogance, or conceit. This does not mean that they stagger along as though they are unwell in order to make a pretentious display of humility, for the Master of Mankind ﷺ would walk as though he were descending from on high, as though the earth were being rolled up for him. Some of the early Muslims spoke unfavorably about the affectation of weakness when walking. It is related that ʿUmar saw a young man walking very slowly and said, "What is the matter? Are you ill?" He replied, "No, Commander of the Faithful." So ʿUmar swung his whip at him and told him to walk with vigor. The meaning of **walk humbly** here is to walk with dignity and serenity, as the Messenger of God ﷺ said, "When you go to pray, do not go running there, but walk with dignity. Join the prayer whenever you arrive, and complete what you may have missed afterwards." ʿAbd Allāh ibn al-Mubārak related that Ḥasan al-Baṣrī said of this verse, "The believers are humble folk. By God, their hearing, sight, and limbs are so humble that you would think them ill, though they are not; they are healthy, by God, but they harbor fear within them, fear that others do not harbor. They are kept from the herebelow by what they know of the hereafter. They say, **Praise be to God, Who has dis-**

---

1   Q Furqān 25:63-64.

pelled grief from us,[1] yet by God, what grieves them is not what grieves other people. Their souls are not burdened by anything they might do in order to reach Paradise, but fear of Hell makes them weep. The one who is not consoled by God's consolation will be torn up with grief for the world. The one who sees God's favor only in his food and drink is short on knowledge, and bound to suffer."[2]

The Prophet ﷺ is reported to have said, "I saw people from my Community who have not yet been created, and who will come after this day. I love them, and they love me. They extend sincere counsel and generosity to one another. They walk with God's light gently among people, with discretion and reverence. They are safe from people, and people are safe from them, by virtue of their patience and forbearance. Their hearts echo with the remembrance of God. Their mosques are filled with their prayers. They are merciful to their young, and respectful to their elders. They comfort one another. The wealthy among them look after the poor, and the strong look after the weak. They visit their sick, and attend their funerals." Thereupon a man in the group said, "Are they kind to their slaves?" The Prophet ﷺ turned to him and replied, "No! They do not own slaves. They serve themselves. They are too noble to ask God for luxury, because of how lowly the herebelow is in the eyes of their Lord." Then the Prophet ﷺ recited: **The servants of the**

---

1 Q Fāṭir 35:34.
2 Ibn Kathīr, *Tafsīr* 6/121-122.

All-Merciful are those who walk humbly upon the earth.[1]

Humble yourself to God's folk, and humble yourself to all of God's creatures. Venerate a thing, and you will draw spiritual replenishment from it, and its true reality and inner secrets will be unveiled to you. Humility to creation is the essence of true might, true nobility, and true knowledge.

Sidi Abū Madyan, may God sanctify his secret, said of humility:

I was humbled in the land when you captured me,
Passion's pangs all around me, below and above;

If I had two hearts, I would keep one to live,
And let the other be tormented by your love.

The one who was better than me and you, may God bless him and give him peace, would let a slave-girl of Medina take him by the hand and lead him around where she wanted. He would show mercy to the young and affection to the old, and kiss infants. He ﷺ would mend his own sandals and patch his own garments, and was at his family's service. When he entered Mecca for the Conquest, he entered humbly with his noble head bowed in deference to God. The Niche of his heart was vast enough to accommodate the magnificence of the Real, and he saw how all things began and ended there, may God bless him and grant him peace.

---

1   Ibn ʿAjība, *al-Baḥr al-madīd,* 5/146.

The Lamp

In the terminology of the Karkarī Order, the Lamp (*miṣbāḥ*) is the secret of the heart's kernel, the disclosure-site of the breath that blows as the dark concealment of night gives way to bright dawn of gnosis, through "I loved to be known."

The Lamp is a luminous dot that falls into the servant's heart from a name or attribute, by the hand of a Shaykh who has arrived and can guide others to arrival. Its meaning flows through the disciple and lifts the veil that covers the inner vision, so that he wallows in the glorious lights of eternity, and his inner vision is drawn like a magnet toward the meadows of the spiritual world.

It is a wakeful inrush (*wārid*) that God casts into the heart of those who seek His Presence at the beginning of the path, rousing them from the sleep of heedlessness. The *wārid* allows them to arrive at the Real so that they may free themselves from the shackles of "where" and the prison of illusion.

It is the she-camel of meaning, and its Lights are the mount of gnostic truths and secrets which carry the disciple across the deserts and wastelands of his soul, stage by stage, purifying him from the pollutants of "where" and cleansing him of the dross of sensation. Upon it he travels from the worlds of alterities to the worlds of Lights and secrets.

The night of separation and distance is the garb of the heedless, for they take consolation in the external sensory world and are caught up in the games and diversions of the herebelow. It has tempted them with its delights, and the enemy has made it appear attractive to them, involving himself in their wealth and family, and making them forget the covenant of **Am I not your Lord?**.[1] He made them forget the honor of **I have breathed into him of My spirit**,[2] and the trust of, **I am placing a vicegerent upon the earth**.[3] Therefore they are always plunged in the night of separation and distance.

Sidi al-Ḥarrāq said, may God sanctify his secret:

Before today I wallowed
In separation and despair,

Always full of sorrow
In the dark night of "where".

Darkness implies remoteness and distance from direct knowledge of God; it is the disclosure-site of separation between the servant and the vision of the Lights of the attributes. When the night of the self falls upon a person and he longs for the glimmers of nearness, he finds consolation in the stellar Lights of the attributes. After looking for long enough, he

1   Q Aʿrāf 7:172.
2   Q Ḥijr 15:29.
3   Q Baqara 2:30.

becomes sick with desire and yearning, as God says: **Then he cast a glance at the stars and said, "Truly I am sick."**[1]

The serpent of passion sunk its fangs into my liver,
And no doctor or healer can tend it,

Save for the Beloved in whom I am enraptured,
For he has the antidote to mend it.

He yearns for the Lamp of the attributes that shines from the eastern sky of the Essence. He yearns for the Lamp of guidance that shines from the eastern sky of divine nurture, the Lamp of Lights that dispels the darkness of alterities. When this yearning becomes strong and his resolve solidifies, he tastes the inner meaning and wakes from the slumber of heedlessness, breaking the idol of his "I" with the axe of invocation. He depends no longer on his own selfish interests and caprices, nor on his knowledge, works, or states.

When the celestial lamp descends from the heavens of the unseen to the page of his yearning heart, bringing with it the Lights of guidance, the spirit is invigorated by the melodies of spiritual subtleties. It will behold physical forms to be **drunk, though drunk they are not**,[2] such are the marvels of witnessing.

---

1   Q Ṣāffāt 37:88-89.
2   Q Ḥajj 22:2.

The bond of prophethood is a Lamp of Light
In the heart's Niche, by revelation hanging.

By God, as Isrāfīl blows the Trumpet,
So is the spirit blown into my being.

When He discloses Himself to speak to me,
I see Moses upon Sinai standing![1]

The luminous Lamp is the army of the heart, bedazzled in the presence of the Real. To quote Ibn 'Ajība:

It unveils and clarifies things so that their beauty is clearly distinct from their ugliness; for it is the nature of the opened inner vision to judge beauty as beautiful and ugliness as ugly. The heart then approaches what it affirms to be beautiful, and turns away from what it affirms to be ugly. Or one could say that it approaches that wherein lies its welfare, and turns away from that wherein lies harm.

Consider, for example, a man who goes into a gloomy house containing scorpions and snakes, and also piles of gold and silver, but it is too dark for him to tell which is which, so he does not know what to avoid and what to grab. But if he fetches a lamp, he will be able to tell them apart and know what to avoid and what to trust. Just so, the heart of the sinful believer does not distinguish between the bitterness of sin and the sweetness

1   Attributed to Ḥallāj.

of obedience, but if it is illuminated by the Light of godconsciousness, it will be able to recognize what is good and bad for it, and tell truth from falsehood. God says, **O you who believe! If you reverence God, He will make for you a criterion;**[1] that is, a Light to tell truth from falsehood.[2]

One of al-Iskandarī's aphorisms reads, "Light is the army of the heart, just as darkness is the army of the soul. When God wants to help His servant, He replenishes his with armies of Light and severs his link to darkness and alterities." Sidi Ibn ʿAjība, may God sanctify his secret, says:

The soul, intellect, heart, spirit, and secret are all names for one single thing, which is the lordly luminous subtlety that has been placed in this dark corporeal shell. The reason it has different names is that it has different states and passes through different stages. It is like rainwater that falls upon the roots of a tree and then ascends through its branches, emerging as leaves, then light and blossoms, then forming fruits, which then grow until they are fully formed. The water is the same, but it has different names according to its stages…

This is the nature of the interaction of the heart with the soul. The "war" between them is a metaphor for the difficulty that lies in transporting the spirit from the abode of darkness, which is the seat of the soul, to the abode of Light, which is the heart and what lies beyond it. The heart battles the soul to

---

1   Q Anfāl 8:29.
2   *Īqāẓ al-himam,* p. 131.

return it to its origin, while it is always trying to sink back down to the earth of human nature, where its appetites lie. The heart has the Lights of inrushes to help it and draw it nearer, until it ascends to the presence that it is its original home. These Lights are in this sense its armies, strengthening and supporting it against the darkness of the soul. They are the first inrushes.

But when the soul inclines toward base appetites and indulges in them, they become its armies in a similar sense. They are darkness, for they veil it from the truth and prevent it from beholding the suns of gnosis. When the soul charges with its armies of darkness and appetite toward a sin or base desire, the heart meets it head-on with its armies of Light, and battle breaks out between them. If God wishes to help and succor His servant, he replenishes his heart with the armies of Light and cuts off the support of other-than-God from his soul, so that the Light overpowers the darkness and the soul is defeated. If God wishes to thwart His servant, He succors his soul with alterities and cuts off his heart from the support of the Lights. The one He succors obeys His command as it should be obeyed, while the one He forsakes does the opposite.

Shaykh Zarrūq ﷺ said, "The replenishments of Light are three in number: the first is certainty untainted by doubt; the second is knowledge accompanied by inner vision and lucidity; the third is inspiration that flows alongside witnessing. The replenishments of darkness too are three: the first is weak certainty; the second is the dominance of ignorance in the soul; the third is self-pity. All of this boils down to whether one is pleased with one's soul or not."[1]

The true nature of the Lamp is that it is a luminous force that transcends color, quantity, direction, perspective, and delimitation. It is like water which takes on the color of its glass vessel; hence God Almighty says, **The Lamp is in a Glass**. The levels of the Lamp can only be apprehended through the colorations of the heart-glass.

Suhrawardī said, may God sanctify his secret:

He purified them, so their hearts became pure for Him;
The Niche and the Lamp glowed in their Light.

They savored the moment of their wondrous nearness;
The cups were delicate, the wine a delight.

Dear friend, it is not right to blame the lover
If upon him the dawn of union shines bright,

Nor to find sin in those compelled by passion
To reveal the secrets they tried to hold tight.

They give themselves gladly, without hesitation,
For they know that in selflessness victory lies;

---

1   *Īqāẓ al-himam,* p. 130.

The herald of truth did call out to them,
And they set out at once in answer to his cries.

They sailed upon the ships of fervor,
Seeking only to reach His door,

Across the ocean of their aching tears,
Finding the key upon its shore.

Their only joy is the thought of their Beloved,
So joy is theirs, always and forever.

They left themselves behind and reached Him,
And cried out in dazzled awe together.

The curtains of subsistence were lifted for them;
He made them extinct, and away they were blown.

If you cannot match them, at least imitate them;
To imitate the saints is a victory on its own.

Arise, regretful one, and bring the cups,
To pass around a vintage sweet,

Of the grapes of grace in the jug of spirit,
Not trodden beneath any farmer's feet.

It is the wine of eternal love,
Wherein the mourner may find repose.

Noah in his Ark did drink a fair draught,
And sigh with delight as the waters rose.

The spirits pour forth into His dominion,
Nothing but Him can they abide;

Their bodies and hearts alike aglow,
As if the Niche and the Lamp were inside.

Betray not the Name of their Beloved,
Unless you would risk your blood and your hide!

The Glass

In the terminology of the Karkarī Order, the Glass (*zujāja*) is the subtlety of the heart that contains and protects the Lamp of eternity from the winds of temporality, the turbidity of the senses, and the delimitations of "where." It is the manifestation of the unseen world's descents into the visible world. The Glass is locus of the divine gaze and the treasury of the spiritual world, the manifestation of the secret, and the reality that reflects the ocean of union within the drop of separation. It is the vast container of the Lamp of Muḥammadan Light, transparent and encompassing, still and in motion. It is the supreme isthmus, the mirror that reflects the Lights of eternity in the substance of temporality, the container of the unseen and the manifestation-site of the visible. It is the tablet bearing symbols that stitch the realm of separation back to its original state. It is the sublime spokesman for the supreme judge, of whom the Beloved ﷺ said, "Ask your heart, and ask your soul," three times, and then proclaimed: "Righteousness is what the soul feels at ease with, and sin is what disquiets the soul and unsettles the breast—even if people give you their opinions again and again."[1]

1   Aḥmad, *Musnad*, 17647.

The Glass is the third symbol in the verse of unveiling, for it is the mirror that reflects the Lights and secrets of the Lamp. Since the Lamp is a pure spiritual reality that is hallowed beyond shapes, and it loved to be known, it descended in the manner of a symbol, by becoming reflected within the imaginal Glass of divine immanence, in order for you to clearly behold the inward meanings within the sensory realm, and to understand transcendence in the guise of immanence: "as if you see Him."

The Glass is thus a container that reveals the condition of the Lamp and its characteristics, levels, descents, determinations, and properties. It is an expression of the Lamp's integral union in the spectral language of separation that subsists through the uncreated names of God. And because the Lamp is free from the touch of temporality, the Glass becomes manifest in different modes within time and space, and so discloses itself in every moment through a distinct name, and in every place through a distinct form.

Consider the following example to illustrate this: the Glass is a formal container, and the Lamp is a supra-sensory and non-delimited water without form or color; yet when it makes contact with the Glass of your heart, it takes on its color and shape. Your eternal secret then becomes uncovered, and your hidden rank becomes manifest from behind seventy veils, disclosing the purpose for which you were created in pre-eternity. The Prophet ﷺ said, "Conceal whatever you please; for by God, whenever any servant male or female harbors a secret, God garbs them in its robe; if good then good, and if bad then bad. If one of you were to do a good deed behind seventy veils, God would make that goodness manifest so that people spoke well of him; and if one of you were to do an evil deed behind seventy veils, God would make that evil manifest so that people spoke ill of him."[1]

The descents of the Lights of the Lamp through the levels of the Glass:

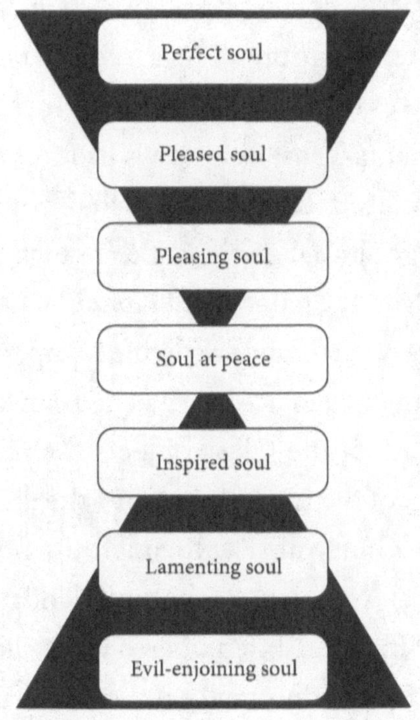

---

1   *Ḥilyat al-awliyā'*, 5/42.

The soul at peace is the isthmus of the seven souls, and each soul has its own color from the spectrum that distinguishes it from the others in the Glass. Collectively, they are a colorless spirit. Strive to understand this.

Another subtle point is in order: the patched cloak (*muraqqaʻa*) is the sensorial descent of the imaginal Glass into the visible world. For the Lamp, as I have explained, is a force that has no limit and no location, while the Glass has an illusory limit in the world of imagination and variegation. The limit of the Glass is demarcated by its distinct characteristics, levels, and determinations. The same is true of the patched cloak which takes on a spectrum of colorful shapes that cover the disciple's Lamp-heart as it draws its force from the flow of the Olive-mediator. The patched cloak thus manifests the Hā'-nature of the Shuʻayb-heart, which branches out into twelve parts according to the letters of *lā ilāha illā Allāh*. The disciple who wears the patched robe is a divine Lamp in a human Glass.

The Glass, then, is a Furqānic patched cloak. The differentiated multiplicity of the Glass reflects the nondifferentiated Qur'ānic union of the Lamp-heart. For the differentiated multiplicity of the Glass subsists through the nondifferentiated union of the Lamp, just as the nondifferentiated union of the Lamp is reflected in the differentiated multiplicity of the Glass. The patched cloak is thus concealment in manifestation, and manifestation in concealment. Glory be to the One Who made differentiated multiplicity a sign of nondifferentiated union, and nondifferentiated union a foundation of differentiated multiplicity!

Dear God, let it be that witnessing the union of Your Qur'ānic reality does not veil us from service to differentiation of Your Furqānic reality; and that our service to the differentiation of Your Furqānic reality does not veil us from witnessing the union of Your Qur'ānic reality. Amen.

The Resplendent Planet

In the terminology of the Karkarī Order, the Planet (*kawkab*) is the manifestation of the universal soul. It is the locus wherein the dots of reality converge with the demarcations of imagination, so that the sensory takes shape through the imaginal, and the supra-sensory becomes sensory, the spiritual becomes physical, and the circle becomes a disc.

God says, **And a sign unto them is the night: We strip the day therefrom, and behold, they are in darkness. And the sun runs to a dwelling place of its own. That is the decree of the Mighty, the Knowing. And for the moon, We have decreed mansions, till it returns like an old palm stalk. It befits not the sun to overtake the moon, nor the night to outstrip the day. Each flows in an orbit.**[1] Ibn ʿAjība comments on this:

A sign unto them is the night of heedlessness, from which **We strip the day** of wakefulness, and vice versa. The servant is always going back and forth between wakefulness and heedlessness, until the **sun** of gnosis rises over him and settles in his heart, and thereafter never sets. He alludes to this when He says, **the sun runs to a dwelling place of its own**; its **dwelling place** is the heart of the gnostic. **And for the moon** of gnosis,

---

1   Q Yā Sīn 36:37-40.

We have decreed mansions through which it shrinks and grows as its branches and orientations shrink and grow until the **sun** of gnosis rises over it and blots out its light, after which there is neither growth nor shrinkage. Qushayrī said, "The **sun** is like the gnostic whose gnosis is always shining, the possessor of mastery who is entirely uncolored, standing high in the heavens of his felicity, never eclipsed or shrouded by clouds. The **moon** is like the servant who passes through different phases and transformations, always subject to variegation. He experiences expansions that raise him to the brink of arrival, but then he tires and falls back to contraction in his distress at losing that pure state. He regresses until his heart slows and nearly stops beating altogether,[1] but then God has mercy on him and graces him with the ability to recover from his slump and wake from his agonies. Once again his state grows in purity to the point that he almost attains perfection, until yet again he falls short and plummets. So it goes, until he reaches whatever end was destined for him.[2]

Dear disciple, may God grace you with success, know that before God cast the Light of His attribute into your heart via the Olive-Mediator, the Mediator stored it for you in the Hā' of the Name Allāh by the secret of God's words, **Each swims**

---

1   The original Arabic text reads: "his heart is unsettled from its proper time and place." Assuming there is no typo in the Arabic edition, this seems to suggest that the heart slows until it stops beating altogher, and then God wakes it up and makes it beat again.

2   *Al-Baḥr al-madīd,* 6/149.

in an orbit. You revolve in the orbit of a Kāf of Immanence, from which you cannot escape without his authoritative permission. Your supreme goal is to fill your orbit with Lights so that the circle becomes a disc and the Glass becomes a Resplendent Planet, by your Shaykh's spiritual power which flows through you.

God likens the circumference of the heart to a moon because of how it receives Lights from the sun of the Lamp-spirit. The mansions of its route are determined by the Mediator so that you may learn the true meaning of servanthood through the secret of "As if you see Him." The heart will then reach its unification through total orientation toward the presence of union, remembrance, contemplation, and witnessing, producing both spiritual state and station. The newborn **crescent** of the beautiful attributes will appear in the sky of certainty like a spiritual infant. It will be nurtured as it ascends through the stages of contraction and expansion, the Lights of the attributes, and the meanings of inrushes. When it stands high in the sky of gnosis and faces the station of the innermost secret, it will be disclosed as a resplendent planet and a full **moon**—in form, not in essence. The "I" will become manifest—and how tremendous is the "I"!—and the subtleties of divine mercy will approach it. These mercies will teach it the innermost secrets of reality. The "I" will then become aware of its own deficiencies, and its true meaning will be disclosed to it so that it realizes that it is a shadow cast by the **sun** behind it. The "I" will approach this **sun**, little by little. And the closer it draws, the more it will be erased, until its essence is annihilated in the **sun's** essence. Such is the station of true poverty.

Allow me to explain this further so that you understand. The **moon** first appears as a newborn crescent shaped like a bow. It then grows until the fourteenth day, which corresponds to the levels of the fourteen luminous letters, the oath-letters of the Qur'ān. It then diminishes for another fourteen days, which correspond to the shadow letters. There remain two hidden levels, which are governed by the *hamza* (glottal stop). Thus the heart turns between Light and darkness. The Resplendent Planet is the stage of the three middle days when the full moon is seen in plain view.

The beauty of the Planet is so dazzling that in this station there is risk of the manifestation of ego. The heart becomes so absorbed in the sweetness of beholding the spiritual world in this sublime station that the disciple may become confused. For even though he tastes the flavor of spiritual truths and experiences the rapture of yearning for the secret's qualities, the waves of the "I" come roaring forth and he cries, **This is my Lord!**,[1] and he worships his own desire without realizing it. Then when it sets and the Planet is veiled, he realizes that its lights were borrowed from the **sun** of the spirit, not from the horizons of the soul at peace. It is then that he repents and cries, **If my Lord does not guide me, I shall surely be among the people who are astray!**[2]

1   Q An'ām 6:77.
2   Q An'ām 6:77.

The Blessed Tree

In the terminology of the Karkarī Order, the Olive Tree (*shajara zaytūniyya*) is the unqualified liminal reality between God and creation. This Tree sustains itself and contains its own oil within it, and the seal of the Chosen Prophet courses through its branches. It is beyond the constraints of necessity and possibility, and its disclosure-site is the Perfect Man, who is the manifestation of all-comprehensive oneness, and the vicegerent who brings together the dispersion of engendered being.

The Tree is mentioned several times in the Holy Qur'ān. The Almighty says, **"O Adam! Dwell thou and thy wife in the Garden, and eat from wheresoever you two will, but approach not this tree, lest you two be among the wrongdoers." Then Satan whispered to them, that he might expose to them that which was hidden from them of their nakedness. And he said, "Your Lord has only forbidden you this tree, lest you should become angels, or among those who abide forever."**[1]

Thus he lured them on through deception. And when they tasted of the tree, their nakedness was exposed to them, and they began to sew together the leaves of the Garden to cover themselves. And their Lord called out to them, "Did I not

1   Q Aʿrāf 7:19-20.

forbid you from that tree, and tell you that Satan is a manifest enemy unto you?"[1]

Hast thou not considered how God sets forth a parable? A good word is as a good tree: its roots firm and its branches in the sky.[2]

And a tree issuing forth from Mount Sinai that produces oil and a seasoning for eating.[3]

And when he came upon it, he was called from the right bank of the valley, at the blessed site, from the tree, "O Moses! Truly I am God, Lord of the worlds!"[4]

And if all the trees on earth were pens, and if the sea and seven more added to it [were ink], the Words of God would not be exhausted. Truly God is Mighty, Wise.[5]

God was content with the believers when they pledged allegiance unto thee beneath the tree. He knew what was in their hearts and sent down Tranquility upon them and rewarded them with a victory nigh.[6]

It is the Blessed Olive, from whose Light the Light of the Cosmos is kindled. It is the Tree of Eternal Life and of the Everlasting Kingdom. It is the Tree of the Pledge of Contentment,

1   Q Aʿrāf 7:22.
2   Q Ibrāhīm 14:24.
3   Q Muʾminūn 23:20.
4   Q Qaṣaṣ 28:30.
5   Q Luqmān 31:27.
6   Q Fatḥ 48:18.

the Tree of the Secret of Secrets. "I loved to be known" is its seed, and the knowledge of the unseen and the secrets of eternity are its fruits. We said of it in a poem:

Love is its seed, and passion its clay;
Secrets perfume the earth on which it grows.

Its scent is ardor, desire its sweet grass;
Its fragrance pervades the night breeze as it blows.

Its song is the spirit of water in its substance;
Upon the string of Oneness its melody is hewn.

Its notes are unified, their keys mysterious;
The levels of the Aeon are enfolded in its tune.

Its chant is eternal, its ipseity obscure;
It echoes always, the Omnipotent's reflection.

Its drunkenness is sober, its wine manifest,
Poured into the cup of keen inner vision.

To drink from that cup spells death for the soul;
Its secret revived 'Uzayr, as is known.

Through all its levels it is engraved with a secret;
Its symbol is the Ṭā Sīn of the Corners and the Black Stone.

Once there was a man who suffered from an illness that no physician was able to treat. Then he had a dream of God's Messenger ﷺ, who advised him to look for a cure in the fruit of the "Neither Nor" tree. The man had no idea how to interpret this dream, nor did any of the learned men of his day, until at last God blessed him with an encounter with man of spiritual realization, who immediately answered, "That is easy. Your cure lies in the olive tree, which God says is **neither of the East nor of the West.**"

Let us begin with the first instance wherein it was disclosed itself to Adam ﷺ, as God says: **"O Adam! Dwell thou and thy wife in the Garden, and eat from wheresoever you two will, but approach not this tree, lest you two be among the wrongdoers." Then Satan whispered to them, that he might expose to them that which was hidden from them of their nakedness. And he said, "Your Lord has only forbidden you this tree, lest you should become angels, or among those who abide forever." And he swore unto them, "Truly I am a sincere adviser unto you." Thus he lured them on through deception. And when they tasted of the tree, their nakedness was exposed to them, and they began to sew together the leaves of the Garden to cover themselves. And their Lord called out to them, "Did**

I not forbid you from that tree, and tell you that Satan is a manifest enemy unto you?" They said, "Our Lord! We have wronged ourselves. If Thou dost not forgive us and have Mercy upon us, we shall surely be among the losers."[1]

Hearts enflamed with passion catch the singular fragrance of the Tree of the Secret of Secrets (*shajarat sirr al-sirr*),[2] and the desire for knowledge and the sweetness of love is aroused within them. Love usually spells tribulation: it humiliates the proud, impoverishes the rich, and causes all manner of torment and struggle. The Beloved Prophet ﷺ said to a man of the Helpers who told him that he loved him, "If you love me, then ready yourself for tribulation. By Him in Whose hand is my soul, tribulation comes more swiftly to those who love me than water flows down from the mountaintops to the lowlands." He then said, "Dear God, if anyone should love me, grant him temperance and modest means; and if anyone should hate me, grant him abundant wealth and children!"[3]

When the Lord said to Adam ﷺ, **O Adam! Dwell thou and thy wife in the Garden,** this was meant as a herald of trial and tribulation and a forbiddance of pride and indulgence, as though He were saying, "Adam, everything in the Garden has been granted unto you except for this Tree, for it is the Tree of

---

1   Q Aʿrāf 7:19-23.

2   In the context of Shaykh al-Karkarī's writings, the "sirr al-sirr" is a reference to the second secret of the Path, called the Lām al-ʿIshq/Lām al-Qabḍ, which is the second Lām of the divine name Allāh.

3   Bayhaqī, *Shuʿab*, 1397.

Love, and love spells tribulation. Dwell with your wife in the Garden in peace, for I created it for you to dwell there, **and eat from wheresoever you two will** of the rivers, trees, and comforts of the Garden, **but approach not this tree**, the Tree of Love, so as to avoid tribulation, **lest you two be among the wrongdoers**, wronging yourselves; for love is fire and light, and he who will not brave its fire will not have its light. Anyone who desires its light must let its fire burn away his ego and all that he is, so that his self remains through the selfhood of his Lord; and it is then that he will find the light of love illuminating him, as God says, **He loves them, and they love Him.**[1] The All-Merciful planted the Tree of Love with His hand for Adam, just as He stirred Adam's clay with His hand for the sake of the tree. Though He forbade it to him, Adam was still eager to take it, for it is man's nature to crave what is denied him. Yet the tree was not meant for anyone other than Adam and his progeny. Adam's essence was tested with the tribulation of having to forgo this special favor and to look to others instead, in order to make manifest the truth of how he was created for it, and it for him.[2]

God disclosed His beauty in them in order to inflame their passion, and revealed to them the secret of the secret through His most subtle decree. They yearned for a glimpse of the tree, and when they drew near to it the desire of passion overwhelmed the true reality of passion, and so they ate from it and

1   Q. Mā'ida 5:54.
2   Najm al-Dīn Rāzī, *Tafsīr al-ta'wīlāt al-najmiyya.*

touched it. By this they learned the most secret of secrets and the subtlest decree, and they became so full that the Garden could no longer hold them due to the weight of the Lights of those secrets and the powerful gravity of lordship. Thus He said, **lest you two be among the wrongdoers** by entering the bounds of the protected pasture of lordship and beholding the secrets of divinity. Had God not prevented their tongues from divulging those secrets, knowledge of the divine decrees would have filled the world. This is why some exegetes say that this tree was the Tree of Knowledge of the Decree and Predestination...

The Accursed One knew that it was the Tree of Eternal Life and Kingship, and since it was forbidden to him, he wanted to touch it in order to claim lordship for himself through its power. Yet he could not do so, since he did not have the requisite preparedness for this. This tormented him, for he could see how replete it was with the treasures of the unseen. So he decided to direct Adam toward it instead ... but his desire was mixed with envy of Adam, and so he sought to ensnare him in it, knowing how perilous it was. But God protected Adam and Eve from that danger.

Then Satan whispered to them, that he might expose to them that which was hidden from them of their nakedness. When God wishes to divulge one of His secrets to His servant, He allows the Devil to whisper to him some pretext that causes the secret to be divulged. And so the servant is elevated by the knowledge of that secret, and the harm passes to the Devil while the benefit goes to the knowing servant. This is how it was with Adam and his Enemy. The Enemy wanted to cause him to fall from his level, yet instead his honor only grew, while the Enemy himself fell even lower because of his envy. He became forever banished, while Adam became accepted for all eternity. Thus God says, **Evil plotting besets none but those who plot,**[1] and says of Adam, **Then his Lord chose him, and relented unto him and guided.**[2]

Moses ﷵ and the Tree:

God says, **And when he came upon it, he was called from the right bank of the valley, at the blessed site, from the tree, "O Moses! Truly I am God, Lord of the worlds!"**[3] So God's Confidant ﷵ was called by the Voice of the divine Attributes, "Moses! Remove Moses from Moses, and annihilate your attributes in Mine!" Our shaykh Sidi Aḥmad al-ʿAlawī said, may God sanctify his secret:

Annihilate yourself and be present in Him and for Him;
Subsist through Him, protected by the kindness of God.

Remove yourself from yourself and remain through Him;
When you leave yourself, you will find nothing but God.

---

1   Q Fāṭir 35:43.
2   Q. Ṭā Hā 20:122. Baqlī, *ʿArāʾis al-bayān,* 1/422–423.
3   Q Qaṣaṣ 28:30.

There is nothing in existence but the self-disclosures of God, who discloses Himself to whom He wills, when He wills, as He wills.

The Confidant ﷺ approached the carpet of the All-Merciful from the realm of engendered being and ephemerality. He was called from the **bank** of the eternal **valley**; the courtyard of beginninglessness; the Tree of the Essence; by the Voice of the Attributes: **O Moses! Truly I**, alluding to distance in nearness and nearness in distance, to absence in presence and presence in absence, to divine selfhood, and to visionary unveiling: **Truly I am God.** That is, "Come out of yourself inasmuch as you are yourself, for I am God, and I shall sustain you. Look upon Me with eyes from Us, until you see divinity and know the truth!"

It has been said that there is a vast difference between these two trees; for the Tree of Adam was trial and tribulation when it manifested, while the Tree of Moses spelled the commencement of his prophetic mission and his message. Yet if those who say this knew the true nature of the Tree of Adam, they would not have said such a thing about Adam; for the Tree of Adam symbolizes the Tree of Lordship, which is why God says: **approach not this tree.** Adam was adorned with the divine attributes, and so he desired the Essence itself, but God denied it to him and said, "This thing is not for you," for eternality by its nature cannot become unified with ephemerality. God said this, but He manifested His eternality in the Tree, and Adam became intoxicated and could not restrain himself from it. He ate from it the seed of lordship, and so his spiritual state grew too large for the Garden to contain, and he had to fall down to the quarry of the lovers.[1]

The Beloved Prophet ﷺ and the Tree:

God says, **God was content with the believers when they pledged allegiance unto thee beneath the tree. He knew what was in their hearts and sent down tranquility upon them and rewarded them with a victory nigh.**[2] The eternal love from the Covenant of **Alastu** transcends the vicissitudes of space and time, error and sin. The levels of those who took this pretemporal covenant are not marred by heedlessness or forgetting. They perpetually dwell in the bliss of the gardens of nearness, resting peacefully beneath the Tree of the Secret, enjoying the fruits of its secrets and enraptured in the dazzling Lights of its seeds. Contentment is their attribute, love and yearning their qualities. Victory is their gift, lordly knowledge their spoils. God created them for His love and connected them to the Tree of inner meaning, in whose Light they love one another.

A noble hadith says, "Among God's servants are some who are not Prophets, though the Prophets and martyrs envy them." Someone said, "Tell us who they are, that we might love them." The Prophet ﷺ replied, "They are people who love one another through the Light of God, nor for ties of blood or kinship. Their

---

1   *'Arā'is al-bayān*, 3/86-87.
2   Q Fatḥ 48:18.

faces are Light, upon pulpits of Light. They will not fear when others do, nor grieve when others grieve." Then he recited, **Behold! Truly the friends of God, no fear shall come upon them, nor shall they grieve.**[1] Ibn ʿAjība ﷺ says:

God was content with the believers, who orient themselves toward God, **when they pledged allegiance unto thee,** O knower of God, **beneath the tree** of your saintly aspiration. **He knew** the sincerity **in their hearts, and sent down tranquility upon them,** until they found repose in the hardships of spiritual training and discipline, **and** He **rewarded them with a victory nigh,** which is arrival at the presence of eye-witnessing, **and abundant spoils that they will capture** in the form of endless spiritual victories, unveilings, secrets, and ascensions.

God has promised you abundant spoils that you will capture after the victorious spiritual opening, namely the return to subsistence, abiding in subsistence, broadened spiritual stations, and advancing in ascensions of unveiling; **then He hastened this for you,** meaning the station of annihilation; **and He has restrained the people's hands from you,** protecting you from obstacles, so that you may turn toward your Lord; **that it may be a sign for the believers** who stay behind and do not join you on the journey, that they may follow you guidance, **and that He may guide you upon a straight path,** the path of arrival at the holy Presence and the locus of divine intimacy.

---

1   Q Yūnus 10:62. *Ṣaḥīḥ al-targhīb,* no. 3023.

And others of which you were not capable of realizing in this world, **God has encompassed them**, stored them for you until the Day of Resurrection; this means the station of **upon a seat of truth before an Omnipotent King.**[1]

Rūzbihān Baqlī said: **God was content with the believers**, that is, He was content with them in pre-eternity according to His beginningless knowledge, and will remain content with them forever, because His contentment is an attribute without beginning or end, unchanged by contingencies or the passage of time, nor by obedience or defiance. They remain forever among His chosen ones, and their rank will never fall due to slips, human nature, nor base desire; for those who have divine approval are protected by His attentive care and are immune to the traits of those who are distant from God. They have become characterized by the attribute of divine contentment, and so they are content with God just as He is with them.[2]

There is but one Tree, and the forms of disclosure are manifold, according to the dictates of divine wisdom. The one who acknowledges its rightful due and pledges allegiance beneath it to the Muḥammadan Reality will become a recipient of the Intercession, and indeed by its blessing he too will become an intercessor for others. It is the Good Tree, **its roots firm** within the hearts of non-delimitation, **and its branches**[3] extend into the differentiated heavens of the prophets. The Handful of Light

1   Q. Qamar 54:55.
2   *Al-Baḥr al-madīd*, 7/144.
3   Q Ibrāhīm 14:24.

is dispersed throughout these prophetic presences, and is passed down from our father Adam ﷺ to our forefather Abraham the Intimate Friend of God ﷺ. The **Good Tree** is the presence of the supreme congress of saints, disclosed by the words of the Prophet ﷺ who proclaimed beyond the Lote Tree, "Peace be upon us and upon God's righteous servants." For every Prophet or Messenger wishes to be among them, knowing as they do that all of the laws and dictates of prophethood and messengerhood will end at the Resurrection when the reward and punishment is settled, while the properties of sainthood will last forever because they are connected to the attributes of uncreated reality, not the rulings of the illusory realm. The Sacred Law is meant to give order to the herebelow, and the herebelow is really an illusion. This is why the Prophets all prayed to be included among the righteous folk, as God says: **And who shuns the creed of Abraham, but a foolish soul? We chose him in the world and in the Hereafter he shall be among the righteous.**[1]

My Lord! Thou hast given me something of sovereignty, and taught me the interpretation of events. Originator of the heavens and the earth! Thou art my Protector in this world and in the Hereafter! Take me as a submitter unto Thyself, and admit me to the company of the righteous.[2]

---

1   Q Baqara 2:130.
2   Q Yūsuf 12:101.

And he smiled, laughing at her words, and said, "My Lord! Inspire me to give thanks for Thy blessing wherewith Thou hast blessed me and my parents and to work righteousness pleasing to Thee, and cause me to enter, through Thy Mercy, among Thy righteous servants!"[1]

And We bestowed upon him Isaac and Jacob, and We established prophethood and scripture among his progeny. We gave him his reward in this world, and in the Hereafter he shall truly be among the righteous.[2]

It is a Tree whose **oil would well-nigh shines forth, even if no fire had touched it.** Now fire causes light to shine because of the correspondence between the two, and this causal connection between fire and light is decreed by divine wisdom in the physical realm. However, the oil of the Olive's Secret shines even without fire's touch. Moreover, his words **well-nigh** are decreed by divine wisdom. They share the characteristics of the Kāf of Immanence, so that God's wisdom may conceal His power, and lest the secret of predestination be revealed and the dictates of the Law become annulled.

1   Q Naml 27:19.
2   Q ʿAnkabūt 29:27.

The Olive

In the terminology of the Karkarī Order, the Olive (*zaytūna*) is the soul prepared to be kindled by the reality of **from among your own**,[1] after being cleansed of the "I" by the Tree of "He." It is the path of ascension from the luminous corporeal temple to the mosque of spiritual union.

God mentions the Olive six times in the Holy Qur'ān, alluding to its actualization of the levels of faith mentioned in the Ḥadīth of Gabriel, who came to teach us our religion in the guise of a questioner, although he knew the answers well. He manifested as a meeting of opposites in order to rouse you from your sleep of heedlessness, and said in the form of a questioner: "Tell me of faith." The holy Prophet replied, "It is to believe in God, His angels, His scriptures, His Messengers, the Last Day, and to believe in fate both good and evil."[2]

The disciple who has achieved realization of the pillars of faith is an Olive. He has passed away in the unseen wāw that connects to the Hā' of Ipseity, forming the word *Hu*, "He." So noble is this Olive that God Himself swears by it when He says,

---

1   **A Messenger has indeed come unto you from among your own. Troubled is he by what you suffer, solicitous of you, kind and merciful unto the believers.** Q. Tawba 9:128.

2   Muslim, *Ṣaḥīḥ,* 12.

By the fig and the olive, by Mount Sinai, and by this land made safe![1] Anything by which God swears is an object of reverence for both the exoteric scholars and the gnostics who have verified inward Truth. However, the latter revere the objects that God swears by more, for they understand that the concealed Book is to be found in the setting-places of the stars,[2] and they know the hidden secrets of the letters.

The Olive is the disciple who moves from the stage of the Resplendent Planet to the stage of the Olive, having erased all directions and abandoned his corporeal home for the mosque of ultimate union. The Olive-stage is the path that is not delimited by proximity or distance, and our Sufi camp recognizes it as the ascension from the corporeal temple to the mosque of spiritual union. God says: **Glory be to Him Who carried His servant by night from the Sacred Mosque to the Farthest Mosque, whose precincts We have blessed, that We might show him some of Our signs. Truly He is the Hearer, the Seer.**[3] Ibn ʿAjība comments that the reason He says **His servant** rather than "His Prophet" or "His Messenger" is to indicate that anyone whose servanthood is perfected will have a share of the Ascension. Their minds and spirits will ascend to what is beyond the Throne, and plunge into the oceans of invincibility

1   Q Tīn 95:1-3.

2   **I swear by the setting-places of the stars, and truly it is a magnificent oath, if you but knew. Truly it is a Noble Qurʾān, in a Book concealed. None touch it, save those made pure, a revelation from the Lord of the worlds.** Q Wāqiʿa 56:75-80.

3   Q Isrāʾ 17:1.

and the Lights of the spiritual world, each one in accordance with the degree to which they have let go of their own attributes and adopted God's.[1]

It is here that the disciple is required to follow the Sunna of the Beloved ﷺ who taught us to erase the directions on route to the mosque, saying: "Dear God, put Light in my heart, Light in my tongue, Light in my hearing, Light in my sight, Light above me, Light below me, Light on my right, Light on my left, Light in front of me, Light behind me. Put Light in my soul, and magnify my Light, and amplify my Light. Give me Light, and make me Light." Bukhārī and Muslim provide various narrations for this ḥadīth.

Note that the Light in this hadith begins with the essence of a person: the heart, then the hearing, then the sight; that is, the illumination of the corporeal body. It then proceeds to the erasure of the spatial directions, which imply confinement. If the disciple masters this, he becomes an Olive attached to the Tree of Transcendence, like the Resplendent Planet hanging from the Tree of the vast universe. He becomes a true servant, with his name, trace, and essence annihilated in the Real, so that no name describes him, no outline defines him, and no essence confines him. He tastes knowledge of non-delimitation, by

---

1   *Al-Baḥr al-madīd*, 7/75.

virtue of the waters of life that permeate the branches of the Tree. His Planet shines bright and draws from the Moon of the Muḥammadan laws and the Sun of Aḥmadan realities. Thus the disciple is nurtured between transcendence and immanence, necessity and possibility, delimitation and non-delimitation.

The Permission

In the terminology of the Karkarī Order, the Heart (*qalb*) is the locus of God's gaze, the quarry of knowledge, and the Inviolable House wherein evil thoughts and dualistic whispers are forbidden. It is the Ancient House of preeternity beyond the contingencies of place and time, and the seat wherein lies the secret that contains the divine.

Another term in the Order is Permission (*idhn*), which is a ray of divine approval. This ray shines from the sun of God's will, and reflects upon the mirror of fate. It is thus the isthmus between an act and its effect. It is through permission that mastery is gained and preparedness is attained.

Following the Light Verse, God Almighty proclaims, **it is in houses that God has permitted to be raised and wherein His Name is remembered, He is therein glorified morning and evening.**[1] "Permission **to be raised**" is the sixth symbol in the Verse of Spiritual Opening. When God is pleased with a heart, He raises it from the earth of the animal soul to the heaven of the holy spirit. Therein lies the Lote Tree of Lights and sublime realities, which is the end of outward forms, levels, and locations. It is there that the corporeal elements are erased in the

1   Q Nūr 24:36.

body of the Chosen One, so that nothing remains but the Muḥammadan Reality, which would burn up if it went any further. The heart becomes **a place of visitation for mankind and a sanctuary,**[1] from which God discloses Himself to His servants through His attributes and subtle graces. He discloses to the repentant with forgiveness; to the fearful with security; to the lover with affection; and to the yearner with nearness. He becomes the Kaʿba for the seekers to circumambulate, the Qibla for the devotees who are sought, and a Mosque for the beloveds who prostrate to none but the One.

The heart that is permitted to rise is the mother of all hearts, just as Zamzam is the mother of all waters, Sinai is the mother of all mountains, and the Sacred House is the mother of all houses. It is the center, and all others are the periphery. It is the primal origin, and all others are its shadows. It is the house inhabited by the Supreme Name, disclosing through all possibilities and impossibilities. All things upon the earth turn and rush toward it without even realizing it, due to its countless distinct entifications in the sensory world. Whatever the soul loves or desires, it is a manifestation of the disclosures of the one who possesses the Kaʿba-heart. Whoever wishes to approach God

---

1   And [remember] when We made the House a place of visitation for mankind, and a sanctuary, "Take the station of Abraham as a place of prayer." And We made a covenant with Abraham and Ishmael, "Purify My House for those who circumambulate, those who make retreat, and those who bow and prostrate." Q Baqara 2:125.

must go through Olive-mediator's door. God says, **It is not piety that you should come to houses from their rear, but piety is he who is reverent and comes into houses by their doors. So reverence God, that haply you may prosper.**[1]

One does not enter the divine presence from the backdoor, by way of egoic fantasies or psychic delusions. Whoever approaches from anywhere but the front door, his prayers and offerings around the house will be nothing but whistling and clapping: **Their prayer at the House is naught but whistling and clapping. So taste the punishment for having disbelieved!**[2] The only way in is to enter through the door of the Shaykh who has attained and can lead others to their own attainment. It is this Shaykh who can lift the veils from their hearts, cleanse them of the haze of sensoriality, and purify them with the water of the unseen. He cuts deep into their hearts with the luminous pickaxe of the Supreme Name until springs gush forth from them. This will teach them to revere the attributes of lordship when they disclose themselves at the level of servanthood, and to perfect the properties of servanthood within the disclosures of lordship. To this effect, Sidi al-ʿAlawī, may God sanctify his secret, says:

1   Q Baqara 2:189.
2   Q Anfāl 8:35.

The true Shaykh is he who is generous with his secret,
Putting the disciple's welfare above his own.

He will lift up the veils that cover his heart,
Preventing him from reaching the highest station.

He will enter God's presence, from which he was severed,
And see the Real manifest wheresoever he turns.

He will be annihilated to all the worlds,
Not even the delights of the Garden will tempt him.

That, by God, is the Shaykh unrivaled,
Alone in his time, unique in the world.

He is the Piercing Star, should you attempt to approach him.
And if you value your own soul, he is more precious still.

God says, **And [remember] when We made the House a place of visitation for mankind, and a sanctuary, "Take the station of Abraham as a place of prayer." And We made a covenant with Abraham and Ishmael, "Purify My House for those who circumambulate, those who make retreat, and those who bow and prostrate."**[1] Ibn ʿAjība writes in his Qurʾān commentary, *The Vast Ocean*:

---

1   Q Baqara 2:125.

The heart is the **house** of the Lord. God Almighty said to one of His Prophets, "There has occurred to Me a house I might live in." He replied, "Lord, what house could accommodate You?" He replied, "Neither My earth nor My heaven can contain Me, but the heart of My believing servant can." When the heart is purified from alterities and filled with Lights, and when mysteries and secrets become firmly rooted in it, it becomes **a place of visitation** and a **sanctuary** for God's servants. All who reach it and **circumambulate** it are secure from misguidance, error, evil thoughts, and false beliefs. All who enter it with love are secure from banishment and exile, and are numbered among God's most excellent servants...

Their expressions differ, but Your splendor is one;
All are referring to that same beauty.

God promised His Prophets and chosen ones to cleanse their hearts of other-than-God, so that they reject everything apart from Him and they become open to the **circumambulation** of mystical inrushes and Lights, and the **retreat** of mysteries and secrets. Their outer beings are humbled before its glory, and their hearts and spirits yield to its resplendent beauty.[1]

Through His permission, God made the heart a Ka'ba for the presence of union; a House inviolable to other-than-Him and beyond all duality. The affairs of humanity in this life and

---

1   *Al-Baḥr al-madīd*, 1/139-139.

the next are supported by it, if they only knew, yet: **Alas for the servants! Never did a messenger come unto them, but that they mocked him.**[1]

This heart is the morsel of flesh that dwells in the universal human body. Consider how the Beloved Prophet ﷺ said, "All of us are a servant to You."[2] In reality we are all a single servant, and the Seal is the heart of that servant.

Dear God, fill our hearts with love for You, and love for the one who loves You, and make our love for him more beloved to us than every other beloved; for to love him is truly to love You. Amen!

1   Q Yā Sīn 36:30.
2   Muslim, *Ṣaḥīḥ*, 741.

The Name

In the terminology of the Karkarī Order, the Name *Allāh* is the manifestation-site of the Named, the original undifferentiation of the names, and the foundation and innermost secret of transcendent meanings. To utter the Name is to actualize its meaning, for the Name does not part from the Named, being neither It nor other-than-It. The Name is thus the guide and the path to the Essence through the levels of existence. It is an absolute reality that gives expression to our inability, as ephemeral beings, to describe the Eternal. The Name is embodied in the six aforementioned symbols, and it descends through the manifest attribute of Light into the realm of possibility.

Know, may God grace you with success, that the servant is incapable of describing the Real, for there is nothing like unto Him. How could the noneternal describe the eternal? How could that which is fleeting describe the Everlasting? It is only proper to describe God as He describes Himself and as His Prophet described Him. To add anything to this is to err and wrong oneself. The six symbols, then, are the foundations of the Path. It is through them that one reads the all-encompassing Name *Allāh*, which is the seventh symbol that encompasses all foundations. The six symbols, then, are enwrapped within the Name just as waves are enwrapped within the sea. Thus God says, **Say: He.**[1] When you recite **Say**, you are uttering a command, as if you were telling your listener to speak, who in turn says **Say**, issuing that command to another, and so on in an infinite circle, like so:

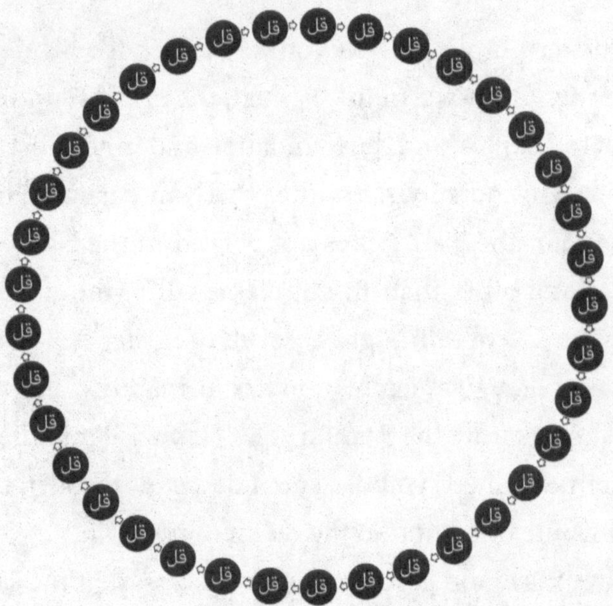

The word remains as is; spoken without a speaker. For the circle of speech is annihilated as the end melts into the beginning. The divine ipseity, the "He-ness," forms a center for this circle of annihilation, with the Wāw hidden inside the *Hā'* of *Huwa*, expressing this separation between the word and the speaker:

1   Q Ikhlāṣ 112:1.

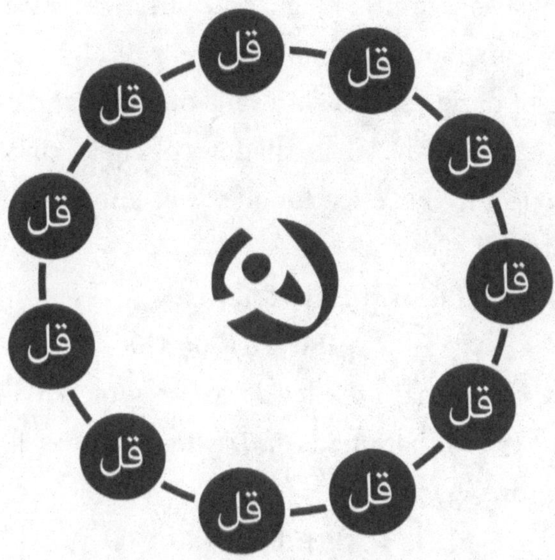

The word *qul*, **Say**, is a luminous word formed from the letters *Qāf* and Lām. The letter *Qāf* pertains to the spiritual world, which is written as it is pronounced as قف, *Qāf-Fā'* without an *Alif*. Thus its numerical value is 100 for *Qāf* plus 80 for *Fā'*, totaling 180. This represents a half-circle of the higher unseen realm, since a half-circle is 180 degrees:

Likewise, the letter Lām is written as it is pronounced as لم, *Lām-Mīm*, with a value of 30 for *Lām* plus 40 for *Mīm*, totaling 70. The Lām is always combined, as it is in the name *Allāh*.

There are seventy veils of Light and darkness between God and creation. One Lām represents the veils of Light, another Lām the veils of darkness: seventy veils of Light, and seventy veils dark; or let us call the latter "shadows of Light", since that shows more respect to the letter, for all of our knowledge is centered on courtesy.

Thus the value of *qul* is as follows:

$$180+70+70=320$$

There still remain the levels of the soul, which are represented by the Muḥammad *Mīm*, whose value is 40. This gives us the following total:

$$180+70+70+40=360$$

The word *qul*, then, expresses a circle of annihilation without beginning or end; speech without speaker. The study of the Name begins with *huwiyya*, "He-ness," and the word *huwa* (He) is the center of the circle of annihilation, such that the *Wāw* is in the center of the *Hā'*, like so: ه

The *Hā'* has five levels, which are the levels of Islam. The *Wāw* has six, which are the levels of faith. This makes 11 in all: annihilation in the station of submission, and annihilation in the station of faith.

Annihilation is not merely a word to be idly uttered by the tongue. It is a matter of diligently observing the details of the obligatory rituals with presence and witnessing. To testify (*shahāda*) is to witness (*mushāhada*); prayer (*ṣalāh*) is a connection (*ṣila*); zakat is a purification (*tazkiya*) for the soul throughout the levels; fasting means to abstain from seeing anything but the Real; the pilgrimage is Arafat, meaning to know (*'arafa*) Him directly in every disclosure and meaning—to see Him in all that you see.

Thus do you become annihilated in the levels of submission and in the levels of faith, all of which are matters of the unseen, and then to enter the station of spiritual excellence through the *Kāf* of Immanence: *ka'annaka tarāh*, "as if you see Him."

The Supreme Name is non-delimited, but it descends into the levels of immanence in the verse of spiritual opening through the name *al-Nūr*. This is why God says, **The likeness of His Nūr**, not "the likeness of Allāh," for there is nothing like unto Him. **The likeness of His Light is as**, *ka*—immanent transcendence—for it is not possible to qualify the Real, but one can qualify His Light in the same manner as He qualifies it in His Holy Book: **God is the Light of the heavens and the earth. The likeness of His Light is as a niche, wherein is a lamp. The lamp is in a glass. The glass is as a resplendent planet kindled from a blessed olive tree, neither of the East nor of the West. Its oil would well-nigh shine forth, even if no fire had touched it. Light upon light! God guides unto His Light whomsoever He will, and God sets forth likenesses for mankind, and God is Knower of all things. In houses that God has permitted to be raised...**[1] The name *Allāh*, signifying the Essence, descends into the name *al-Nūr* which signifies the attributes, through the seven levels that God qualifies in the noble verse, as follows:

---

1   Q Nūr 24:35-36.

Niche, Lamp, Glass, Resplendent Planet, Tree, Olive, and Permission to raise the house of the heart. These seven foundations constitute the invocatory path of the Supreme Name. They are expressed in eternity by the self-effacing prostration in the presence of,

"Peace be upon us, and upon God's righteous servants."

Chapter III

The Verses of Light in the Qur'ān

Spiritual Hypocrites: Wax Without Honey

Their parable is that of one who kindled a fire, and when it lit up what was around him, God took away their light, and left them in darkness, unseeing.[1]

With these words, God provides us with a marvelous parable and a tangible image to ensure that the comparison hits home. This is a parable of the one who treads the Path of the Sufis as a mere authority-follower rather than a verifier of the truth. He is like a branch that sprouts leaves but does not bear fruit. Or like someone whose earthly body sits between the sun of lordship and the moon of servanthood, causing a fated eclipse that blocks the rays of lordship from reflecting upon the moon of servanthood. Since the earthly body comes between the spirit and the soul, the lunar soul remains dark and cannot draw from the Lights of the solar spirit. May God spare us from such a fate!

The attributes of hypocrisy come down to a contradiction between the inner being and the outer being. The tongue outstrips the heart so that the person pretends to possess what is beyond his station, and speaks of things that lie beyond his

1   Q Baqara 2:17.

knowledge. Our blessed Messenger ﷺ likens the hypocrite who recites the Qur'ān to basil, saying: "The hypocrite who recites the Qur'ān is like basil: it smells good, but tastes bitter."[1] Likewise, the outer being of the hypocrite is full, while his inner being is empty. He is like one who kindles the fires of pretension and speaks above his station, mingling empty claims with inward meanings, until God takes away the inward meanings and leaves him only with empty claims—Glory be to the One who is free of all idolatrous association.

God says, **Their parable is that of one who kindled a fire, and when it lit up what was around him, God took away their light, and left them in darkness, unseeing.** They are like the one who keeps the company of the knowers of God, asking them to kindle the Lights of the fire of passion only so that he may beautify his outward appearance, though the true fire of passion burns within the interior of the knowers, not their exterior. The spiritual hypocrite seeks to kindle the fire of fervor that torments the hearts that roam dazzled in God's spiritual realm. He desires the fire of love, but only so that the attributes of the Sufi Camp may be visible upon him. He forgets that fire is kindled for its Light, not the fire itself, and so he does not perceive the fire as Moses the Confidant ﷺ did, as God says: **He saw a fire and said unto his family, "Stay here. Verily I perceive a fire. Perhaps I shall bring you a brand therefrom, or find**

---

1   Muslim, *Ṣaḥīḥ*, 1334.

guidance at the fire."[1] Moses was enraptured by the fire of divine magnificence and glory, for he had served the Shuʿayb[2] of the heart for ten years. And it is through that blessing that, upon seeing the fire, his penetrating sight was drawn to the magnetic Lights of the divine attributes, whose beauty was dressed in the flames of the divine acts. Moses understood the fire's inward meaning by the blessed mediation of Shuʿayb, thereby removing his shoes. He knew that the flames of the divine acts mirror the Lights of the attributes, and that the Lights of the attributes manifest the Tree of the eternal secret. **Then when he came to it** with true resolve and yearning, his recompense was, **Truly I am God; there is no god but I.**[3]

As for the spiritual hypocrite, he does not perceive the fire of the divine acts, for he did not serve the Mediator for eight years, nor did he complete ten years.[4] He desires the outward appearance without the inward knowledge. Like their predecessors, the spiritual hypocrites are always looking to outward appearances, as God says: **And they say, "What ails this Messenger, who eats food and walks in the markets? Why is there not an angel sent down unto him to be a warner with him?"**[5] There-

---

1   Q Ṭā Hā 20:10.

2   Jethro.

3   Q Ṭā Hā 20:14.

4   **He said, "I desire to marry you to one of these two daughters of mine, on condition that you hire yourself to me for eight years. But if you complete ten, that will be of your own accord. And I desire not to be hard upon you. You shall find me, if God wills, to be among the righteous." Q Qaṣaṣ 28:27.**

5   Q Furqān 25:7.

fore, when they seek the knowledge of the Sufi Camp, they seek only the outward aspect of it, not the inward. Yet the exterior of our knowledge is fire: the fire of tribulation and purification, the fire that makes raw gold pure. When the Beloved was asked which people suffer the most tribulation, he replied, "The Prophets, then the learned, then the righteous. One of them might be so afflicted with poverty that he has only one garment to wear, and so afflicted with lice that they kill him. One of them might rejoice more greatly in tribulation that you rejoice in gain."[1]

The Shaykh of our Shaykh Sidi al-ʿAlawī said, my God sanctify his spirit:

Avoid our Camp's science, unworthy one!
Keep the orphan's property out of reach.

God detests the one who replaces
Honest work with vainglorious speech.

Is there any use in praise won through boasting,
Any profit in counterfeit glory?

Can flattery cure an ailing patient?
Can any but loved ones console the lonely?

1   *Mustadrak,* 108.

You may well learn to talk their talk,
But that's a hornet's wax, not a bee's honey.

Spiritual hypocrites speak words that are wax without honey, for the bee of luminous faith does not stir within their depths. Their hearts are empty ruins; **they are like leaning timbers.**[1] How could a person whose heart is **darkness upon darkness** dare to speak about **the Light of the heavens and the earth?** Only Light recognizes Light, and only the one whose heart is a Shining Planet can speak of God's Light. The Path of God is not a matter of boastful words spoken in zawiyas and mosques; the Path is love and bedazzlement in the Lights of God. If you have no Lights, you are dead even as you live, nonexistent even as you exist. Our Path is not about elaborate words and phrases. If eloquence were the standard, then Aaron ﷵ would have surpassed Moses ﷵ, who said, **And my brother, Aaron, is more eloquent than me in speech. So send him with me as a helper to confirm me, for I fear they will deny me.**[2]

There are also hypocrites on the Path who see the fires of the divine act illuminating all around them and suppose that they have attained spiritual perfection, and so they deny the Mediator and say, **I have only been given it on account of knowledge I possess.**[3] They deny the Mediator, and so God denies them; they profess to do without the Mediator, and so God does with-

---

1   Q Munāfiqūn 63:4.
2   Q Qaṣaṣ 28:34.
3   Q Qaṣaṣ 28:78.

out them. The Lights return whence they came, and God leaves them in the darkness of their own souls and the gloom of their hypocrisy: **God took away their light, and left them in darkness, unseeing.**[1]

I urge you then, may God have mercy upon you, to remain wherever God puts you and be content with what God apportions you. He who desires more must serve the masters, for service to them is the essence of love, and to be near them is to be blessed in this life and the next; and upon their mention, mercy descends. Live with them as a servant, and you will die as a master. Beware of claiming the spiritual stations of this Camp, for not all that glitters is gold. The Master of the Lovers, Ibn al-Fāriḍ, said:

> *Thus do I advise you about love, yet should you ignore me,*
> *I would not blame you; choose for yourself what you desire.*

> *If you would live happily, die a martyr for love;*
> *And if you cannot, then there are those who are worthy of love.*

> *He who does not die of love has not lived in it;*
> *If you want the bee's honey, you must endure its stings.*

> *Grab the coattails of passion and shed all bashfulness;*
> *Tread not the path of worshippers, though they be noble.*

1   Q Baqara 2:17.

Tell the one who dies of love, "Now you have earned it."
And tell the pretender, "Not all that glitters is gold!"

The Meaning of the Saint and Sainthood

God is the Friend (Walī) of those who believe. He brings them out of the darkness into the light. As for those who disbelieve, their friends are the false gods, bringing them out of the light into the darkness. They are the inhabitants of the Fire, abiding therein.[1]

In the terminology of the Karkarī Order, the saint (*walī*) is a heavenly fruit that emanates the perfume of divine unity into the heart of every lover. He is a servant-master, a disclosure-site of the names and attributes, and an upholder of the scales of divine oneness. He is the middlemost prayer, the master of the age, and the Aeon itself. If not for the courtesy of servanthood, the *walī* would be entirely unknowable and beyond description.

Sainthood (*wilāya*), for its part, is the dot of the isthmus in a state of perfect equilibrium. It is the shadow of prophethood, and the place of the spirit's visionary ascent to the highest peaks of the all-encompassing celestial sphere.

When God chooses a servant for sainthood, he brings him out of the darkness of nonexistence into the Light of eternity; out of the darkness of illusion into the Light of understanding; out of the prison of servanthood into the freedom of lordship.

---

1   Q Baqara 2:257.

He pulls the garb of human darkness from him, and clothes him in the pre-eternal Lights of the attributes, upon the carpet of eye-witnessing. He becomes with Him and for Him, subsisting beneath His attributes. God erases from him the darkness of sensoriality and regard for created beings with the Light of vision and eye-witnessing. He sees how the cosmos is an out-pouring from the seas of divine invincibility upon the meadows of the spiritual world, and from the meadows of the spiritual world to the vessels of the physical world.

Sidi Ibn ʿAṭāʾ Illāh says in the *Aphorisms*, "The cosmos is all darkness, and is only illuminated by the manifestation of the Real therein. If someone sees the cosmos but does not see Him in it, or with it, or before it, or after it, then he is lacking Light, and is veiled from the suns of mystical knowledge by the clouds of ephemera." Sidi Ibn ʿAjība says in his commentary on this aphorism:

When it comes to witnessing God, people are of three categories: the masses, the elite, and the elite of the elite. This is why Ibn ʿAṭāʾ Illāh says in the aphorism, "If someone sees the cosmos but does not see Him in it, or with it, or before it, or after it, then he is lacking Light, and is veiled from the suns of mystical knowledge by the clouds of ephemera." Those who are in the station of subsistence see God the very instant their gaze falls upon the cosmos; they affirm the ephemera through God, and see nothing except through Him. Yet because of their perfection, they affirm the Mediator and that which it mediates; they witness God upon witnessing the Mediator, without giving precedence to one over the other, and without regard to the container or the content.

Shaykh Mulay 'Abd al-Salām ibn Mashīsh ﷺ said to Abū al-Ḥasan al-Shādhilī ﷺ, "O Abū al-Ḥasan, sharpen your faith-inspired inner vision, and you will find God in everything, and upon everything, and with everything, and before everything, and after everything, and above everything, and beneath everything, and near everything, and encompassing everything—with a nearness that befits Him, and an encompassment that suits Him. Pass beyond containment, boundary, place, and direction; beyond companionship and spatial proximity; beyond the confines of created being. Erase it all with His attributes: the First, the Last, the Manifest, the Hidden, and with 'He, is He, is He (*Huwa Huwa Huwa*).' God was, and there was nothing with Him; and He is now as He ever was."

Another of them said, "I never saw anything without seeing God in it."

The disciples who walk the Path behold the cosmos, then they behold the Maker with it, and the cosmos disappears from their vision the moment they behold Him. Such is the state of the people of high aspiration. Those in the station of annihilation, however, behold God before beholding creation, in the sense that they do not see creation at all, for to them it is unreal; in their drunkenness, they are oblivious to the Mediator and to divine wisdom, drowning in the sea of Lights. All ephemera are effaced for them. One of them said regarding this station, "I never saw anything without seeing God before it."

The veiled people who rely on proof and argument behold only the cosmos, and do not see the Maker whether before it or after it. They find proof for His existence in the existence of the cosmos. This applies to the Muslim masses, the people of the right hand, and they are the ones who are "lacking Light," deprived of it and veiled from the suns of mystical knowledge by the clouds of ephemeral things. Those suns have risen and their Light has shone forth; but the sun must have clouds, and a beautiful woman must have a veil. May God reward the poet who said:

The lifting of her veil is what veils her;
How strange it is that appearances conceal![1]

God's Messenger ﷺ said, "God created His creation in darkness, then cast some of His Light upon them. Those whom the Light touched were guided, and those whom it missed went astray."[2]

The saints are God's Light on earth. They are His beloveds and chosen ones. Their hearts are the Niche for the Lights of guidance; if you know them and keep their company, you will be guided; if you miss them, you will stray from the path without realizing it.

1   *Īqāẓ al-Himam,* pp. 63-64.
2   Ibn Ḥibbān, *Ṣaḥīḥ* 6303.

The first thing that is made beloved to the servant on the path of sainthood is solitude and isolation. This was the Sunna of our Master the Messenger of God ﷺ, whose prophethood began with a love for solitude, inspiring him to spend several nights at a time engaged in worship in the Cave of Ḥirā'. If you wish to recite in the Name of your Lord, you must make a retreat in the Ḥirā' of your heart, and pass away from your attributes and divest yourself of your ego. Clear out from your heart all the objects of your love, beginning with your own soul that lies between your sides, for it is your worst enemy. God says, **And when you have withdrawn from them and all that they worship save God, then take refuge in the cave. Your Lord will spread forth something of His Mercy for you, and make you incline to ease in your affair.**[1]

Withdraw, and God will **spread** the **mercy** of His Lights upon you, and guide you to a Shaykh who will show you His secrets. He will give you to drink the wine of non-delimitation from the cup of delimitation, until you become drunk and oblivious to existence. He will plant the olive seed of necessity in the receptive soil of your heart, and will water it with the waters of love, producing **fruits** of Light for you **at all times.** He will teach you how to craft the elixir of Lights, which is an antidote for the poison of the darkness of other-than-God.

God says: **God is the Friend of those who believe. He brings them out of the darkness into the light. As for those**

---

1   Q Kahf 18:16.

who disbelieve, their friends are the false gods, bringing them out of the light into the darkness. They are the inhabitants of the Fire, abiding therein.[1] God befriends the saints, just as the latter befriend false gods. God says, **By the soul and the One Who fashioned it, and inspired it as to what makes it iniquitous or reverent.**[2] The false god is your own evil-enjoining soul; it is your caprice, and the quality of divisiveness that manifests within you. Those who befriend idols conceal the Lights of innate disposition with the darkness of heedlessness and base desire. They blindly follow others and pursue their caprices. They are the people who say, **We follow what our fathers followed.**[3] They are the ones who call to the misleading paths described in the noble hadith, "God's Messenger ﷺ drew a line, and then drew several lines on either side of it. Then he said, 'This is God's straight path, and each of the others has a devil upon it, calling to it.' Then he recited, **This indeed is My path made straight.**"[4]

The protégés of false gods are bandits who waylay the path to God's Light, drawing people away from the Lights of His innate disposition into the darkness of conjecture. Yet how could God ever be known through conjecture? How could He ever be known through darkness?

1   Q Baqara 2:257.
2   Q Shams 91:7-8.
3   Q Luqmān 31:21.
4   Nasā'ī, *Kubrā* 10662; Q. An'ām 6:153.

The protégés of false gods are the idols of our time. They rival God by dressing up falsehood as truth. Their words are sweeter than honey, but their hearts are sourer than a bitter gourd. They have hearts of wolves, but they are dressed in sheep's clothing. They encourage their disciples to hope for swift spiritual openings and replenishment, but these are no more than empty promises.

Light is a Divine Proof

O mankind! Verily there has come unto you a proof from your Lord. And We have sent down unto you a clear Light. As for those who believe in God and hold fast to Him, He will cause them to enter into His Mercy and Bounty, and will guide them unto Himself upon a straight path.[1]

Sidi al-'Alawī said, may God sanctify his secret:

The dove of union cooed in the midst of separation,
And so by God's power, we set forth for unity.

We are the kings of the earth in nearness to Him;
For His love, we sacrificed both self and family.

We stand in sunlight while others are in darkness;
Wheresoever He discloses, keen is our sight.

Light upon Light from God have we been gifted,
For He guides the worthy to the Friend's holy Light.

---

1   Q Nisā' 4:175-175.

God's proof to His servants is the Master of Creation ﷺ, then his brothers, the saints who come after him. They are the heirs of the Prophets, guides to God, for the Lord has made them an isthmus between eternity and noneternity. They are the doves of union who witness the Light of the attributes, and God's proof against His servants, upholding righteousness in the dispersive realm of separation, purified from the pollutants of sensoriality and the illusions of other-than-God, following in the footsteps of His Messenger ﷺ.

And since the blessed being of the Beloved Prophet ﷺ is itself a demonstrative proof, a pure Light, and a holy Handful, he was not confined by spatial direction, and front and behind were the same to him, as he said, "Do you see this qibla that I face over yonder? By God, your humility does not escape my notice, nor does your bowing. I can see you behind my back."[1] He was free of the imperfections of human nature, and hence God said of him: **Thou threwest not when thou threwest, but God threw.**[2] And the saints follow in his footsteps, their essences loci for his manifest Light.

God said of the ever-truthful Prophet Joseph: **She indeed inclined toward him, and he would have inclined toward her, had he not seen the proof of his Lord.**[3] The proof of his Lord was that Gabriel the Mediator appeared to him bearing the proofs of the Lights of eternity to his heart, so that through the

---

1   Bukhārī, *Ṣaḥīḥ*, 418.
2   Q Anfāl 8:17.
3   Q Yūsuf 12:24.

needle's eye of Zulaykha he beheld a glimpse of union, and Zulaykha vanished in the Lights of divine Oneness.

The proof of God is Light that can be seen by the one whose vision is sharpened by the eternal Lights through the mediation of a Shaykh who lifts the veils of alterity and otherness from his heart, as Sidi al-ʿAlawī said, may God sanctify his secret:

He will lift up the veils that cover his heart,
Preventing him from reaching the highest station.

The one who has not witnessed the Light has no proof; and if he has no proof, his worship is illusory. The Almighty says, **Whosoever calls upon another god along with God, for which he has no proof, his reckoning is with his Lord.**[1] If you do not have the proof of Lights, you are dominated by hidden idolatry, for alongside God you worship the Zulaykha of your soul and immediate gratification. The Prophet ﷺ said, "Idolatry is more hidden than a black ant crawling upon a boulder on a dark night." How could you hope to see it? You must have the Lights of divine Oneness if you are to discover the ant of your hidden idolatry, so that the secrets and subtle ailments within you may gradually be revealed and treated by those Lights. When they shine forth brightly, the maladies of turbidity (*tawḥīl*) will be erased; and it is then that you will truly voice God's oneness (*tawḥīd*). Ibn ʿAjība says in his Qurʾān commentary:

---

1   Q Muʾminūn 23:117.

Verily there has come to you a proof from your Lord: Those who are able to bestow upon you divine knowledge and guide you to Him, namely His saints, have **come to you** bearing a manifest **proof** that none but the blind could fail to see. **And We have sent down unto you** from the secret of Our holiness and the ocean of Our omnipotence **a clear Light** by which you may witness the secrets of the Essence and the Lights of the attributes; that is, witness the disclosures of the Primal Muḥammadan Handful. **As for those who believe in God and hold fast to Him** as they journey to Him, **He will cause them to enter into His Mercy**, which is the presence of holiness, **and Bounty**, which is infinite ascension through the mysteries of the gnostic sciences, **and will guide them unto Himself**, unto arrival at Him, which means witnessing Him in that Light, **upon a straight path** that leads to Him in the shortest possible time. Or it could be that the verse is chronologically inverted, and that it means, "He will guide them to Him upon a straight path that they will travel until they arrive at Him, whereupon He will admit them into the mercy of His presence and the bounty of increased intimate knowledge of Him." God knows best.[1]

---

1   *Al-Baḥr al-madīd*, 2/137.

Light is Guidance from the Darkness of Error

O People of the Book! Our Messenger has come unto you, making clear to you much of what you once hid of the Book, and pardoning much. There has come unto you from God a Light and a clear Book, whereby God guides whosoever seeks His Contentment unto the ways of peace, and brings them out of darkness into Light, by His Leave, and guides them unto a straight path.[1]

The saint is one of God's Lights: a subtlety in density, divinity in humanity, heart in vessel. He is God's deputy and representative among His creation. Those who follow his Lights, which are kindled from the Niche of prophecy, will be guided to **the straight path.**

God begins by speaking of guidance to the **ways of peace**, which are the Lights of the beginning stages of the Path, and then says, **and brings them out of darkness into Light**; that is, pulls them out of the mires of darkness into the rivers of Aḥmadan-Muḥammadan Light. Anyone who is granted this is certainly **guided unto a straight path.**

So there are two instances of guidance. The first is for those who experience the disclosures of the Lights of the divine attrib-

---

1   Q Māʾida 5:15.

utes and acts, namely the **ways of peace.** The second is for those who experience the secret truths of the Essence, namely the **straight path**, the path of the Singular Alif, the Alif of divine Oneness.

As for how He connects the **clear Book** with **the Light** before it, there is a particular secret and meaning to this, which is that **the Book** is a setting place, and **the Lights** are the stars that set therein. God says, **I swear by the setting-places of the stars! And truly it is a magnificent oath, if you but knew.**[1] The treasured meaning buried in this verse is that when God loves a servant, He causes the star of love to rise to the heaven of his tranquil spirit, where its Lights illuminate the hidden gnostic sciences within the orchards of his heart. There, beyond the veils of passion, the trees of divine mystery appear to him, and the bird of his spirit alights upon the branch of eternity. Then when the breeze of the All-Merciful blows, his heart trembles upon experiencing these unveilings, and his inner core quakes upon witnessing the heralds of the spiritual opening. His spirit returns, drunken and dizzy after being buffeted by the powerful waves of the sea of Beauty and Majesty, bearing the calm waters of the ocean of divine equilibrium. He pours these waters upon his fervent heart, and the tree of Oneness grows, bearing the fruits of God's exclusive singularity. He no longer wanders lost in the remote plains of detachment, nor speaks out of impulsive caprice and chaotic thought, but only out of the

---

1   Q Wāqiʿa 56:75-76.

inspiration of witnessing. Then when he draws nigh and approaches from the vast horizontal periphery to the essential center of the ocean invincibility, and the hand of omnipotence casts him into the waters of ultimate reality, it is then that he is truly garbed in the robe of, "I become him." There, he subsists between the two bows, without beginning and without end, beyond all qualification, separation, union, proximity, or distance. He realizes the secret of sincerity.

Ibn 'Ajība says:

By the star when it rises, your companion has neither strayed nor erred; nor does he speak out of caprice.[1] God swears by the star of knowledge, when it rises over the horizon of the heaven of sober hearts, that the possessor of this heart—in which the star of knowledge in God has risen, and upon which the suns of reality shine—has not strayed or erred, nor does he speak out of caprice, for he is engrossed in witnessing God, and nothing discloses to him but God. **It is naught but a revelation revealed**: that which is disclosed therein is nothing but revelation revealed through divine inspiration, **taught to him by one of awesome power,** namely the divine inrush, **possessed of vigor** and might, for it is from the presence of the All-Conquering, and so it overpowers all that it encounters. **It stood upright when upon the highest horizon** of the heaven of the unseen, **then drew nigh and came close** to the heart, **till it was within two bows' length** or the heart **or nearer. Then He**

---

1   Q Najm 53:1-3 ff.

revealed, through the mediation of that inrush, **to His servant what He revealed** of the mysteries and secrets of reality, and the unveilings of unseen decrees. **The heart lied not in what it saw**, for it was true, but the subjugation of servanthood veiled it from exact knowledge of the moment of its occurrence.

And indeed he saw him another time: the heart saw the mysteries of the Essence of God another time, in the world of invincibility outside the circle of cosmic disclosures; these are the subtle mysteries that surround the Lights of the spiritual and physical worlds, **at the lote tree of the boundary**, the tree of the Muḥammadan Handful where all the knowledge of the learned and the spirits of the martyrs reach the end, for even the thoughts of the gnostics cannot reach beyond it; **by which lies the Garden of the refuge**, to which the thoughts of the gnostics and the secrets of the firm-rooted knowers return home; **when there covered the lote tree that which covered**, when the cosmic tree was covered with annihilation and erasure as the suns of reality shone mightily forth.

The gaze swerved not; the inner vision did not swerve from witnessing those mysteries, nor was it veiled from them by earth, heaven, Throne, or Footstool, for those worlds are subtle in the gaze of the gnostic.

Nor did it transgress the limit of servanthood such that it aspired to the periphery by the magnificence of lordship; for the periphery cannot be reached, whether in this world or the next, and there is only an endless ascension through unveilings, and a perpetual deepening of the sweetness of witnessing.

Indeed, he saw the greatest of the signs of his Lord. This pure heart saw the greatest wonders of its Lord, for it contained Him Whom neither earth nor heaven can contain.[1]

1   *Al-Baḥr al-madīd,* 7/236.

The Revealed Scriptures are Light

*Truly We sent down the Torah, wherein is a guidance and a Light,
by which the prophets who submitted judged those who are Jews,
as did the lordly ones and the sages, in accordance with such of
God's Book as they were bidden to preserve and to which they
were witnesses. So fear not mankind, but fear Me! And sell not
My signs for a paltry price. Whosoever judges not by that which
God has sent down—it is they who are disbelievers. And therein
We prescribed for them: a life for a life, an eye for an eye, a nose
for a nose, an ear for an ear, a tooth for a tooth, and for wounds,
retribution. But whosoever forgoes it out of charity, it shall be an
expiation for him. Whosoever judges not by that which God has
sent down—it is they who are wrongdoers. And in their footsteps,
We sent Jesus son of Mary, confirming the Torah that had come
before him, and We gave him the Gospel, wherein is a guidance
and a light, confirming the Torah that had come before him, as a
guidance and an exhortation to the reverent.*[1]

The circumstance behind the revelation of these verses was
related by Abū Hurayra, who told of how a Jewish man and
woman committed adultery, and so the Jews said to one another,

1   Q Mā'ida 5:44-46.

"Let us go to that Prophet, for he has been sent with a lighter law than ours. If he rules something less than stoning, we shall accept it, and clear our consciences before God, for we will be able to say, 'One of Your Prophets ruled so.'"

So they went to God's Messenger ﷺ, who was sitting in the mosque with his Companions, and said, "Abū al-Qāsim! What say you of a man and woman who commit adultery?" He did not answer immediately, but went to their Torah school and stood by the door, and said, "I ask you by God, Who revealed the Torah to Moses: what does the Torah tell you should be done with the adulterer?" They replied, "His face should be tarred, and he should be flogged, and then the two of them should be paraded about on a donkey, riding backwards."

A young man there remained silent, and when the Prophet ﷺ saw this, he encouraged him to speak up. The young man said, "By God, the truth is that the Torah prescribes stoning." The Prophet ﷺ said, "When was it that you first decided to replace God's ruling with a lighter one?" He replied, "A man committed adultery but was excused from stoning because he was a kinsman of a king of ours. Then a man from another family committed adultery and was to be stoned, but his people were adamant that unless the first man was stoned, their kinsmen would not be stoned either. So they came up with this new punishment and agreed on it." The Prophet ﷺ said, "I shall judge by what the Torah says," and they were stoned.

Al-Zuhrī said, "We have been told that this verse was revealed in connection with this: **Truly We sent down the**

Torah, wherein is a guidance and a Light, by which the prophets who submitted judged; and the Prophet ﷺ was one of them."[1]

The Psalms are the disclosure-site of the divine acts, the Torah of the attributes, the Gospel of the names. The Holy Qur'ān contains them all, for it is their meeting place; the union-site of the acts, attributes, and names. It manifests the sciences of the Oneness of the Essence, and so is the disclosure-site of union, while the other heavenly Scriptures have it dispersed within them. Or one could say that the Qur'ān is the setting-place, and the Scriptures are the disclosure-site of the star, as God says, **I swear by the setting places of the stars ! And truly it is a magnificent oath, if you but knew. Truly it is a Noble Quran.**[2]

In the terminology of the Karkarī Order, the Holy Qur'ān is an attribute subsisting through the eternal Essence, transcending letters, delimitation, and sounds. It is the highest remembrance, the greatest world, manifesting in the setting-places of the stars. It is the disclosure of God's singular identity, sent down in the formal human character of the Perfect Man, our master the Messenger of God ﷺ. The Qur'ān is the universal Scripture, which is why it rules over all others, for it comprises the properties, attributes, and names.

1 *Asbāb nuzūl al-Qur'ān,* p. 199.
2 Q. Wāqi'a 56:75-77.

A noble ḥadīth states that ʿUmar ibn al-Khaṭṭāb once took the Prophet ﷺ a book he had received from one of the People of the Book and read it to him. The Prophet ﷺ became angry and said, "Will you let yourself be misled by it, Ibn al-Khaṭṭāb? By Him in Whose hand is my soul, I have brought it to you fresh and clean. Do not ask them about anything, for they might tell you something true and make you deny it, or tell you something false and make you believe it. By Him in Whose hand is my soul, if Moses were alive now, he would have no choice but to follow me."[1]

God did not leave anything out of the Book, for His Holy Book contains tidings of everything that exists whether great or small, obvious or subtle, outward or inward. Everything from the heights of the Throne to the depths of the earth is gathered within it. All the sensory things of the material world are written in its lines; all the meanings of the spiritual world are recorded in its dotted characters; all the unseen mysteries of the invincible world are concealed in its unqualified ink.

It is related that someone asked Shaykh Fakhr al-Dīn al-Rāzī ﷺ about the Qurʾān and how God describes it as **clear Arabic.**[2] He replied, "Indeed, but the Arabic of our Lord is not like your Arabic." The questioner elaborated, "But the Qurʾān contains some letters that are extraneous, because if they were removed the meaning would be the same, since the letters do not add any meaning." The Shaykh ﷺ said, "So you theorize—

1   Aḥmad, *Musnad* 15156.
2   Q Naḥl 16:103.

but it would be better if you provided some concrete examples to prove your assertion." The man said politely, "When God Almighty tells the story of Korah (Qārūn), He says, **We gave him such treasure that the keys to it would truly be a heavy burden for a group of strong men.**[1] The word 'truly' (*inna*) here is extraneous, since it does not add any meaning and the verse would stay the same thing without it." The Shaykh said, "What was that group of strong men who would have struggled to carry those keys?" This question puzzled the man since it seemed irrelevant to his concern, but he answered, "The books say that they were carried upon mules." The Shaykh said, "How many mules?" The man replied, feeling even more puzzled, "I do not know." The Shaykh said, "The answer is found in the word *inna*, the one you would like to see removed. For it is composed of *Alif* and *Nūn*, which have the values one and fifty respectively, meaning that it would have taken fifty-one mules to carry the keys to Korah's treasure. If we removed it from the Qur'ān, this information would be lost. You might ask why knowing this information is useful. The answer is that it speaks to the perfection of the Creator, Who says, **We have neglected nothing in the Book.**[2] Likewise, our master 'Abd Allāh ibn 'Abbās said that if he lost his camel's halter, he could find it in the Qur'ān. This is why we say that the language of the Qur'ān is the Arabic of our Lord, not the Arabic of our own understanding."

1   Q Qaṣaṣ 28:76.
2   Q An'ām 6:38.

This is one of the features of the Holy Qur'ān, which is why it brings together all the Scriptures that preceded it, embodying their meanings and laws, manifesting their secrets and subtleties.

Al-Baqlī says in his commentary:

Regarding **the lordly ones and the sages**, the meaning of "lordly one" (*rabbānī*) is the one who is related to the Lord (*Rabb*) through gnosis, love, and affirmation of unity. When the seeker reaches God through these stages and becomes rooted in beholding His Beauty and Majesty, adorned with His attributes and bearing the Lights of His Essence, and becomes annihilated to himself and subsistent with his Lord, he becomes **lordly**. It is like when iron is placed in the fire. The iron is prepared to receive the fire, though it does not become fire itself; rather, when it comes into contact with the fire, it glows red hot and becomes fire-like. In the same way, the gnostic is illuminated by the disclosure of the Lord, and so becomes lordly, spiritual, and luminous, characterized by the world of spirit and divine invincibility. His speech is from the Lord, to the Lord, and with the Lord. The ardent lovers of God are those who stand in His Presence, those who behold the unveiled Face of God.

The "sages" (*aḥbār*) are those who hear directly from God without intermediary, and differentiate between truth and falsehood by the Light of God. It is said that the lordly ones are those who return always to God no matter what state they are in, while the sages are those who have knowledge of God and His signs. It is also said that the lordly ones are those who know

God, and the sages are those who know the laws of God. Ibn Ṭāhir said that the lordly ones are the Companions, who took the Word of the Lord from the highest envoy and most intimate mediator, while the sages are the scholars of the Muslim community who put their knowledge into practice.

Whosoever judges not by that which God has sent down— it is they who are disbelievers: the one who has direct knowledge of the command from God in his every breath and movement receives the revelation of inspiration from God, which descends into his heart. He might even speak to him and address him directly, as the Prophet ﷺ said, "Among my community are Those Who Are Spoken To (*mukallamūn*), and 'Umar is one of them."[1] If he then does not judge by what God sent down to his heart by raising it from doubt to certainty, from darkness to Light, from defiance to compliance, from falsehood to truth, from idolatry to monotheism, from injustice to justice, and from disobedience to obedience, the verdict of these three verses[2] will be laid down upon him. He will be guilty of ingratitude in that he is not thankful for the blessing of discoursing with God, wrongdoing in that he does not apply his knowledge to his action, and iniquity in that he violates God's will for His creation.[3]

---

1   A similar version of this ḥadīth is found in Bukhārī, *Ṣaḥīḥ*, K. Aḥādīth al-Anbiyā', 3469: "In the communities before you, there were people who were inspired [*muḥaddathūn*]. If there is one in my community, it is 'Umar."

2   The commentator is referring to Q 5:47 as well here.

3   *'Arā'is al-bayān*, 1/314.

Light and Darkness are the Secret of Polarity

Praise be to God, Who created the heavens and the earth, and made darkness and light. Yet those who do not believe ascribe equals to their Lord![1]

Al-Bayḍāwī says in his commentary on this verse:

The Almighty here declares that He is deserving of praise for these tremendous boons, whether He is praised for them or not, for they constitute an conclusive argument against those who ascribe equals to their Lord. He said "heavens" in the plural and "earth" in the singular, even though there are as many earths as heavens, because their levels are essentially different and diverse in their effects and motions. He mentioned the heavens first because of their nobility and high station, and also because they were created first.

And He made darkness and light: He brought them into being; the difference between "creating light" (*khalq*) and "making light" (*jaʿl*) is that "creating" in Arabic implies apportionment, while "making" implies "placing into a container."[2]

---

1   Q Anʿām 6:1.
2   *Anwār al-tanzīl*, 1/477.

So the Almighty praises Himself by Himself, knowing as He does that creation cannot possibly praise Him enough. He says, **All praise belongs to God**, for His praise is eternal and without beginning, and only the beginningless can praise the beginningless. The attributes and names praise none other than the Essence by disclosing the qualities of Beauty and Majesty, and manifesting Its self-subsistence and perfection.

The treasured meaning buried in this verse is that one of the ways in which He praises Himself is by creating binaries: He creates the heavens and the earth, the heavens of duties and the earth of self-interests, the heavens of luminous veils and the earth of dark veils, the heavens of the unseen and the earth of disquietude, the heavens of luminous rays and the earthly quarry of separative entities. And He manifests Himself between these polarities, and discloses Himself between the contradictory things, so that you may know that **naught is like unto Him.**[1] Al-Ṭabarī and al-Shawkānī, may God have mercy on them, note in their commentaries that Ibn ʿAbbās ﷺ said when a man asked him about the meaning of the verse, **The Command descends among them,**[2] he replied, "Can you be sure that if I tell you, you will not disbelieve?" Tell me, by your Lord, how can you know the truth when you are mired in darkness upon darkness? You lay claim to divine knowledge and to the highest spiritual station, yet you are still dreaming and have

1   Q Shūrā 42:11.
2   Q Ṭalāq 65:12.

not yet woken, nor broken free from the bondage of heedlessness. You believe that you possess agency, influence, motion, stillness, and power, yet you are heedless, heedless, heedless!

You need Light by which to discern your darkness, and by which to know meaning of the opposites. You will not know your darkened soul without the Light of God's spirit that is blown into you. God says, **When I have proportioned him and breathed into him of My Spirit, fall down before him prostrating.**[1]

There is a subtle point in the verse under discussion, which is familiar to the folk of spiritual taste, regarding the meaning of the words "make" and "create." The Holy Qur'ān here uses **created** for the heavens and the earth, and **made** for darkness and Light. The secret to this is that Light and darkness are of the world of pure meaning, which is why God says about the spirit-nature of Adam ﷺ, **Thy Lord said to the angels, "I am making (*jā'il*) a vicegerent upon the earth,"**[2] but said about his clay-nature, **Truly the likeness of Jesus in the sight of God is that of Adam; He created (*khalaqa*) him from dust, then said to him, "Be!" and he was.**[3] Thus "making" pertains to spirits, and "creating" to bodies.

When Light predominates in a person, he pertains more to the spiritual world than to the physical, for he accepts the God's call as conveyed by the Message, and believes in the unseen. When darkness predominates in a person, he pertains more to

1   Q Ṣād 38:72.
2   Q Baqara 2:30.
3   Q Āl 'Imrān 3:59.

his idolatrous animal nature, for he rejects the teachings of the Message and denies the unseen.

Al-Baqlī said, may God sanctify his secret:

And [He] made darkness and light; that is, the One who created the spirit and the heart made in the spirit the Light of intellect and gnosis, signs and objects of contemplation, and made in the heart the darkness of the evil-enjoining soul, in order that servanthood be made manifest in the abode of trial. He also kindled in the heart the Light of faith from the lamp of the unseen, and established in the soul the darkness of base desires from the world of doubt. He also kindled the Light of the spirit by the Light of witnessing, and plunged the heart into the darkness of struggle. Some say that darkness is in the bodies, and Light in the spirits. Others say that He made darkness the acts of the body, and Light the states of the heart.

Al-Wāsiṭī was asked about the wisdom of manifesting the cosmos and God's words, **He created the heavens and the earth**, and replied, "He does not need the cosmos, for to Him it makes no difference whether the cosmos is manifested or not. If it be argued that He created it in order to manifest His lordship, my answer would be that His lordship was already manifest, and indeed it cannot be manifest to any other than Him, for no other has the power to bear it. On the contrary, He both manifested the cosmos and veiled the cosmos with itself, lest His lordship be manifested to any other. None but the Real can bear the Real."

When asked the same question, another master replied, "It was a necessary consequence. Understand the consequence, and you will understand the wisdom of the cosmos's manifestation. One of the pre-eternal attributes of God is knowledge, and one of the objects of His knowledge is the existence of the cosmos exactly as it is. He therefore manifested the cosmos according to both His prior essential knowledge and His pre-eternal will that the cosmos come into being. How could the cosmos not be manifested, when the divine knowledge and will decreed in pre-eternity that it would? It is impossible that the cosmos could remain nonexistent. Moreover, His Essence is the source of His attributes, which are the source of His acts. The meanings of the Essence therefore manifested in the attributes, and those of the attributes in the acts. His transcendent power bore the acts and set them down in the primordial substance at the particular time ordained for this, which He calls **the day He created the heavens and the earth.**[1] It is also true that in pre-eternity, He loved those who love Him and longed for those who long for Him, that the treasures of the Majesty of Essence and Beauty of Attributes might be made manifest and communicated to His beloved ones, as He said: 'I was a hidden treasure, and I loved to be known.' The cosmos was made manifest to honor the beauty of the yearners, and express His pre-eternal love for the lovers."[2]

<hr>

1   Q Tawba 9:36.
2   *'Arā'is al-bayān,* 1/344-345.

The Excesses of Transcendentalism (*tawḥīd*)
and the Mires of Perplexity (*tawḥīl*)

They did not measure God with His true measure when they said, "God has not sent down aught to any human being." Say, "Who sent down the Book that Moses brought as a Light and a guidance for mankind, which you make into parchments that you display, while hiding much? And you were taught that which you knew not, neither you nor your fathers." Say, "Allāh," then leave them to play at their vain discourse.[1]

The story behind the revelation of this verse is that Mālik ibn al-Ṣayf came to challenge the Prophet ﷺ. The Prophet ﷺ said to him, "I ask you by Him Who sent down the Torah to Moses: does it say in the Torah that God hates a fat scholar?" Mālik, who was himself a fat scholar, became enraged and said, "By God, God has not sent down aught to any human being!" His companions were aghast at this and said, "Woe betide you! Not ever to Moses?" He replied, "By God, God has not sent down aught to any human being!" This verse was then revealed.[2]

---

1   Q Anʿām 6:91.
2   Qurṭubī, *Tafsīr*, 8/455.

This blessed verse describes the condition of those who make the divine Lights into abstract meanings that are too transcendent to appear in imaginal forms and are beyond immanent comparability. They proclaim God's transcendent incomparability, but in a cold sterile way that He Himself does not employ, nor did the Prophet ﷺ. Instead of taking guidance from the Book of divine Unity (*tawḥīd*) in all its fullness and drawing guidance from its clarity, they clung to a few disparate pages of it, wallowing in the mire of perplexity (*tawḥīl*). They selected what conformed to their desires, and explained away anything that contradicted them. The result was that they went so far in asserting His transcendence that they made Him seem distant from His servants, though He Himself affirms that He is close to them: **When My servants ask thee about Me, truly I am near,**[1] and He inspired His Prophet to say, "God created Adam in His own image."[2] It is entirely expected, then, that His attributes should manifest upon His servants beyond any dualism, for in reality nothing exists but Him. In trying to declare Him transcendent, they instead compared Him to His creation, and distanced Him from themselves. Sidi al-ʿAlawī, may God sanctify his secret, said of such people, "The people furthest from God are those who most fervently declare His transcendence."

You affirm His transcendence with your mind, but liken Him to creation with your heart. Is that transcendence? You do

---

1   Q Baqara 2:186.
2   Bukhārī, *Ṣaḥīḥ,* 5786.

not measure Him with His true measure, for you do not know Him. If you knew Him, you would be aware that every atom subsists through His Essence, exists through His attributes, and manifests through His names.

The treasured meaning buried in this verse is that if you knew Him, you would be aware that He is the All, glorified and majestic! You would see that He is the act and the effect, manifested in the world of possibility. Thus He says of Himself, **God is the Light of the heavens and the earth**, and says, **Who sent down the Book that Moses brought as a Light and a guidance for mankind**, linking Light with guidance. The one touched by the Light will be guided, and the one it misses will go astray and remain in the turbidity of those parchments, comparing God to creation even as he imagines that he is declaring His transcendence, straying ever more distant even as he imagines that he is drawing nearer. He condemns figurative interpretation and then engages in it himself; he calls an argument weak in one instant, and then employs it in his favor the next. All this is occasioned by his darkened caprice. If he surrendered himself to God, it would be better and more enduring for him.

He denies the attributes of God's Messenger ﷺ even as the Jews denied them and erased them from the Torah. God describes him in the Holy Qur'an as Light, and as a Lamp, saying, **a luminous lamp**.[1] Yet you see such a person arguing vehemently that the Beloved ﷺ is but a human being and a serv-

---

1   Q Aḥzāb 33:-46.

ant. Indeed he is a human being, but not like other human beings, just as a diamond is a stone unlike other stones. And indeed he is a servant, but what servant? The foremost of all servants, the best of all servants, the most righteous of all servants ﷺ.

God issued a command to His Prophet regarding such people and others who share their viewpoint, saying: **Say, "Allāh,"** that is, proclaim aloud the levels of God's unity and the meanings of His exclusive singularity, **then leave them to play at their vain discourse.** Leave them in their sensory illusions, relativistic fantasies, and materialistic mirages, their vain discourse (*khawḍ*). The word *khawḍ* literally means a pool of putrid mud, a mixture of water and dust; for the water of transcendence and the dust of immanence are mixed up for them, and their vision is blind to the Lights of guidance when it discloses in the human realm of the senses. They play in their mire, restricting esoteric meanings to the constraints of time by declaring that the beatific vision is for the hereafter alone. Such are the children of the lower world, which is but **play and diversion.**[1]

Sidi al-ʿAlawī said, may God sanctify his secret:

Messenger of God, you are Light given form,
Light upon Light, the Qurʾan embodied.

---

1   Q Anʿām 6:32.

We added to this description of God's Messenger ﷺ:

Seeker of knowledge, meaning, and virtue,
The door to beatitude is wide open to you.

Cleave to the Prophet, the door of the All-Merciful;
Blessings of God upon the Light of Testimony!

The Supreme Gate, the Pillar and the Sanctuary;
Blessings of God upon the Light of Eternity!

Disciple, if you would approach the Secret,
A needy dervish, a lover of the Lord,

Light is the path to the presence of the Mighty,
The only remedy by which you may be cured.

Najm al-Dīn al-Rāzī[1] says in his commentary:
Who could produce a book like the one Moses ﷻ was sent with; a book whose nature is to illuminate hardened hearts with the Light of God and guide them by that Light to God and His religion? Who but God Himself could do so? The books that others produce cannot do this. Yet **you make [it] into parchments that you display!** God sent down a Book to illuminate

---

1   The disciple of Najm al-Dīn Kubrā the founder of the Kubrawiyya Order (d. 1256).

your hearts and guide you to God that you might know Him, and that God might behold its Light in your hearts, yet you made it into parchments by writing it down instead of placing it into your hearts by adorning yourselves with the Book's qualities. Thus it was inevitable that you would **display** it by rendering it down to something you recite and narrate, **while hiding much**, namely the many truths in it which pertain to its infinite Light and guidance.

And you were taught that which you knew not, neither you nor your fathers. This alludes to the status of Muḥammad ﷺ and his religion, wherein lies the culmination and perfection of all other Prophets and religions, as God says: **We sent among you a messenger from among you, who recites Our signs to you and purifies you, and teaches you the Book and Wisdom, and teaches you what you knew not.**[1] What the Prophet ﷺ taught them of the Book lay in God's words: **Say, "Allāh," then leave them to play at their vain discourse**; and the Wisdom he taught them was the secret that is conveyed from master to disciple, from innermost secret to innermost secret. **Say, "Allāh"** with your innermost secret in solitude, completely unmindful of anything but Him, **then leave them,** all creation, **to play at their vain discourse** with one another, until on the Day of Woe they cry out, **We engaged in vain discourse with those who do the same!**[2]

1   Q Baqara 2:151.
2   Q Muddaththir 74:45; Aḥmad ibn ʿUmar Najm al-Dīn al-Rāzī, *al-Taʾwīlāt al-najmiyya.*

Light is Life, and Darkness is Death

Is he who was dead, and to whom We give life, making for him a Light by which to walk among mankind, like unto one who is in darkness from which he does not emerge? Thus for the disbelievers, what they used to do was made to seem fair unto them. And thus have We made great ones among the guilty in every town, that they may plot therein. But they only plot against themselves, though they are unaware. And when a sign comes unto them, they say, "We will not believe till we are given the like of that which was given to the messengers of God." God knows best where to place His message. Humiliation before God and a severe punishment shall soon befall the guilty for that which they used to plot. Whomsoever God wishes to guide, He expands his breast for submission. And whomsoever He wishes to lead astray, He makes his breast narrow and constricted, as if he were climbing to the sky. Thus does God heap defilement upon those who do not believe.[1]

The story behind the revelation of this verse, according to Ibn ʿAbbās, was that it refers to Ḥamza ibn ʿAbd al-Muṭṭalib and Abū Jahl. What happened was that Abū Jahl hurled some refuse upon

---

1   Q Anʿām 6:122-125.

God's Messenger ﷺ, and when news of this reached Ḥamza, who was not yet a believer at that time, he set off angrily for Abū Jahl with his hunting bow in his hand, and struck him over the head with it. Abū Jahl cried out, "Abū Yaʻlā, can you not see what has become of us? We have lost our minds, and allowed our gods to be profaned, and forsaken the ways of our forefathers!" Ḥamza replied, "Who is more mindless than you? You worship stones instead of God! I bear witness that there is no god but God, alone without partner, and that Muḥammad is the Servant and Messenger of God!" God then revealed this verse.[1]

In the terminology of the Karkarī Order, there are two kinds of death: compulsory death when the subtle lordly spirit parts with the human body; and voluntary death, which is a majestic bridge built with many bricks, the first of which is turning away in repentance from other-than-God and breaking free from the dictates of instinctual nature into the spiritual realms, riding upon the celestial steed of the Muḥammadan Lights.

In the terminology of the Karkarī Order, life is an azān that invites the believer to subsistence and heralds the prayer of pre-eternity. It is the secret of the singular substance that encompasses all manifestations of Oneness within the realm of divine self-disclosure.

The treasured meaning buried in these verses is that **he who was dead** means the one who was dead because of his caprice and appetites and his regard for himself and his deeds; the one

---

1   Wāḥidī, *Asbāb al-nuzūl*, p. 227.

to whom We give life is the one who is reinvigorated by the luminous breezes of nearness and connection, and has become oblivious to created things. He turns away from temporality and orients himself toward the Light of our Prophet 'Adnān and the attributes of the All-Merciful. God blesses him with the company of the Folk of God, allowing him to pledge allegiance to them outwardly and inwardly, and thereby revive his heart with the Light of eternity. He washes him with the water of life in the bowl of faith, and opens the eye of his heart with the Lights of subsistence, so that he sees meaning in matter, subsistence in annihilation. His hearing becomes God's hearing, his sight God's sight, his hand God's hand, his foot God's foot. His luminous image is perfected, so that he is in the image of the All-Merciful, as is described in the authentic hadith. He becomes **a Light walking among mankind**, a star for the people of earth by which they may be guided through the darkness of the land of outer Law and the sea of inner Reality. Is this one better, or the one who wanders in the **darkness** of his senses, veiled by himself from himself, dead in the form of the living, asleep in the form of the waking, confined by his human dust-nature in his corporeal earth, **darkness upon darkness**?

Ibn 'Ajība says, may God sanctify his secret:

In the beginning, the spirit remains upon the innate disposition that God instilled in it, which is knowledge and affirmation of lordship. As it develops, it may undergo several deaths, and then be revived after each one according to God's will. It might die of unbelief and then be revived by faith. It might die of sin and wrongdoing and then be revived by repentance. It might die of selfishness and appetite and then be revived by asceticism, piety, and spiritual discipline. It might die of heedlessness and laziness and then be revived by wakefulness and contrition. It might die of regard for sensoriality and the prison of created being and matter, and then be revived by regard for meaning and meditative escape into the realm of witnessing and vision. After this, it will never die again. God knows best.[1]

Al-Baqlī said, may God sanctify his secret:

One of them said that the verse means, "one who is dead by regard for deeds, to whom We give life by regard for neediness."

Qāsim said, "He gives life to His saints by the Light of awareness, just as He gives life to bodies by spirits."

Sahl said that it means, "one who is dead by ignorance, to whom We give life by knowledge."

Ibn ʿAṭāʾ said that it means, "one who is dead by separation from Us, to whom We give life by connecting him to Us, making for him a Light too, not like him whom We leave in darkness."

The Master (Qushayrī) said, "For this camp, faith means the life of the heart in God. When heedless people are inspired with remembrance, they become alive after having been dead. If the people of remembrance are ever beset by forgetfulness, they die after having lived. The one who is amid the Lights of nearness, beneath the rays of gnosis, and inside the spirit of inner vision cannot be rivaled by the one amid the mysteries

---

1   *Al-Baḥr al-madīd,* 2/304.

of darkness, nor can the one trapped in the prison of blights possibly rival him."

A subtle notion occurred to me regarding the interpretation of this verse, namely that by "dead" is meant the one who is annihilated in the world of tawḥīd denial, but then having witnessed the thunderbolts of divine majesty and glory, God gives him life by the spirit of subsistence so that he witnesses His endlessness, and is revived from the wasteland of denial by the Lights of knowledge, and walks with the aid of secrets and spirits in the Lights of subsistence, never again to be veiled from the Lights of the beauty of His Face. Every dead heart is revived by him, and every soul that is bereft of obedience to its Lord and beguiled by the darkness of its appetites is made tranquil upon beholding him.[1]

Ibn Ḥibbān narrates in his *Ṣaḥīḥ* that God's Messenger ﷺ said, "God created His creation in darkness, then cast some of His Light upon them. It hit those He willed, and missed those He willed; and He knew who it would miss and who it would hit. Those whom any of His Light hit were guided, and those whom it missed went astray." 'Abd Allāh ibn 'Amr said after relating this, "This is why I say that the pen has dried."[2]

If God wishes to guide someone according to His pre-eternal will, He expands his breast with the Lights of nearness and makes him taste the sweetness of yearning, so that he yearns to

---

1   *'Arā'is al-bayān,* 1/396.
2   Ibn Ḥibbān, *Ṣaḥīḥ,* 6303.

meet Him and becomes cold towards the abode of delusion. The Prophet ﷺ was asked about the verse, **Whomsoever God wishes to guide, He expands his breast for submission.**[1] They asked, "Messenger of God, how does God expand his breast?" He replied, "It is a Light that He casts into it, so that it expands for him and grows more spacious." They said, "Is there any sign by which this may be recognized?" He replied, "Turning towards the abode of eternity, and turning away from the abode of delusion, and preparing for death before meeting it."[2]

If this Light of guidance is cast into a person's heart, he yearns for the gardens of nearness and becomes detached from other-than-God. His entire being is attracted towards the beauty of the attributes upon the carpet of witnessing. You see him always enraptured and impassioned in solitude. He converses with the trees, and speaks with the stones, and holds discourse with the stars. He turns his face unto Heaven, the hands of his heart outstretched, that God might turn him towards a qibla **well pleasing** to him.[3]

1   Q An'ām 6:125.
2   Ibn Kathīr, *Tafsīr*, 3/335.
3   Q Baqara 2:144.

Following the Light is an Act of Helping
God's Messenger ﷺ

Those who follow the Messenger, the unlettered Prophet, whom they find inscribed in the Torah and the Gospel that is with them, who enjoins upon them what is right, and forbids them what is wrong, and makes good things lawful for them, and forbids them bad things, and relieves them of their burden and the shackles that were upon them. Thus those who believe in him, honor him, help him, and follow the light that has been sent down with him; it is they who shall prosper.[1]

Al-Bukhārī narrates in his *Ṣaḥīḥ* that ʿAṭāʾ ibn Yasār said, "I met ʿAbd Allāh ibn ʿAmr ibn al-ʿĀṣ and asked him, 'Tell me about the description of God's Messenger ﷺ in the Torah.' He replied, 'Indeed, by Allah, he is described in the Torah in some of the same ways as he is in the Qurʾān: **O Prophet, We sent you as a witness, a tiding-bearer, a warner, and a refuge for the unlettered. You are My servant and my messenger. I have named you the reliable one, who is neither coarse, nor vulgar, nor loud-mouthed in the marketplace; one who does not repay one ill turn with another, but forgives and pardons.**

1   Q Aʿrāf 7:157.

God will not take him back until He has straightened the crooked nation by him so that they say, "There is no god but God." By this will be opened blind eyes, deaf ears, and covered hearts."[1]

Ibn ʿAjība says:

Shahr ibn Ḥawshab related that Kaʿb al-Aḥbār, who was from the Ḥimyar people of Yemen, told him the story of how he came to Islam. Kaʿb's father was one of those people of the Torah who believed in God's Messenger ﷺ before his coming. Kaʿb recalled, "My father was one of the most learned scholars of the Torah and the other scriptures of the Prophets, and he did not conceal from me anything that he knew. When death came to him, he called me and said, 'Dear son, you know that I never kept any of my knowledge from you—but I kept from you two pages containing the description of a prophet who will be sent, and whose time is nigh. I was reluctant to tell you of him, for I could not be certain that after I died you would not follow one of those false pretenders. I cut them out of my book and placed them in that alcove over there, and plastered them over. Do not take them out until that Prophet emerges. When he does, follow him and look at them, and God will grant you abundant goodness.'

"When my father died, I could hardly wait for the mourning to be over so that I could look at the pages. I found there written, 'Muḥammad is God's Messenger ﷺ, the Seal of Prophets;

1   Bukhārī, *Ṣaḥīḥ*, 2125.

no Prophet will come after him. He will be born in Mecca, and emigrate to Ṭayba. He is neither coarse, nor vulgar, nor loud-mouthed in the marketplace. He who does not repay one ill turn with another, but repays the ill with good, and forgives and pardons. His Community are the Praisers, who praise God for every honor and in every circumstance. Their tongues are hum-bled with magnifications. God will help their Prophet against all who oppose him. They wash their loins with water, and wrap garments about their waists. Their bear their scriptures in their hearts, and eat their offerings in their bellies yet still receive reward for them. They are as merciful to one another as parents to their children. They will be the first community to enter Par-adise on the Day of Resurrection. They are the forerunners, the ones brought near, the interceders, the ones interceded for.'"[1]

The treasured meaning buried in this verse is that you should follow the Prophet's ﷺ Lights which emanate from His blessed Glass. So subtle is his Glass that its outer side and inner side are one; hence God praised the coming together of its parts, saying: **Truly those who pledge allegiance unto thee pledge allegiance only unto God. The Hand of God is over their hands.**[2] That is, follow his Lights until you attain the sweetness of witnessing and the pleasure of nearness and con-nection, so that the shackles of the veils that bound your hearts are removed from you. You were once trapped in spiritual

---

1 *Al-Baḥr al-madīd,* 2/402.
2 Q Fatḥ 48:10.

struggle without witnessing, worship without effect, but then He made you taste the fruit of your deeds in this world, and lifted the veils of other-than-God and duality from your hearts through the simplest of works.

Upon my word, this is the sign of the Shaykh and true Heir: He enables you to attain in the blink of an eye, and lifts the veils of your heart merely by the pledge of allegiance without any difficulty or toil, due to the power of his luminosity and the greatness of his innermost secret. He gifts you a Light borrowed from the firebrand of Prophethood through the quality of sainthood, and you taste the sweetness of witnessing and drink from the river of love. You obtain the key to the treasury of the attributes, filled with subtleties of witnessing and lofty ranks, and you are saved from delusional provocations.

As for the false Shaykh of the present age, he prescribes to you thousands upon thousands of invocations, but this produces no effect upon the heart; and then he asks you what you have felt, or what dreams you have dreamed. We do not deny the value of spiritual exertion or the station of dreams, which after all constitute a forty-sixth of prophethood as a hadith states, and no one would deny it but one who rejects revelation itself. But what about the other forty-five parts? My answer is that they are the stations of witnessing and firsthand vision.

The verse brings together the stations of nearness and effort, as well as the proper conduct of the disciple.

The first is following, which cannot be achieved by anyone who violates the Law of the Beloved ﷺ. How could anyone hope to draw near to God when he is filled with pollution? Flesh nourished on the unlawful will inevitably be condemned to the fire of distance. The Prophet 爨 said, "O people! God is pure, and He accepts only what is pure. God has commanded the believers the same as He commanded the Messengers, saying: **O messengers! Eat of the good things and work righteousness. Truly I know what you do.**[1] And He says, **O you who believe! Eat of the good things We have provided you.**[2]" Then he spoke of a man who travels a long road, dusty and disheveled, raising his hands to the sky, "O Lord, O Lord!" Yet his food is unlawful, his drink unlawful, his clothing unlawful, nourished upon the unlawful—how can he expect to be answered?[3]

The second is faith in the Mediator—faith that is sure and certain, so that not an atom of doubt remains in the heart.

The third is honoring, meaning reverence and veneration of the Mediator.

The fourth is help, whether it be with one's possessions, life, family, or children. An authentic hadith states: "Once when we were with the Prophet 爨, he took 'Umar ibn al-Khaṭṭāb by the hand. 'Umar said to him, 'Messenger of God, you are more beloved to me than everything but myself.' The Prophet 爨 said, 'No, by Him in Whose hand is my soul; not until I am more

1   Q Mu'minūn 23:51.
2   Q Baqara 2:172.
3   Muslim, *Ṣaḥīḥ,* 1015.

beloved to you than your own self.' 'Umar said to him, 'Then now, by God, you are more beloved to me than my own self.' The Prophet ﷺ said, 'At last, 'Umar!'"[1]

The fifth is following the Light of the moon of divine Oneness. The Prophet ﷺ said, "You will see you Lord even as you see this moon—you do not doubt your vision of it."[2] This is the sign of the Heir. The one who follows his Light, which is borrowed from the Light of prophethood, will be a helper of God by God. He will not be dominated by distance from God, and will escape the shackles of temporality, and the provocations of the soul and Satan, and attain witnessing of the All-Merciful by the Light of 'Adnān ﷺ.

---

1   Bukhārī, *Ṣaḥīḥ*, 6632.
2   Bukhārī, *Ṣaḥīḥ*, 523.

The Light of God Cannot Be Extinguished

They desire to extinguish the Light of God with their mouths. But God refuses to do aught but complete His Light, though the disbelievers be averse.[1]

The treasured meaning buried in this verse is that if someone desired **to extinguish the light** of the sun by blowing on it, or to conceal its light with the hands of obfuscation and doubt, he would be wasting his time as well as failing to benefit from its light. So how could the Light of eternity, sent down into pure hearts and manifested in luminous minds, giving rise to dazzling miracles and wonders, be extinguished? How could the solar Light of existence that shines over all creation be blotted out? How could the Light of God, whose rays shine upon every brow, be smothered? Everyone subsists by it and loves it whether they know it or not; for even though they deny His Light or confine it to the hereafter, they physically subsist by it and they yearn for it. Their hearts long to behold the Light through the senses and in physical space, and they yearn for its presence in the shadows of this perishing world.

God's norm is to allow darkness to overcome Light, and for

---

1   Q Tawba 9:32.

there to be an endless struggle in the world of meaning and imaginal form between good and evil, being and nonbeing; **But God refuses to do aught but complete His Light, though the disbelievers be averse.**

In the physical world, God's norm is to allow those with illuminated hearts to be overpowered by those with darkened hearts. Sometimes this means people who claim to follow the Sufi way but who associate sainthood with lineage and are forever saying, "My father was this, my grandfather was that," the fake Shaykhs of this era who believe that Sufism is nothing but fancy words, lineages, shawls, and turbans. Abū Hurayra related that God's Messenger ﷺ said, "Whenever a man follows a path in pursuit of knowledge, God smooths for him the path to Paradise. If a person's deeds slow him down, his lineage will not speed him up."[1]

A man is judged by religion alone;
Lineage is no replacement for piety.

Humble Salmān was raised by Islam,
And noble Abū Lahab laid low by idolatry.

Our master Salmān ﷺ hailed from Persia, yet the Beloved Prophet ﷺ said of him, "Salmān is one of our Household." Abū Lahab grew up in Mecca in the proximity of God's Messenger ﷺ,

---

1   Abū Dāwūd, *Sunan*, 3160.

but never saw him for who he truly was; all he saw was the orphan lad in the care of Abū Ṭālib. And God revealed about him: **May the hands of Abū Lahab perish, and may he perish!**[1] Our master ʿAlī said, may God ennoble his countenance:

All people share the same constitution:
Their father was Adam, Eve their mother.

The mothers of men are but vessels
Made to receive heredity from their fathers.

If they should have any noble pedigree,
They rejoice, though it is but water and clay.

No matter what pride you take in your origin,
The glory of ours it could not outweigh.

Virtue is the preserve of the folk of knowledge,
For they provide guidance to all who strive.

A man's worth lies in the good he does;
The ignorant are the enemies of the wise.

Seek knowledge, and accept no substitute,
For people are dead, but the wise are alive.

1   Q Masad 111:1.

People who place all value in lineage and heredity—those who desire temporal power, **like leaning timbers,**[1] highwaymen who waylay the seekers of truth, calling to injustice and deviant paths—are always overpowering God's true Folk by reviling them, attacking them, and accusing them of engaging in sorcery or madness. Praise be to God, praise be to God, praise be to God! We are accused of the very things that the Best of Creation ﷺ was accused of. Al-Baqlī says:

Such is the way of those who follow … those who don the garb of Shaykhs and realized gnostics … who say, "We are the sons of Shaykhs, the chiefs of the Path." Yet far be it for someone who has not experienced the taste of connection with God, and whose heart is attached to other than God, to be one of God's friends!

Junayd said, "How could they extinguish the solar Lights of the attributes, which shine forth from their faces and glisten on their cheeks? These Lights are firmly fixed in the spheres of divine oneness and the heavens of subsistence, and they grow ever brighter. For He is infinite, and there is no end to His attributes."[2]

The Prophet ﷺ said, "God created His creation in darkness, then cast some of His Light upon them. It hit those He willed, and missed those He willed; and He knew who it would miss

---

1   Q Munāfiqūn 63:4.
2   *'Arā'is al-bayān,* 2/12.

and who it would hit. Those whom any of His Light hit are guided, and those whom it missed go astray."[1]

The same divine Light that was diffused upon the spirits in the pre-temporal world of the seed is also diffused upon the bodies in this visible world. The darkened souls, however, are averse to it, and the more they try to extinguish God's Light by blowing upon it, the stronger and brighter it shines. It manifests through them, though they do not realize it; indeed, they are the ones who make it manifest, though they know it not. For things become apparent through their opposites. Study the life of the Best of Creation, and notice how it was none other than Abū Lahab himself who spread the name of the Master of Mankind through the marketplaces during the pilgrimage season, saying, "Do not listen to that bewitching nephew of mine!" See how God made the enemy spread His religion. A noble hadith says, "God may aid this religion by means of a wicked man."[2]

The story of the conversion of Ṭufayl ﷺ is the best example of this. Ibn Isḥāq says:

God's Messenger ﷺ offered his people counsel and called them to leave their present state and attain salvation. When God protected him from Quraysh, they began to issue warnings about him to the people and to those Arabs who visited them from outside the city. Ṭufayl ibn ʿAmr al-Dawsī, who was a noble man and a talented poet, related that he arrived in

<hr>

1   Ibn Ḥibbān, *Ṣaḥīḥ*, 6303.
2   Muslim, *Ṣaḥīḥ*, 166.

Mecca while God's Messenger ﷺ was there, and some men of Quraysh walked up to him and said, "Ṭufayl, you have come to our city while a man in our midst is causing trouble. He has divided our community and caused discord among us. He speaks like a sorcerer, dividing men from their fathers, brothers, and wives. We fear that you and your people will suffer the same fate. Do not speak to him or listen to anything he says."

Ṭufayl recalled, "By God, they kept at me until I had agreed not to listen to him or speak to him. I even put cotton in my ears when I went to the mosque so that I would not hear a word he said, for I did not wish to hear. Then I went to the mosque, and found God's Messenger ﷺ standing inside praying by the Kaʿba. I stood nearby, and God would not allow me to avoid hearing some of what he said; and what I heard was beautiful. I said to myself, 'Woe betide me! By God, I am a talented poet, and I can tell beauty from ugliness. Why shouldn't I hear what this man has to say? If what he says is beautiful, I will accept it. If it is ugly, I will reject it.' So I waited until God's Messenger ﷺ went home, then followed him. When he went inside, I went in after him and said, 'Muḥammad! Your people say things about you. By God, they made me so afraid of you that I put cotton in my ears so I would not hear what you said. But God insisted on making me hear you, and I heard something beautiful. Present your message to me.' God's Messenger ﷺ presented Islam to me, and recited the Qur'ān. By God, I had never heard anything more beautiful, nor more just. I embraced Islam and uttered the testimony of truth. Then I said, 'Prophet of God, I am a man of authority among my people. I shall return to them and invite them to Islam. Pray to God to make for me a sign that will assist my cause with them. ' He said, 'Dear God, make for him a sign!'

"Then I returned to my people. When I reached a ridge overlooking their homes, a **Light** appeared before my eyes like a Lamp. I said, 'Dear God, not in my face! I fear they will think my face has been mutilated for renouncing their religion.' So it moved to the end of my whip. As I went down to them from the ridge, the people began to notice the Light on my whip, as if there were a candle attached to it. I reached them by morning. My father, an elderly man, approached me. I said, 'Away, father, for I am no longer yours, nor you mine.' He said, 'Why, dear son?' I replied, 'I have embraced Islam and followed the religion of Muḥammad ﷺ.' He said, 'Then dear son, my religion is yours.' I said, 'Then go and bathe and wash your clothes, then come to me, and I will teach you what I have learned.' He went and bathed and washed his clothes, then came to me. I presented Islam to him, and he embraced it.

"Then my wife came to me. I said, 'Away, for I am no longer yours, nor you mine.' She said, 'Why?' I replied, 'Islam has come between us, for I have followed the religion of Muḥammad ﷺ.' She said, 'Then my religion is yours.' I said, 'Then go to the shrine of Dhū Sharā and cleanse yourself from it.'" (Ibn Hishām explained that Dhū Sharā was the idol of the Daws tribe, who kept a shrine to him where there was a waterfall running from a mountain.) "She said, 'Do I have anything to fear from the wrath of Dhū Sharā?' I replied, 'I guarantee you do not.' She went and bathed there, then returned to me. I presented Islam to her, and she embraced it.

"Then I called the people of Daws to Islam, but they were slow to accept it. I went to God's Messenger ﷺ in Mecca and said to him, 'Prophet of God, Daws are being stubborn with me. Pray against them!' He said, 'Dear God, guide Daws! Return to your people and call them, and be gentle with them.'

"I remained among the Daws calling them to Islam. Meanwhile, God's Messenger ﷺ emigrated to Medina, and the battles of Badr, Uḥud, and the Trench took place. Then I went to God's Messenger ﷺ along with those of my people who had converted. God's Messenger ﷺ was at Khaybar at the time. Seventy or eighty households of Daws settled in Medina, and then we went to God's Messenger ﷺ at Khaybar, and he included us in the share of the spoils along with the other Muslims."[1]

---

1   Ibn Hishām, *Sīra*, 383-385.

Light is the Moon of Outward Law
and the Sun of Inward Reality

He it is Who made the sun a radiance, and the moon a light, and determined for it stations, that you might know the number of years and calculation. God did not create these, save in truth. He expounds the signs for a people who know.[1]

In the terminology of the Karkarī Order, the outward sun is the disclosure-site of Muḥammadan laws and lordly edicts; and the inward sun is the disclosure-site of axial perfection which annihilates psychic doubts. It is the sign of divine realities, the symbol of the Real, the dot of the secret, the disc of the spirit, the circle of pure meanings.

The moon in the terminology of our Order is the exemplification of God's Light in the imaginal realm, and the determination of divine oneness as a distinct entity through the Lights of Lordship, and the true reality of the human soul. The treasured meaning behind this verse is that it proclaims the glory of the One Who made the **sun** of lordship descend from the heights of divinity down to the cosmic heaven. The **sun's** lordly **radiance** reflects upon the **moon** of servanthood, whose **Lights** are

1 Q Yūnus 10:5.

determinations of **the stations** of godly virtue—so that we **might know the number of the years** of the levels, and **calculate** of the locations of the spiritual stations. **God did not create these, save in truth and for truth.**

The spirit of Command is a radiant **sun** that illuminates the **moon** of the heart, which is turned about between the fingers of the All-Merciful; that is, between the veils of Light and darkness, between the awe of majesty and the vigor of beauty, between the night of contraction and the day of expansion, between the levels of witnessing and unveiling and the obscurities of secrets and disclosures. Thus the root is known from the branch, and the trunk from the shadow, and the levels of **stations** and mysteries of disclosure become clear.

Al-Baqlī says:

He made the **sun** of the Essence a **radiance** for the gnostic spirits, so that they may perceive the wellsprings of beginninglessness and endlessness. And He made the **moon** of the attributes a light for passionate hearts, so that they may behold the glorious qualities of beauty and majesty. The spirits are annihilated by the glory of the Essence in the Essence itself, and the hearts subsist to behold the attributes in the attributes themselves. The **sun** of the Essence is never veiled at any time from the inner vision of the spirits, and therefore they look right at it, and it never leaves them, for it is the station of *tawḥīd* and gnosis...

The **moon** of the attributes appears to the hearts when they are expanded, and is hidden from them when they are contracted. Thus the hearts are turned about in the Lights of the attributes. Just as the **moon** is hidden by the rays of the sun, and grows and shrinks, hearts experience the same as the attributes go between obscurity and clarity. The **moon** of the attributes passes through stations in the hearts of the lovers to manifest experiences and states, and to demonstrate the number of breaths that they ought not let pass by without the concentration of gnosis and pure love, and the moments wherein they ought to vigilantly await divine inrushes. This is what is symbolized in His words, **that you might know the number of years and calculation.**

Some say that they are different **suns**: the **radiance of the sun** of gnosis manifests upon the body and adorns it with the Lights of service, and the **moons** of consolation sanctify the innermost secret with the Light of Singular Oneness, which enter it in the stations of oneness (*tawḥīd*) and exclusive singularity (*tafrīd*). Others say that ... the **sun** of divine grace grants humanity the radiance of obedience, and the **moon** of oneness instils Light in their innermost secrets, so that they turn about in the **radiance** and obedience and the Light of oneness, to the stations of the folk of true faith.[1]

---

1   *'Arā'is al-bayān*, 2/67.

Light is the Antidote for the Blindness of Inner Vision

*Say, "Who is the Lord of the heavens and the earth?" Say, "God."
Say, "Then have you taken, apart from Him, protectors who have
no power over what benefit or harm may come to themselves?"
Say, "Are the blind and the seer equal, or are darkness and light
equal?" Or have they ascribed unto God partners who have created the like of His creation, such that that creation seems alike
to them? Say, "God is the Creator of all things, and He is the One,
the Paramount."*[1]

The treasured meaning behind this verse is that the standard of truth is plain and obvious. **Light** and **dark**, the Light of
virtue and the darkness of sin. The one whose inner vision is
blind is not equal to the one whose inner vision is illuminated
by the **Light** of eternity. **Blindness** is a black spot that covers the
pupil of the heart's eye, preventing it from beholding the **Light**
of eternity in the mirrors of contingency. There are two kinds
of **blindness: blindness** of outer vision, and **blindness** of inner
vision. **Blindness** of outer vision, for the one who bears it
patiently, is good in the herebelow and the hereafter. Anas ibn
Mālik ﷺ related that he heard the Prophet ﷺ say, "God says, 'If

1   Q Raʿd 13:16.

I test My servant through his two beloved ones,'" meaning his eyes, "'and he bears it patiently, I will reimburse him for them in Paradise.'"[1]

As for **blindness** of inner vision, it is a curse in the herebelow and a torment in the hereafter. God says, He will say, **"My Lord! Why hast Thou raised me blind, when I used to see?"**[2] The one who sees only the external vessels of the sensory world and the expressions of illusion is not truly able to see. When the veil of physical space is lifted and he sees how his heart's eye was blind to the luminous meanings that dwelled in the corporeal vessels, he will be told, **"You were indeed heedless of this. Now We have removed from you your cover; so today your sight is piercing."**[3]

So if you believe that you are doing well, though you are wallowing in the mire of your illusions, you must keep the company of God's folk until it becomes clear to you that you are oblivious to the truth and far from God. You must seek the people of Light, so that they might adorn the eye of your heart with the kohl of the Lights of remembrance taken from the Olive Tree that exists beyond the bounds of "where," and grace you with the seed of Lights so that the darkness of your caprice, your folly, and your where-ness is obliterated, and your wretched darkness becomes clear to you.

1   Bukhārī, *Ṣaḥīḥ*, 5329.
2   Q Ṭā Hā 20:125.
3   Q Qāf 50:22.

Al-Baqlī says:

Say, "Are the blind and the seer equal, or are darkness and light equal?" The one whose heart's eye is blocked from beholding the vision of eternity and the **Lights** of beginninglessness cannot be **equal** to the one whose spiritual vision beholds God's Beauty by His eternal **Light**, and is not veiled by base human nature or the objections of others. Nor can the rising **darkness** of the servant's smoky soul **equal** the shining **Lights** of the spirit as they rise to the heights of intimate holiness. Nor can the one who beholds God's Beauty through His eternal Light, and is not veiled by base human nature or the objections of others, be equal to the one who beholds the outline of the world through exoteric knowledge. Nor can the **Light** in the faces of the gnostics be **equal** to the jealousy that shows in the faces of the pretenders.

Abū 'Uthmān said, "The one who is adorned with the **Light** of grace and guided to the path of service cannot equal the one who is blind to them and deprived of them. Can the one who dwells in the **Lights** of divine grace be **equal** to the one who languishes in the **darkness** of his own devices?"[1]

Anyone who desires the Light of spiritual excellence must seek out the gnostics who live according to the Law of the Prophet ﷺ, and engage in continuous remembrance in the dead of night, and the beginning and the end of the day, and endure hunger, wandering, and lack of sleep. Otherwise, there is no

---

1   *'Arā'is al-bayān*, 2/231-232.

hope. Continuous remembrance is the cure for the blindness of separative entities, the antibiotic for the germ of heedlessness, the proven antidote for the one who seeks the divine Presence and nearness to it. The one who desires true life must find a Shaykh to illuminate his heart and bring him out of the darkness of his illusions and caprices, and from the confines of his limited corporeal form into the infinite space of his nondelimited spirit. Such a Shaykh will plant the seed of luminous existence in the depths of his heart, and water it with remembrance and meditation so that it bears the leaves of virtuous states and the fruits of lordly secrets. He will dress him in the robe of "I become his sight with which he sees," so that he knows with certainty that the **blind and the seer are** not **equal.**

Light is the Door to Gnosis

Alif. Lām. Rā'. [This is] a Book that We have sent down unto thee, that thou mightest bring forth mankind out of darkness into light, by the leave of their Lord, unto the path of the Mighty, the Praised—God, unto Whom belongs whatsoever is in the heavens and whatsoever is on the earth. Woe unto the disbelievers for a severe punishment. Those who prefer the life of this world over the Hereafter, and who turn from the way of God and seek to make it crooked; it is they who are far astray. And We have sent no messenger, save in the language of his people, that he might make clear unto them. Then God leads astray whomsoever He will and guides whomsoever He will. And He is the Mighty, the Wise. We indeed sent Moses with Our signs, "Bring thy people out of darkness into light, and remind them of the Days of God. Truly in that are signs for all who are patient, thankful."[1]

The treasured meaning behind these verses is that God's **Book** which connects eternity to noneternity, and brings together meanings and secrets, manifesting the opposites through the eternal attributes and the noneternal modality of the letter. God sent it down from the locations the stars into the

---

1   Q Ibrāhīm 14:1-5.

heaven of the Perfect Man, to bring the community of witnessing out of the darkness of souls and regard for multiplicity into the Light of the innate disposition of "Yea, we bear witness," **by the leave of their Lord**, meaning the **leave** of lordship that derives from the pre-cosmic Cloud with no air above or below, to the path of the Singular Alif that has no beginning. The purpose of the **sending down** of the Book is **guidance** from the **darkness** of unbelief and misguidance to the **Lights** of submission and providential care. The Prophet ﷺ said, "By God, for God to guide a single man through you would be better for you than a fortune of the finest red camels."[1] What could be greater than to be guided to knowledge of oneself and its levels and stations? For God Almighty says, **Whosoever is rightly guided is only rightly guided for the sake of his own soul, and whosoever is astray is only astray to its detriment.**[2] To know the true nature of one's soul is immense beyond measure and priceless beyond counting, for by knowing oneself in the levels of servanthood, one knows one's Creator in the stages of lordship. Guidance is therefore from you and to you, from your sensoriality to your meaning, from your earth to your heaven, from the darkness of your soul to the Light of your Creator, Who shaped you. The mercy gifted from the locations of the stars of guidance came with the scripture of providential care, so that you might discern the path and recognize your true friend upon it.

1   Abū Dāwūd, *Sunan*, 3178.
2   Q Yūnus 10:108.

Ibn ʿAjība says, may God sanctify his secret:

The Prophet ﷺ brought his Community out of many darknesses and into many Lights. The first was out of the darkness of unbelief and idolatry into the Light of faith and submission; then out of the darkness of ignorance and blind conformity into the Light of knowledge and active verification of truth; then out of the darkness of sin and disobedience into the Light of repentance and rectitude; then out of the darkness of heedlessness and indolence into the Light of consciousness and effort; then out of the darkness of self-interest and desire into the Light of renunciation and temperance; then out of the darkness of regard for causality and reliance on convention into the Light of witnessing the Causer and breaking the habitual course of nature; then out of the darkness of reliance on saintly miracles and the sweetness of worship into the Light of beholding the Worshipped; then out of the darkness of reliance on outward sensation into the Light of beholding the secrets of inner meaning, when you become oblivious to creation through witnessing the Creator. That is the final darkness that remains in the soul; when it emerges from it, the soul becomes a spirit and a divine secret. The possessor of that spirit becomes a spiritual and lordly gnostic. After that, nothing remains but perpetual ascension through the witnessing of secrets. This is the status of the axial saint and readiness for direct prophetic instruction;

he becomes a Muḥammadan saint who brings other people out of those darknesses into these Lights.

As for the one who does not reach this station, he may still help to bring others out of some of these darknesses. The warriors who strive in jihad bring people out of the darkness of unbelief into the Light of faith; the scholars bring people out of the darkness of ignorance into the Light of knowledge; the ascetics and worshippers bring their followers out of the darkness of sin into the Light of repentance of rectitude. As for the darkness that remains, none can bring others out of it except for the lordly spiritual masters who receive direct prophetic instruction, by the leave of their Lord, and guide them upon **the path of the Mighty and Wise**, which leads to everlasting glory. Woe to those who reject such people and pursue their selfish interests and caprices, preferring the life of the herebelow to the hereafter; for they are far astray from God's Presence.[1]

---

1   *'Arā'is al-bayān,* 3/354.

The Mediator is Light

Or like the darkness of a fathomless ocean, covered by waves with waves above them and clouds above them—darknesses, one above the other. When one puts out one's hand, one can hardly see it. He for whom God has not appointed any Light has no Light.[1]

In the terminology of the Karkarī Order, the ocean (*baḥr*) is a material symbol of knowledge. Those who recognize this ocean have no knowledge of it, and those who have no knowledge of it recognize it. It has no floor that one may stand upon, and no color that one may refer to. Its drops are separative entities that are integral to its union. Its sandy shores lie within its inner dimension, while its unseen dimension is manifest in its visible realm. Its carrion is lawful, and its water pure. Its waves are illusory images of cosmic forms.

The treasured meaning behind this verse is that the secret of divine foreordination is obscure and profound, elusive and difficult to understand. We are like a feather blown in its wind, not knowing where we may fall. Those who are not blessed with the merciful Lights of union have no share or station, nor any Light or faith; and the one who has no faith has no nearness; and the

1   Q Nūr 24:40.

one who has no nearness has no knowledge; and the one who has no knowledge is **a mirage upon a desert plain.**[1] God says: **He for whom God has not appointed any Light has no Light.** This verse may also be read as: **He who does not appoint [the name] Allah as his Light, has no Light.** That is, **he who does not** make the invocation of the Singular Name of the Essence as a Light for himself, has no Light.

The invocation of the Name requires permission, and permission requires the Mediator. The Mediator, then, is the rope that links you to the world of Lights, the window between the worlds of spirit and body. The one who has no Mediator has no Light; the one who denies the Mediator denies the Name without realizing it; and the one who denies the Name cannot hope to attain any knowledge of the Named.

Even the one who was better than all of us, the Master of Creation, took Gabriel as a Mediator to accompany him to the Lote-Tree of the Farthest Boundary of imaginal forms. If it were possible to do without the Mediator, the Beloved ﷺ would have done without it.

Many people invoke the Singular Name for years but remain in **layers of darkness.** The cause of this is that the chain of their Mediator is severed, and they do not keep up the constant search for knowledge of God. If they had sincere aspiration and firm resolve, they would keep on searching until they found the

---

1   Q Nūr 24:39.

real master, and not pledge themselves to just anyone simply because he made a few grandiose claims. As one poet put it:

The thirsty man does not stop until he drinks,
Nor the hungry man until he finds food.

The one who invokes the Name without a Mediator will remain lost in the dark wilderness of his soul, forbidden from entering the city of spiritual Lights, for he denies the Moses of his heart.

Al-Baqlī says, may God sanctify his secret:

He for whom God has not appointed any Light has no Light: that is, the one who is unaccompanied by the Light of divine knowledge that results from the unveiled witnessing of God which shines in his spirit until the end of his journey to God, will not have any Light of gnosis, or Light of witnessing, or Light of arrival. The gnostic who is sincere in witnessing the Real requires a million Lights in every instant, so that he may look upon the beauty of eternity, recognize the paths of the attributes, and reach the wonders of the Essence through the Light that has no beginning and no end. Qāsim[1] said, "He for whom God has not appointed any Light at the moment of apportioning, has no Light at the moment of creation."[2]

---

1   Al-Baqli frequently refers to "al-Qāsim said" in his tafsir when listing opinions of other Qur'ān commentators. Al-Sulamī has these same quotes from "al-Qāsim" in his tafsir too, and they seem to refer to Abū al-ʿAbbās al-Qāsim al-Sayyārī (d. 342/953), a Sufi and scholar of Merv mentioned in Qushayrī's *Risāla*.

2   *ʿArāʾis al-bayān*, 3/19.

Light is a Prayer from God For His Servants

He it is Who prays for you, as do His angels, that He may bring you out of darkness into light. And He is ever Merciful unto the believers.[1]

The circumstance behind the revelation of this verse was that when God revealed, **Truly God and His angels pray for the Prophet. O you who believe! Pray for him, and invoke greetings of peace,**[2] Abū Bakr said, "Whenever God gives you goodness, He includes us in it." Then God revealed, **He it is Who prays for you, as do His angels, that He may bring you out of darkness into light. And He is ever Merciful unto the believers.**[3]

The *Tafsīr* of al-Qurṭubī notes that al-Naḥḥās related that the Israelites asked Moses ﷺ, "Does your Lord pray?" This shocked him, but then God revealed, "My prayer is that My mercy outruns My wrath." Ibn ʿAṭiyya said, "Some narrated that

---

1   Q Aḥzāb 33:43.
2   Q Aḥzāb 33:56.
3   Wāḥidī, *Asbāb al-nuzūl,* p. 376.

the Prophet ﷺ was asked, 'Messenger of God, what is God's prayer upon His servants?' He replied, 'Glorious, Holy! My mercy outruns My wrath.'"[1]

Ibn 'Ajība says:

The Israelites said to Moses ﷺ, "Does our Lord pray?" This weighed heavily upon Moses ﷺ, but then God revealed to him, "Tell them that I do pray, and that My prayer is My mercy, which envelops all things."

The Ḥadīth of the Ascension includes: "I said, 'My God, I felt ashamed before I came to you, and I heard a voice call with a cadence like that of Abū Bakr, "Halt! Your Lord is praying!" I was amazed at two things: had Abū Bakr reached that station before me? And surely my Lord has no need to pray?'

"God replied, 'I have no need to pray to anyone, but I say, "Glory be to Me! My mercy outruns My wrath." Recite, Muḥammad: **He it is Who prays for you.** My prayer is mercy for you and your Community.' Then he said, 'As for your Companion, I created a being in his form to call to you with his voice, so that you would not feel ashamed, lest you be too awestricken to understand what is required of you here.'"[2]

In the Karkarī Order, prayer (ṣalāt) is a flood of witnessing that cannot be qualified. It is expressed by the unseen bow-shaped semicircle of lordship that hovers above the bā' of servanthood. This form of prayer transcends number, time, and all

1   Qurṭubī, *Tafsīr*, 17/169.
2   *Al-Baḥr al-madīd*, 6/35.

levels of corporeal existence, to the extent that all atoms vanish in the process of performing it and the All comes into manifestation. What remains is the nearness of Him Who has no likeness, beyond the circle made from the two arcing bows of lordship and servanthood, where only the rule of the One remains. This prayer takes place beyond the furthest Lote-Tree that is messengerhood, at the beginning of the Lote-Tree that is sainthood, and within the reality of "Peace be upon us, and upon God's righteous servants."

Prayer is the bliss of annihilated ascension through witnessing the attributes and names. His Name of Light discloses itself, and connects the worlds of necessity and possibility. Shaykh al-ʿAlawī says in *The Holy Gifts* (*al-Minaḥ al-quddūsiyya*):

A group of scholars once went to a gnostic in Egypt for the purpose of challenging him. The gnostic said to them, "Scholars, has anyone among you prayed?" Bemused at this, they replied, "Have any of us not prayed?" He said, "Then you must be among those whom God exempts when He says, **Truly man was created anxious; when evil befalls him, fretful; and when good befalls him, begrudging, save those who perform prayer, who are constant in their prayers?**"[1] They were silent, as they had no knowledge of this prayer, for it is one of the secrets of God which He grants to whom He will, and with which He guides those who long for Him. This is why the Prophet ﷺ said, "Prayer has been made the delight of my eye," because it is the

---

1   Q Maʿārij 70:19-23.

locus of nearness and ultimate desire. Outwardly it is prayer (*ṣalāt*), but inwardly it is connection (*muwāṣala*). It is the link between worshipper and Worshipped. Outwardly it is worship, but inwardly it is witnessing.

Due to its great honor and nobility, prayer was divided into obligatory and recommended, and assigned requirements and meritorious additions, so that the one who truly desires to pray may utilize his inner vision and avoid doubts and errors. It is said that it is not permitted to do anything until one knows God's ruling concerning it. This is especially true of this matter, given its tremendous importance, although few know it and most have no experience of it, except for those who pray, **and who are mindful of their prayers,**[1] **and who turn away from idle talk;**[2] and for the gnostics, everything besides Him is **idle.** They are the ones who know this prayer and its requirements, and who accomplish its obligations and recommendations.[3]

Al-Bayḍāwī says:

He it is Who prays for you with mercy, **as do His angels** with prayers for forgiveness for you and concern for your welfare. The meaning of "prayer" here is the common element between these, which is concern for your welfare and manifesting your nobility, which is a figurative use of the term. Or some say it means mercy, a "bending" of affection as a figurative reference to prayer, which involves a literal "bending" of bows and

---

1   Q Maʿārij 70:34.
2   Q Muʾminūn 23:3.
3   *Minaḥ,* p. 106.

prostrations. The prayers for forgiveness and supplications that the angels make for the believers are also invocations of mercy upon them, and are the cause of mercy inasmuch as the supplications of angels are always answered.[1]

The treasured meaning behind this verse is that the prayer of the Lord is beginningless and eternal, transcending changes of time, place, or obedience and disobedience. When God prays for a person in pre-eternity, He selects him for eternity, and his misdeeds will not harm him. Prayer from Him to us is luminous mercy and spiritual replenishment, taking us out of the darkness of the human soul, the blindness of regard for the material world, and the veils of ego, into the Light of the spiritual realms and lordly attractions.

The sign of God's mercy and prayer upon you is that He brings you out of the darkness of our worldly nature into the witnessing of pre-eternal Lights, so that His power brings you to a lordly Shaykh who sets the wick of your heart alight, and you see the lamp of truth in everything, before everything, and after everything, and wherever you turn your face, you see the face of God. When this happens, you will know that God has chosen you.

Al-Baqlī says, may God sanctify his secret:

In the Almighty's words **He it is Who prays for you, as do His angels,** the prayer of God refers to how He chose the servant in pre-eternity for gnosis and divine love; and when He

---

1   *Tafsīr anwār al-tanzīl*, 3/89.

selected him for this, He made his sins forgiven, and made His elite angels pray for forgiveness for him so that he would not need to do it himself, and could be entirely engrossed in God and His love. With this prayer, He brings them out of the darkness of nature into the Light of witnessing. This is born of His pre-eternal selection and His eternal enveloping mercy. Thus He says, **And He is ever Merciful unto the believers**, for He was merciful unto them before they even existed by bringing them into existence and guiding them to Him without any means or cause

Abū Bakr ibn Ṭāhir said, "The sign of God's prayer upon His servant is that He adorns him with the Lights of faith, clothes him in the robe of grace, and crowns him with the crown of truthfulness. He removes misguiding passions and false desires from his soul, and grants him the contentment that was destined for him."

The Master (Qushayrī) said, "Prayer from God means mercy, and from the angels means intercession, that He might protect you from error with the spirit of connection."[1]

1   *'Arā'is al-bayān,* 3/144-145.

The Light of Inner Vision
is the Life of the Inmost Secret

Not equal are the blind and the seeing, nor darknesses and Light, nor shade and scorching heat. Not equal are the living and the dead. Truly God causes whomsoever He will to hear, but thou cannot cause those in graves to hear.[1]

God says **darknesses** in the plural but **Light** in the singular because there are many hidden paths and routes that lead to ruin, upon each of which is a devil who calls to it. As for the path of Truth, it is one luminous Alif. 'Abd Allāh reportedly said, God's Messenger ﷺ drew a line, and said, 'This is God's straight path.' Then he drew lines on either side of it and said, 'These are the other ways, and each has a devil upon it, calling to it.' Then he recited, **This indeed is My path made straight; so follow it, and follow not other ways.**"[2]

The treasured meaning behind this verse is that the believer who swims in the Light of divine oneness and knowledge, and is surrounded by the **Light**s of reality with every breath, is

1   Q Fāṭir 35:19-22.
2   Aḥmad, *Musnad* 4294; Q. Anʿām 6:153.

not equal to the one who is veiled by self-regard , and who remains in the **darknesses** of his caprice, **dead** and inert to the luminescence of his heart, worshipping the Lāt of I, the ʿUzzā of his lower self, and the Manāt of his caprice.

The one who is alive through remembering and seeing the Living, reposing beneath the shade of spiritual opening and consoled by the breezes of love and intimacy, is **not equal** to the one who is **dead** through the **darknesses** of concrete entities, the **scorching heat** of base desires, and the fires of caprice. He is **not equal** to the one who is deaf to the call of the attributes' **Lights** that appear in this world through the imaginal form of the Radiant Lamp ﷺ, nor the one who is buried in the grave of spatial confinement, and lost in the **darkness** of his heedlessness.

The one who is in the shade (*ẓilāl*) is **not equal** to the one who is lost in error (*ḍalāl*). The former is aided by the Alif of Oneness that descends by the **Lights** of the attributes, while the latter is oblivious to it because of his self-regard, and so remains in the **darkness** of his delusion and caprice.

Ibn ʿAjība says:

The **blind** man who sees only the outward appearances of created things is **not equal** to the seeing man whose inner vision is opened so that he may behold the Creator, rather than halting at the sensory cosmos. Nor are the **darknesses** of sin and heedlessness, and the circle of sensoriality, **equal to** the Light of wakefulness, temperance, and gnosis. Nor is the cool **shade** of contentment and resignation equal to the **scorching heat** of self-management and choice. Nor are the **living**, meaning those who know God and remember Him, **equal to the dead**, meaning those who are ignorant or heedless.

Qushayrī said, "Those who are connected to Us are **not equal** to those who are distracted from Us; those who are attracted to Us are **not equal** to those who are veiled from Us; those whom We show Our reality are **not equal** to those whose hearts We make heedless of Our remembrance."[1]

1   *Al-Baḥr al-madīd.*

The Expansion of the Breast
by the Light of Remembrance

What of one whose breast God has expanded for submission, such that he follows a Light from his Lord? Woe unto those whose hearts are hardened to the remembrance of God! They are in manifest error.[1]

The circumstance behind the revelation of this verse was that it was revealed about Ḥamza, ʿAlī, Abū Lahab, and his son. ʿAlī and Ḥamza were among those whose breasts God expanded, while the hearts of Abū Lahab and his son were hardened to the remembrance of God.[2]

The treasured meaning buried in this verse is that the **Light** of expansion is the prior love that descends by providential care into the **breasts** of the people of love to protect them from the dazzling power of the Lights of magnificence, and to guard them from the mountains of pride. The **expansion of the breast** begins with the melting of the ice of hardness or distance by means of an invocation transmitted at the hand of a lordly Shaykh. Then the **breast** is softened through contemplation of

1   Q Zumar 39:22.
2   Wāḥidī, *Asbāb al-nuzūl,* p. 383.

the soul's horizons and the wondrous secrets it contains, then broadened by cleansing it from other-than-God and outward forms. After that, the Shaykh plants the seeds of the **Lights** of eternity, and he waters them with the water of the Unseen, so that the tree of secrets and mysteries grows and produces the fruits of inner realities and subtle graces. The traces of spatial confinement and distractions of the sensory realm are then erased, and the disclosures of the spirit become manifest.

Al-Qurṭubī says in his *Tafsīr*:

Ibn Masʿūd ﷺ reportedly said, "We said, 'Messenger of God, when God says, **What of one whose breast God has expanded for submission, such that he follows a Light from his Lord,** how is the **breast expanded**?' He replied, 'When Light enters the heart, it **expands** and opens.' We said, 'Messenger of God, what is the sign of this?' He replied, 'Turning towards the abode of eternity, and turning away from the abode of delusion, and preparing for death before it comes.'"

In *Nawādir al-uṣūl* (*Rare Sources*), al-Ḥakīm al-Tirmidhī narrated this as a ḥadīth of Ibn ʿUmar, as follows: "A man said, 'Messenger of God, who is the cleverest believer?' He replied, 'The one who remembers death the most, and prepares best for it. When Light enters the heart, it expands and broadens.' They said, 'What is the sign of that, O Prophet of God?' He replied, 'Turning towards the abode of eternity, and turning away from the abode of delusion, and preparing for death before death comes.'"[1]

---

1   *Al-Jāmiʿ li-aḥkām al-Qurʾān*, 18/265-266.

Woe unto those whose hearts are hardened to the remembrance of God! That is, **woe** unto those whose **hearts** are rusted over by the darkness of pride; those who do not find pleasure in remembering God upon the carpet of humility before His servants, and who do not look down upon themselves while exalting others. And what pride is worse than knowing the cure but not taking it, simply because you look down upon the mediation of the physician? What could be more hard-hearted than recognizing the Light of God, but denying it out of pride? What could be more hard-hearted than twisting verses to suit your darkness and caprice? What could be more hard-hearted than ignorantly holding yourself above the Folk of God, those to whom He has given the elixir of Lights and the antidote for the soul, elevating yourself due to your heedlessness and the darkness of your heart, saying, "I" this, and "I" that? If you only knew how distant you are from God, you would go out into the wilderness and weep at how heedless you are, and bewail your hard-heartedness. You would weep in the hopes of chancing upon a divine breeze that would heal your short-sighted regard for the external appearances of created things, and your immersion in gross spatiality. But your ignorance is compounded; for you are ignorant, and unaware of your ignorance.

Al-Baqlī says in his Qur'ān commentary:

What of one whose breast God has expanded for submission, such that he follows a Light from his Lord? In this verse, God describes the excellence of sincere devotees who witness Him and are illuminated by His holy Lights. He brings their spirits into the expanse of His eternity and the plains of His beginninglessness, and shows them the Light of His beauty and majesty. They become illuminated by His light when He clothes them in the robe of His splendor and the radiance of His pride. This is the meaning of the **expansion of their breasts**. After the Light of His disclosure permeates their spirits and minds, so that the Light of servanthood is raised therein...they see the Real by the Light of the Real, and they see everything apart from the Real from the Throne to the earth by His Light.

God then reproaches their opposites for being hard-hearted, ill-intentioned, and veiled from the Light of His remembrance, after having overwhelmed them with His condemnation and deprived them of the Light of submission and faith, and warned them of His punishment: **Woe unto those whose hearts are hardened to the remembrance of God**, due to following their lower souls and turning away from obedience to their Lord. He then makes clear that they have strayed from their connection to Him, saying: **They are in manifest error.**

Some say that the verse means that He **expands their breasts** for knowledge of Him so that they are upon **Light** from their Lord, by means of which they may behold the Unseen, and be present with their spirits and innermost secrets, for submission to Him.

Ja'far al-Ṣādiq said, "He **expands the breasts** of His saints because they are the storehouse of His treasures, the mine of His signs, and the house of His trust. The saint, moreover, holds the key to that house, and God is his guardian, and he keeps it enclosed therein so that none but him may look upon it. Thus the Prophet ﷺ said, 'God does not look upon your forms, but upon your hearts.'"

Al-Shiblī said, "By **expansion**, He illuminates their hearts and makes their tongues speak wisdom. They are perfected with courtesy and ascetic discipline, so that they reach sainthood and drink from the cup of true faith."

Al-Nūrī said, "They surrender their innermost secrets by the Light of nearness, which is the meaning of **expansion**."

Someone else said that **he follows a Light from his Lord** means that he witnesses his Lord with certitude, oblivious to the material and spiritual realms, so that he reaches every station and masters every state.

Al-Wāsiṭī said, "This is a tremendous gift that none can bear save those who are aided by providential care and protection. God's providential care guards the limbs and the body, and His protection guards the inner realities and the spirit."

Someone else said that it means, "He makes Himself known to them until they know Him, and gives them vision until they see Him; and this is when He **expands their hearts** to see the divine Artisan, and blinds them from seeing anything besides Him. By **expanding their breasts**, they recognize Him; by blinding them to all but Him, they see Him."

Yaḥyā ibn Muʿādh said, "Hard-heartedness is caused by pursual of immediate gratification; the heart is punished by rust and hardness."

Al-Ḥusayn said, "The heart is hardened more by comfort than by forgetfulness and hardship. Comfort intoxicates, while hardship reminds."[1]

1   *ʿArāʾis al-bayān*, 3/209.

Light is a Sun That Rises Over the Earth of the Body

And the trumpet will be blown, whereupon whosoever is in the heavens and on the earth will swoon, save those whom God wills. Then it will be blown again, and, behold, they will be standing, beholding. The earth will shine with the Light of its Lord, the Book will be set down, and the prophets and the witnesses will be brought forth. Judgment will be made between them in truth, and they shall not be wronged. Every soul will be paid in full for that which it has done, and He knows best what they do.[1]

The treasured meaning of this verse is that when the **trumpet** of annihilation is **blown** into the realm of outward forms, all will **swoon**. Sensory illusions and spatial dimensions will disappear, and non-divine possibilities will crumble. Then when the **trumpet** of subsistence is **blown** into it, every part will **subsist** through its Lord: hearing will subsist through the hearing of God, and sight through the sight of God, until the soul returns from **the lowest of the low to the most beautiful stature**, which is the image of the All-Merciful. Upon this, the earth of the pleased and pleasing soul will **shine with the Light of its Lord**, and become a non-delimited spirit swimming in the oceans of

---

1   Q Zumar 39:68-70.

beauty, immersed in the pavilions of the spirit and divine invincibility, subsisting through God, for God, and in God.

Al-Baqlī says:

The earth will shine with the Light of its Lord: God will disclose Himself to the **earth** of the spirits of the gnostics, Prophets, and Messengers, and the **earth** of the hearts of the sincere devotees and those brought near. The Light of His beauty will appear to the visions of the passionate lovers. Then the **earth** of the Resurrection will **shine with its Lights** for all, masses and elites alike. Yet you must know, intelligent one, that His attributes transcend space and are not temporal loci. Every atom, from the Throne to the earth, is immersed in His radiant Lights forever and ever.

Sahl said, "The hearts of the believers on the Day of Resurrection will **shine** with the Oneness of their Lord and the emulation of their Prophet ﷺ."

Qāsim said, "The **earth** will **shine** with the saints of God, for upon it they are His Lights, His manifest proofs, the saviors of His servants, and the refuge of His creatures."[1]

Ibn ʿAjība says:

The verse alludes to annihilation and subsistence: the servant will **swoon** and become oblivious to his own existence, and then **subsist** through his Lord. The **earth** of humanity **will shine with the Light** of the existence of the Real, and then the whole world will shine.

---

1   *ʿArāʾis al-bayān*, 3/224.

Al-Wartajbī [Rūzbihān Baqlī] said, "The **trumpet blast** of **swooning** is the overwhelming force of divine Majesty, and the **blast** of resurrection is the manifestation of the Lights of His beauty in the Lights of His majesty. With this, the Light of unveiling is imminent: **The earth will shine with the Light of its Lord.**[1]

---

1   *Al-Baḥr al-madīd*, p. 283.

Light is the Believer's *Kāf* of Immanence

Thus have We revealed unto thee a Spirit from Our Command. Thou knewest not what scripture was, nor faith. But We made it a light whereby We guide whomsoever We will among Our servants. Truly thou dost guide unto a straight path.[1]

The treasured meaning buried in this verse is that the spirit of Command is a Light from the divine Niche that reflects upon the mirror of the servant. This Light is accompanied by God's pre-eternal election as it moves along the ascending pathways of eternity into the realm of temporal manifestation. The spirit of Command is a shining disclosure of the spirit by which the Chosen Prophet ﷺ came to know **scripture** and **faith**; and so too for the gnostics of his Community who came after him and followed his guidance, his noble brothers and loved ones from the folk of Lights, who know that **scripture** is a pure lordly Light. They know the meanings, delineated boundaries, and ink of the letter, and so they recognize how the divine Word transcends the formal shapes of letters, the vibrations of sound, and the manifestations of temporality. By this knowledge, they comprehend the secret of the numbered inscription (*marqūm*),

1   Q Shūrā 42:52.

then the concealed inscription (*maknūn*), and so they know the Book of God, and read it as it ought to be read, believe in it, observe its boundaries, adhere to its laws, and move only by its command. They know that each thing has an inner reality, as the Beloved Messenger ﷺ said to Ḥāritha, "Everything has an reality; what is the inner reality of your faith?" They sought the reality of faith, and learned that it is a Light that flows from heart to heart, just as it flowed from the heart of God's Messenger ﷺ to the heart of Ḥāritha ؓ, so that he saw the unseen worlds in the visible world, and saw the Throne of the All-Merciful plainly before him. When he was martyred, he went to the highest Paradise whose ceiling is the Throne of the All-Merciful. Thus what he saw in this life was none other than his station in the Hereafter. We cited this hadīth in full earlier in the section on the ḥadīths of Light.

When God illuminates a person's heart, he sees the reality of his spiritual station. The Light of faith is for him a balance by which he measures his faith. Therefore the one who has no Light in his heart has no faith. By faith, we mean the reality of faith, not the faith of mere words; for according to the folk of inner vision, the one whose faith is mere words is still floating in the orbit of submission.

So **scripture** is Light, and **faith** is Light. As for the **spirit of Command**, it is the reality of Light: the reality of faith and of scripture. It transcends the vicissitudes of time, and is beyond the locus of temporality. The spirit of Command is a luminous mediator that brings together the sciences of transcendence in the realms of immanence, and reveals to you the secrets of the Essence in the manifestations of the attributes. God addresses you from behind its veils with the voice of spiritual allusion. Its Light is the Kāf of spiritual Excellence. When you enter its orbit, the eye of your heart becomes adorned with the Light of eternity, so that the path of Oneness and the ascending road of Singularity becomes clear.

Al-Baqlī says:

Thus have We revealed unto thee a Spirit from Our Command: that is, just as We singled out the Prophets and Messengers for spirituality and for the spirits of dominion, invincibility, beauty, and majesty, We have singled you out for a spirit of holiness, which We brought into being from among the spirits *ex nihilo*, through an eternal holy disclosure. We have thus favored you to behold holiness and the holy substance, which is marked by the disclosures of My beauty and majesty, clothed in the robes of My attributes, and illuminated by the Light of My Essence. We have singled out your noble spirit by these Lights, and we gave it life by depositing the spirit of My act, the spirit of My attribute, and the spirit of My Essence within it. These, moreover, are the knowledge of the unseen, the unseen of the unseen, and the secret of the unseen; the first knowledge pertains to the act, the second to the attribute, and the third to the Essence. Your spirit therefore contains these unique qualities, and all other spirits emerge from its Light. We sent these unique qualities to your blessed body too, and I blew them into your form just as I blew them into your father's form. So he became the Adam of the world; but as for you, the Adam of the world from the Throne to the earth is manifested from the mirror of your existence, just as the cosmos manifested from your holy substance, which was the first thing I created. Anyone who sees the Light of your holy substance has seen Me, for you are My mirror unto the worlds.

Thus the Prophet ﷺ said, "Whoever sees me, sees the Real; and whoever knows me, knows the Real."[1]

---

1   *'Arā'is al-bayān* 3/272.

Light is the Key to Salvation

He it is Who sends down clear signs upon His servant to bring you out of darkness into Light, and truly God is Kind and Ever-Merciful unto you. And how is it that you do not spend in the way of God when unto God belongs the inheritance of the heavens and the earth? Not equal among you are those who spent and fought before the victory. They are greater in rank than those who spend and fight afterwards; yet God has promised unto each that which is most beautiful, and God is Aware of whatsoever you do. Who is it that will lend unto God a goodly loan, that He might multiply it for him, and his shall be a generous reward?

On the Day when you see the believing men and the believing women with their Light spreading before them and on their right, "Glad tidings unto you this Day: Gardens with rivers running below, therein to abide. That is the great triumph." On the Day when the hypocrites, men and women, will say to those who believe, "Wait for us that we may borrow from your Light," it will be said, "Turn back and seek a Light!" Thereupon a wall with a gate will be set down between them, the inner side of which contains mercy, and on the outer side of which lies punishment.[1]

1   Q Ḥadīd 57:9-13.

A subtle point is in order here, namely that of all the Surahs in the Qur'ān, the Surah of Iron (al-Ḥadīd, 57) is the one in which Light is most frequently mentioned. This is because luminous vision is as sharp and penetrating as iron, and therefore God says: "**You were indeed heedless of this. Now We have removed from you your cover; so today your vision is piercing like iron (*ḥadīd*).**"[1] That is, when the **cover** of spatiality is removed from the **vision** that has been weakened by sensory manifestations, and when that luminous **vision becomes iron-like** by **piercing** through the dimension of space, it finally sees through the secret of the eye that unites opposites and discerns the Oneness of the worlds. For those who know the inner reality of things, the realm of opposites contains **great might**, while for those who know their subtleties, it contains **benefits**.[2]

In the terminology of the Karkarī Order, the servant (*'abd*) is the disclosure of the Master's levels, the manifestation of the attributes' variegation, the locus of descent for the verses of Qur'ānic union, and the criterion the differentiates the verses of Furqānic separation.

The Messenger of God ﷺ said, "When God wants good for someone, He grants him deep understanding of religion. God is the Giver and I am the Apportioner (*Qāsim*)." The servant is thus the heir of Abū al-Qāsim, the beam of the balance of existence. The descent, then, pertains to the servant who is the Per-

1   Q Qāf 50:22.
2   Q Ḥadīd 57:25.

fect Man, in whom all of the cosmos is gathered from the Throne to the earth. He is the sieve of those descents, the one who divides them according to the dictates of cosmic wisdom, which is attached to the will of pre-eternity, by the secret of "I am the Apportioner."

The one who yearns for the Lights of the lordly presence must therefore turn to a Shaykh who possesses the power of the two oceans and the secret of the two abodes; a Shaykh who stands by the door of the Lord and has influence in the Supreme Assembly, that he might lift for him the veils of illusory forms by the Lights of eternity. For when the Day of Reckoning comes, bodies will grow from the roots of their deeds, each body according to what was inscribed in the heart. If a person's heart is Light, his body will be Light; if his heart is darkness, his body will be darkness. Lights, moreover, are of differing degrees, corresponding to the measure of realization in this world. Some will have Light like the sun, others like the full moon, others of differing degrees. Some of them will hear Hell itself say to them, "Pass by swiftly, believer! Your Light is putting out my fire!" For Light is the key to salvation on the Day of Reckoning.

A noble hadith says, "God will gather the first and the last for the appointed meeting on the known Day—standing for forty years, their eyes fixed upon the heavens, waiting for the matter to be decided between them. God will descend **in the shadows of the clouds,**[1] from the Throne to the Footstool. A herald will

1   Q Baqara 2:210.

cry out, 'O mankind! Would it please you that your Lord, Who created you, provided for you, and commanded you to worship none but Him and to not associate any partners with Him, should judge for each of you to follow that which he used to follow and worship in the world? Is this not a just ruling from your Lord?' They will respond, 'Indeed yes!' So every nation will go to what they worshipped and followed in the world. They will go forth, and the likenesses of what they worshipped will appear to them. Some will go to the sun, others to the moon, others to idols of stone, or the likeness of whatever they worshipped. The demonic consort of Jesus will appear to those who worshiped him, and likewise for the worshippers of 'Uzayr. Then Muḥammad and his nation will remain. The Lord will present Himself to them and say, 'Why do you not proceed as the people have proceeded?' They will respond, 'We have a Lord whom we have yet to see.' He will say to them, 'If He comes to you, will you recognize Him?' They will respond, 'Between Him and us is a sign; if we see it, we will recognize Him. He will say, 'And what is that sign?' They will reply, 'He lays bare His shank.'

"At that moment, the shank will be laid bare, and all things will fall prostrate toward Him with their backs, but a group will remain whose backs are like the horns of cattle. They will try to prostrate, but will be unable to do so; **for they had indeed been called to prostrate while they were yet sound.**[1] Then He will say, 'Raise your heads.' They will raise their heads, and He will

---

1   Q Qalam 68:43.

give them their Light in the measure of their deeds. Some will be given Light like a great mountain, shining in front of them; others will be given less than that. Some will be given Light like palm-trees on their right sides; others will be given less than that. The last of them will be a man given Light on his big toe, which will flicker on and off. When his foot lights up he will advance, and when it falls dark he will remain in place.

"The Almighty Lord will be ahead of them, leading them across Hell, and leaving behind traces that are razor-sharp and perilous to walk upon. He will say, 'Cross!' They will cross in the measure of their Light: some will cross in the blink of an eye, others like lightning, others like clouds, others like shooting stars, others like wind, others like galloping horses, and still others like running men. This will continue till the one with Light on his big toe crosses, crawling on his face and hands and feet, clawing with one hand after the other, dragging one foot after the other, the Fire enclosing around him. He will go on until he is saved; and when he is saved, he will stand over it and say, 'Praise be to God, Who has given me something He gave no other; for He saved me from it after I looked upon it!' Then he will be taken to a pool by the door of Paradise, in which he will bathe..."[1]

It is then that the spiritual hypocrites will realize the vital importance of Light, and they will be seized by remorse and regret, and beg the folk of Lights to stop and **lend them their**

---

1   Ṭabarānī, *Kabīr,* 9763.

Light.[1] Yet this cannot be, for in the world it was offered to them freely, but they scorned it, and would not listen to those who reminded them of it, nor respected those who bore it. They will be told mockingly, "**Turn back** to the world, the abode of action, **and seek Light**[2] from the folk of Lights!" Then the wall of **this is the parting between thee and me**[3] will be set down between them, whose **inside is mercy** itself, and **one whose outside lies punishment.**[4] The folk of Lights will be taken to the gardens of mystic knowledge, and darkness will be returned to its source.

Behold, may God have mercy on you, the vital importance of Light in this life and the next. It is the key to salvation. Reflect on how if you do not attain it in this world, you cannot hope for Light in the hereafter. Yes, you will be given the brightness of your deeds, but how soon it will dim, for your deeds in the world were not sincerely offered to God alone, for there were many Qiblas in your heart. The darkness of your inmost secret will soon dominate the brightness of your reward, for it is rooted in the depths of your heart. The brightness will go out, and the hounds of darkness who stand waiting by the Path of Light will snare you. How can you hope to cross, when the Path is Light upon Light?

You must stand—may God have mercy on you—by the door of the folk of Lights, that perhaps they might look upon you

1 Q Ḥadīd 57:13.
2 Q Ḥadīd 57:13.
3 Q Kahf 18:78.
4 Q Ḥadīd 57:13.

with the eye of love, and so that you may borrow Light from their hearts, and thereby transcend the darkness of your soul, and become embraced by the intercession of luminous inner meaning.

Light is the Mercy that Encompasses All Things

O you who believe! Reverence God and believe in His Messenger;
He will give you a twofold portion of His Mercy, and make a
Light for you by which you may walk, and forgive you—and God
is Forgiving, Merciful[1]

Al-Qurṭubī says,[2] may God have mercy on him:

A *kifl* (portion) means a share or an allotment, but the root
meaning of the word is a sheet that is tied around a rider to keep
him from falling, according to Ibn Jurayj. Likewise, al-Azharī
said that it is derived from the garment that a camel-rider wraps
around the hump to keep him from falling. Thus the interpretation of this verse is: "He will give you two shares of His mercy
to protect you from falling into the ruin of sin, just as the *kifl*
protects the rider."

Abū Mūsā al-Ashʿarī said that *kiflayn* (a twofold portion)
means "double" in the language of the Abyssinians. Ibn Zayd
said that "A twofold portion" means the rewards of the herebelow and the hereafter. It is said that when the verse **It is they
who will be given their reward twice over for their having**

1   Q Ḥadīd 57:28.
2   *Tafsīr*, 20/276.

been patient[1] was revealed, the believers among the People of the Book boasted of this to the Companions of the Prophet, and so this verse was revealed.

The treasured meaning behind this verse is that God is addressing those who know through firsthand witnessing, and those in whom the invigorating breezes of faith have penetrated their hearts so that they have come to realize the true meaning of God-consciousness by becoming annihilated to their own annihilation, paying no regard to anything but the Supreme Essence. To such people God gives a twofold portion of His mercy; and His mercy is His Light. Consider how He says, **My mercy encompasses all things.**[2] It is His Light by which all entities and existents subsist. The twofold portion of His mercy is Light upon Light, which is why He then says, **and make a Light for you by which you may walk.**

The verse proclaims that God gives His bounty to whomever He will. God's mercy is not something that can be extracted or attained by effort, let alone lineage; for a noble hadith states, "If a person's deeds slow him down, his lineage will not speed him up."[3]

Sidi Ibn 'Ajība al-Ḥasanī ⍟ says:

On the level of spiritual allusion, this verse refers to the one whose ancestors were particularly distinguished by sainthood, righteousness, learning, or political power, but then the func-

1   Q Qaṣaṣ 28:54.
2   Q Aʿrāf 7:156.
3   Abū Dāwūd, *Sunan*, 3160.

tion of true spiritual guidance manifested in people other than his forebears. If he lowers his head and accepts that this special status was afforded to others, he will be given his reward twice over and will be granted a sublime status in the station of sainthood. The reason that sainthood undergoes such cyclical transference is to demonstrate to the people of established elite status that God's bounty is in His hand alone: **That is the Bounty of God, which He gives to whomsoever He will. And God is Possessed of Tremendous Bounty.**[1]

God describes this Light as **a Light by which to walk through (*fī*) mankind.**[2] Note that it is *fī*, meaning "through," not *bayn*, meaning "among." While ordinary walking among mankind takes place on the surface of the earth, this type of walking takes place on the surface of Light; that is, you flow through the realm of union by the secret of separation. You flow through mankind with the perspicacity of the Lights, reading what is written upon their essences and observing how their letters are arranged. You differentiate those who are near from those who are far, and perceive in them the wonders of the names and the manifestation-sites of the attributes in the courtyard of the acts. This Light allows you to behold the power of the divine in the earthly human realm, so that you return from creation to Creator. Any knowledge that does not refer you back to God is tribulation.

1   Q Jumu'a 62:4.
2   Q An'ām 6:122.

When you walk among people by the Light of God, the temporal disappears in the might of the Eternal, and the Eternal remains transcendent in the plain of endlessness. You behold the act by the quality of the attribute, and the attribute by the quality of the name. These are **two portions of His mercy**. The considerations of separative existence are lifted, and you taste the sweetness of connecting with God. The heart becomes engrossed in the beauty of pre-eternity, and you recognize that all things are but the reality of your soul and your illusory subdivisions. With this, you return to yourself, by yourself, and within yourself; and when your veil is lifted for you, then "There you are, and there is your Lord."

Chapter IV

Luminous Vision in the Sufi Tradition

Sidi al-Būṣīrī
May God Sanctify His Secret

In his famous poem *al-Burdah* in praise of the holy Prophet, the early Shādhilī Sidi al-Būṣīrī (d. 1294) writes:

The specter of my beloved flowed in and kept me awake;
Such is love, ever bringing pain to interrupt pleasure.

The Sufi concept of the flow (*al-sarayān*) denotes a luminous connection from the lover to the Beloved which draws the lover into the presence of intimate union and beauty by means of an angelic specter. This specter functions for him as a spiritual mediator and a door to oneness, and its human manifestation is a lordly Mediator, a Shaykh who has arrived and is able to lead others to arrive at the presence of Lights.

Love is the cause for the self-disclosure of the beloved. For when the pursued pursuer disappears in love, the specter of the Beloved flows into the levels of his heart and captures his inner vision and then his outer vision. Wherever he turns his face, the specter of his Beloved is already there to see. The Beloved captures his senses, and so he sees Him in everything he sees. Love is thus the secret flowing within the Beloved's specter, through which the Beloved captures the imagination and mounts the heart's throne, ruling according to the law of passion. If not for love, dear esteemed reader, inner meanings would never be disclosed in the sensory realm, nor eternity in temporality, nor would the Real be recognized. The Almighty loved to be recognized, and so He created creation. In love He created us, and in love we recognize Him.

When a person witnesses the flow of the Beloved's Light in the illusory appearances of things, he has placed one foot upon the road of recognition and love. When the specter of Lights ever leaves a person, he must renew his repentance to God and turn away from beholding other-than-Him. This Light has its source in the presence of our master the Messenger of God ﷺ. Sidi al-Būṣīrī speaks from this station when he says,:

All of them seek from the Messenger of God
Cupfuls from the ocean, sips from endless rain.

They stand before him according to their limits,
As if they were punctuation marks upon his wisdom.

He it is whose meaning and form were perfected,
And then the Originator chose him as His beloved.

He is peerless, his splendor shared with no other;
The essence of beauty is within him, undivided.

Leave aside what the Christians say of their Prophet,
Then praise him as you wish, and do so wisely.

Attribute whatever honor you will to his essence,
And whatever greatness you will to his status.

For the bounty of the Messenger of God
Is indeed limitless, and no words could express it.

If miracles could match the stature of his greatness,
The mention of his name would revive decayed bones.

He did not test us with things that would thwart our minds,
Concerned for us lest we waver or wander.

Mankind have not the power to understand him;
Whether near or far, none could fathom him.

He is like the sun, seeming small from afar,
But dazzling to the eye when viewed up close.

How could his true nature be grasped in the world
By folk who are asleep, lost in their dreams?

The extent of our knowledge of him is this:
That he is a man, and the best of all God's creation.

All the signs brought by the Prophets before him
Came to them solely through his Light.

He is a sun of bounty, and they are its planets,
Reflecting its Lights to mankind in darkness,

Until finally it rose upon the horizon,
Its guidance filled the world and gave life to the nations.

Marvel at the noble character of this Prophet,
Enveloping such beauty, shining with such radiance!

Exquisite as a blossom, luminous as the full moon,
Generous as the ocean, resolute as time itself.

So majestic was he that even when alone,
It seemed as though troops and courtiers were all around him.

The following is a delicate and puzzling concept that is troublesome to those who have not walked the path of realization: God knew that the vessels of spatiality would be unable to know eternity, nor would they recognize His true worth, and so He took a handful of His transcendent Light, a handful that involved neither separation, division, nor mixture. He then clothed this handful in compassion and mercy, and it was the circle of perfection and the archetypal Mother of the Book. The onset of existence from the hidden treasure thus began with love, and God beheld the affairs of the Essence in the mirror of His names and attributes; for He has no need for any other. Manifestation was concealment itself, and this handful was the disclosure-site for the levels of existence.

The Damascene Sufi Bahā' al-Dīn al-Bayṭār (d. 1910) writes:

God disclosed Himself to Himself through the reality of His name the Loving, which loved to be known; and from His Essence and for His Essence, He chose from His name the Beautiful a mirror and a disclosure-site which would be beloved to Him. The Muḥammadan Light was that disclosure-site, and it manifested from His name the Manifest. That disclosure and manifestation was called "the Breath of the All-Merciful," and this is the very reality of Muḥammad ﷺ. He is the ultimate breath of all spirits because he was the first of them to appear from the Breath of God, through the reality of His name the Hidden and the station of the Treasure.

The Hidden Treasure, which is the Hidden Essence, became manifest in its name the Only through the Muḥammadan Reality. Through it, the realities of the names and attributes were disclosed from the hidden treasure of the Essence. This is the meaning of the Prophet's ﷺ words, "The first thing God created was my spirit." The meaning of "creation" here is the disclosure from the Breath of the All-Merciful; and so he was a **mercy to the worlds.**

The first mercy from him was the mercy of the divine names; the first recipient of mercy was the Loving. The divine names, which are the beauty of existence, loved to behold their own beauty from the perspective of the names the Tender, the Affectionate, and the Witness. Therefore they turned to the All-Merciful and told Him of this, that He might save them from the dictate of the Hidden through His name the Deliverer. He replied, "Let all of you be gathered in My presence by the Gatherer, that I may replenish all of your meanings with My mercy. I am the Intercessor, and My status is sublime." God says, **Say, "Call upon Allāh, or call upon the All-Merciful…"**[1] He is our Sovereign, and we all seek recourse with Him.

So all of the names gathered in His presence—a gathering of Essence and oneness, transcending number, matter, and time. When each name had taken its place and station in that presence, they discussed the matter without any dialogue, boasting of their realities in the presence of the Essence, and clarifying the characteristics of their channels and pathways. They said, "Could existence comprise anything other than us?" the Knowing spoke up: "The Aware is aware of you all, and the guidance of His Light will guide you. It is through the all-gathering existent that your realities will manifest. For he is the Perfect Man ﷺ to which all things refer, and it is he who is comparable to all of your presences, and upon him the traces of your scents will manifest. He will share in your names, and he will know the truths of your tidings. Everything that is in this presence will be

---

1   Q Isrā' 17:110.

in him, for he is the gatherer and culmination of all things. Turn, all of you, to God, that He may effuse that great and noble one from the Light of His Essence!"

Then He spoke through His name the Speaker, and responded through His name the Responder, that His name the Willing willed for the manifestation of the beloved master. The Knowing assented, in accordance with the directives of the Wise Director. Then the Giving set about the task by hoisting the banner of address from the effusion of the Essence, by the decree of the Bounteous, that he come into existence from the presence of generosity and goodness. The Director said, "It is for Me to direct, with the aid of the Wise." The Detailer said, "I know how to detail his signs." The Powerful said, "It is for Me to give existence, and I will provide replenishment from the Willing." Then the Strong came forth and said, "I am the Helper, but the verdict of the Clear must be rendered." The Knowing said, "This is already inscribed in the Book, and the verdict of the Supreme Judge: **The Command of God shall be fulfilled,**[1] has been passed. The rule belongs to God, the High, the Great. Let each of you make manifest one of the realities of the disclosures of My illuminating Essence!"

Then each divine name drew its property from the Bounteous Giver, and the Breath of the All-Merciful poured forth the

---

1   Q Aḥzāb 33:38.

replenishing disclosure. the Generous and Ever-Munificent then disclosed to Himself, thereby making the Light of Muḥammad manifest from its blessed reality. After all the names had dispersed themselves among this human kingdom, they turned with all of the meanings they encompassed towards the Muḥammadan presence, so that it would begin with the Adamic vicegerency, and culminate with the Muḥammadan form. The will of the Eternal was attached before time began, in accordance with what the Knowing knew from the Essence of the Bounteous; and so through the Giver, the Muḥammadan Reality became manifest from the divine Lights of self-sufficiency, clothed in the robe of singularity, wrapped in the garb of divine identity, adorned with the crown of sovereignty, settled upon the throne of all-mercy, subsisting by the levels of divinity, replenishing the realities of existence by the power of divine self-subsistence. With this, the manifestations of witnessing emerged from the unseen realms of the Essence.[1]

Sidi al-Būṣīrī said of this, may God sanctify his secret:

All of them seek from God's Messenger
Cupfuls from the ocean, sips from endless rain.

That is, everyone draws from the presence of the Beloved ﷺ, including the angels brought nigh and the Prophets sent to earth. He is the root of existents and nonexistents, the sea that

---

1 *Al-Nafaḥāt al-aqdasiyya*, 32-34.

whelms all the worlds; for he is the universality of formal bodies. Jābir ﷺ is reported to have said, "I asked God's Messenger ﷺ what the first thing God created was, and he replied, 'It was the Light of your Prophet, Jābir. God created it, then created every good thing in it, and after that He created everything else. When He created it, He placed it before Himself in the station of nearness for twelve thousand years. Then He made it four parts, and created the Throne from one, the Footstool from another, and the Throne-bearers and Footstool-keepers from another.

"'He kept the fourth part in the station of love for twelve thousand years, then made it four parts and created the Pen from one part, the Tablet from another, and Paradise from another.

"'He kept the fourth part in the station of fear for twelve thousand years, then made it four parts and created the angels from one part, the sun from another, and the moon and stars from another.

"'He kept the fourth part in the station of hope for twelve thousand years, then made it four parts and created the intellect form one part, knowledge and wisdom from another, and protection and grace from another.

"'He kept the fourth part in the station of humility for twelve thousand years, and then God the Mighty and Majestic looked upon it, and it broke out in sweat-beads of Light. One hundred and twenty-four drops of Light dropped from it, and from each drop God created the spirit of a Prophet or the spirit of a Messenger. Then the spirits of the Prophets breathed, and from their breaths God created the saints, the martyrs, the saved, and the obedient until the Day of Resurrection.

"'So the Throne and Footstool are from my Light; and the cherubim are from my Light; and the spirit-beings and angels are from my Light; and Paradise and all its bliss are from my Light; and the angels of the seven heavens are from my Light; and the sun, moon, and stars are from my Light; and the intellect and grace are from my Light; and the spirits of the Messengers and Prophets are from my Light; and the martyrs, the saved, and the righteous are the products of my Light.

"'Then God created twelve thousand veils and kept my Light, which was the fourth part, within every veil for a thousand years. These are the stations of servanthood, tranquility, patience, truthfulness, and certitude. God immersed that Light in each veil for a thousand years. After bringing the Light out of the veils, God placed it upon the earth, and it lit up everything from east to west like a lamp on a dark night.

"'Then God created Adam from the earth and placed that Light in his brow, after which it transferred from him to Seth. It continued to pass down from pure to good, from good to pure, until God made it reach the loins of ʿAbd Allāh ibn ʿAbd al-Muṭṭalib, and from him to the womb of my mother Āmina bint Wahb. Then He brought me out into the world and made me the Master of the Messengers, the Seal of the Prophets, a mercy unto the worlds, the leader of the radiant ones. That was how your Prophet was first created, Jābir.'"

The hadith of Jābir is comprehensive, complete, and authentic according to those who know by way of witnessing the Lights, and whom God has revived by His Light, and into whom He has breathed His secrets. As for those who take their knowledge from one dead person to another, they consider it to be a weak hadith.

The Light of our Beloved Prophet is the root of every existent, for it is the first descent from the world of the Named. From this Light all of existence was created, the higher and the lower. And since his Light is universal, the mercy too is universal, and so God says, **My mercy encompasses all things.**[1] This is why his mission is universal for all the worlds, and his wives are the Mothers of the Faithful, and his law abrogates all other laws, and his banner is raised above all other banners on the Day of Resurrection. Adam and all others are beneath his banner. Through him, the entire earth was made a pure place of prayer.

His Light is sought by all. It is variegated in the levels of sensory perception, and so everyone seeks it and every love it. **Thou seest them looking upon thee, but they see not.**[2] His noble essence is the core of all essences, and therefore he experiences the feelings of all; a tradition states that he ﷺ said, "One of you is pricked by a thorn, and I feel the pain," or words to that effect.[3] He ﷺ is the outpouring of Essence's beauty manifesting within the forms of witnessed existence. He manifests in the

---

1 Q Aʻrāf 7:156.
2 Q Aʻrāf 7:198.
3 *Al-Nafaḥāt al-aqdasiyya.*

most beautiful stature, which becomes multiplied in forms throughout the levels of oneness. His ﷺ Light is the nourishment of the spirits that yearn for the fragrance of sealhood; for his blessed essence is the talisman that resolves every puzzle with which the gnostics contend. He ﷺ is the singularity of existence in whose Light all matters and perspectives are enfolded. He is the heart of existence, for one of his names is Yā Sīn, which is the heart of the Qur'ān. All Lights split open from his Light, all forms are multiplied from his Light, and all planes of existence take shape from its traces. Therefore Sidi Ibn Mashīsh, may God sanctify his secret, described him by saying, "Dear God, bless him from whom split open the secrets, and from whom broke forth the Lights, and in whom the inner realities ascend, and into whom descend the sciences of Adam, so that he surpassed all creatures."

Light is an attribute, and an attribute is a subtle reality that cannot be perceived unless it makes itself manifest through delimited existent beings. Those who know by way of sensory perception are oblivious to the Lights because they are veiled by its traces; they exist in sensoriality and through it, and the darkness of existent things is imprinted upon their hearts. Their inner vision is overwhelmed by nonexistents, and their perceptions are trapped within the six directions. As for those whom God has chosen for His love, they are guided to a master whose heart is bathed in the Lights of our master the Messenger of God ﷺ. Such masters have cleansed themselves of the impurity of heedlessness and washed themselves of alterity. The cosmos has vanished from them like a mirage, and through differentiated multiplicity they have returned to sheer unity. They see the cosmos by the Light of its Maker. They stand upon the Radiant Path, their solar hearts shining forever and ever. Their night is day, and their revelry is plain for all to see!

Dear God, illuminate our hearts with Your Light, which transcends boundaries and directions, until neither direction nor boundary remains for us and we see You in every existent, O Source of every existent!

Sidi Ibn al-Fāriḍ
May God Sanctify His Secret

The Sultan of Lovers Sidi Ibn al-Fāriḍ (d. 1235) says, may
God sanctity his secret:

By my glance, I gave my companions cause to suppose
That drinking their wine is the source of my joy,

But I have no need for the cup; it is not the wine
That intoxicates me, but the loveliness of the eye.

The eye is the wine-cup, for it is the door to the spirit. With
it, there is no need for the cups of sensory perception, form,
image, or color. The eye that is sharpened with the metal of
eternity and adorned with the Lights of the presence is the cup
that transcends the six directions, in contrast to the physical
cup which is demarcated by the higher, the lower, and the four
cardinal directions. Those who confuse these two cups harbor
suspicions of divine indwelling (*ḥulūl*) and accuse the great
masters of subscribing to this heresy. The heedless take the sensory realm as a standard to measure transcendent meanings,
and imagine that the spiritual cup to be a physical one. Yet they
can only be excused for thinking so, since their inner vision is

blotted and cannot behold such meanings and subtleties. They suppose that the wine indwells in the cup, by analogy to the material world. If they were to witness the transcendent meaning with the eyes of their hearts, they would not criticize God's folk but would acknowledge their eminence. Yet **that is the Bounty of God, which He gives to whomsoever He will.**[1]

The lordly wine is a transcendent Light that does not indwell in physical entities; it is neither absent from them nor does it dwell within them. All physical entities subsist by this Light, for It is both the entity-in-itself and the trace. To this effect, Sidi Ibn al-Fāriḍ says:

The day my eye falls upon my beloveds,
My yearning is satisfied, my soul recollected.

They remain with me in spirit if they should depart,
For I see the shape of them in my mind and heart.

The manifest joy of my eyes, wherever they abide;
Hidden within my heart, wherever they reside.

One of the signs of love is the dissolution of distance between the lover and the beloved. It begins with yearning that stirs in the heart so that the lover longs for his beloved. This causes him to see the beauty of his beloved in everything, and his beloved

---

1   Q Jumuʻa 62:4.

becomes more beloved to him than anything else. One of the supplications of God's Messenger ﷺ was, "Dear God, I ask You for Your love, and the love of those whom love You, and deeds that will lead me to Your love. Dear God, make Your love more beloved to me than my soul, my family, and cool water."[1] It is related that Qays ibn al-Mulawwaḥ, known as Majnūn, used to kiss a dog that resided by the house of his beloved Laylā between the eyes. When asked why he did this, he would reply, "I kiss its eyes because they looked upon Laylā."

Then comes a spectral disclosure of the beloved which does not leave the eye. The image of the beloved does not leave the lover's eye because his heart is void of everything apart from him. The heart is called a *qalb* because of how quickly it turns (*taqallub*) about among the meanings that are imprinted in it. The image of the beloved erases all other images from the lover's heart, and so it turns about only among the reflections of his beloved's beauty.

Then comes annihilation in the act, so that he sees that all things are from the act and directives of the beloved. His heart finds peace, for he knows the root of the act, and so it makes no difference to him whether he is given or denied, healthy or sick, rich or poor.

Then comes annihilation in the name, wherein the lover loses his identity and recalls only the name of his beloved. This is why when Sayyidunā al-Ḥallāj went into the market and

---

1   Tirmidhī, *Jāmiʿ*, 3436.

they asked him what he wanted, or when he was asked what he would eat, he would reply "God," for he had no answer other than the name of his beloved and the object of his passion. In all of existence he saw nothing but the letters of his beloved's name.

Then comes annihilation in the essence of the beloved, whereupon the heart enters the sacred precinct of love and turns towards the Ka'ba of passion, finding nothing in existence but its beloved. When asked who he was, Majnūn replied, "I am Laylā." His essence was annihilated in love and passion for her, until he saw nothing in himself but his beloved.

These are some of the signs of true love and ecstasy.

Describing this station, Sidi Ibn al-Fāriḍ, may God sanctify his spirit, stresses the importance of sincerity in love in the following verses:

Tell the martyr of love, "Now you have lived up to it."
And tell the pretender, "Take heed! Dark eyes are more than mere kohl!"

Some have attempted passion, but they rejected
My healthy love, and instead fell ill.

They were content with wishfulness, cursed with their selfish interest;
They claimed to dive into the sea of love, but were unwetted.

They journeyed through the night without so much as moving;
They wore themselves out, but advanced not a step.

Their envy made them prefer blindness to guidance,
And so they strayed far from the path I tread.

The one who claims to follow the way of God's Folk will be proved a liar by the testimonies of tribulation. If someone claims to have delved the depths of the seas of love, he must produce its treasures and describe its cool embrace. He must bring forth the pearls of unveiling, and give an account of the worlds of the deep sea.

Friends, enough with academic Sufism, where you read a book or two and then sit down to tell people of the stations of annihilation! Enough with hereditary Sufism as well, the Sufism of "My father was this and my grandfather was that." Enough with spiritual leadership passed down through family succession, and the jabber of cultural Sufism. Brown eyes are not equal to eyes adorned with the spirit's kohl, and darkness is not equal to Light, nor are the living equal to the dead.

The way of truth is obvious and clear, "its night as bright as its day; only the ruined stray from it." The way of truth is Light, so seek someone who can illuminate your heart with the Light of faith; someone who can paint the eye of your heart with the kohl of the absolute; someone who can engrave upon your heart the letters of the Divine Name with the chisel of exclusive singularity.

I am enthralled, whether He speaks or whether He is spoken of,
whether He is absent, or whether He is present.

Both are fair and delightful for me,
But sweetest of all is to look upon Him here.

Friends, the one who hears is not like the one who sees. There is a great difference between hearing of honey and tasting honey, and between tasting honey and making honey. These levels are made foundational to the cosmos by God's wisdom. God says, **above every possessor of knowledge is a knower.**[1] This is a covenant which God made with us in the world of spirits when we said, **Yea, we bear witness**[2] when He sprinkled His beginningless Light upon us; when He gave us to drink of the wine of yearning; when the cups filled with the nectar of witnessing were passed round, and we were immersed in the reality of union itself; when there was no "when."

I swear by the oath of allegiance I gave
Before my soul had been clothed in my clay,

The covenant of old that will ever endure,
With Him Who utterly transcends all change;

And by the rising Lights of Your dawn,
Whose brilliance makes every moon diminish to naught;

1 Q Yūsuf 12:76.
2 Q A'rāf 7:172.

And by the attribute of perfection that is in You,
From which the beauty of everything fair is drawn.

The nectar of witnessing is a luminous flash from the sea of beginninglessness, bringing together the two half-circles of necessity and possibility. It draws from the ocean of the primordial Cloud, and divides the Seven Oft-Repeated verses between Lord and servant. The Beloved Prophet ﷺ said, "Whoever performs a prayer without reciting the Mother of the Qur'ān, it is deficient," three times. Someone said to Abū Hurayra when he related this, "But what about when we are behind the imam?" He replied, "Recite it inwardly, for I heard God's Messenger ﷺ say, 'God Most High says, "I have divided prayer into two halves between Me and My servant, and My servant shall have what he requests." When he says, **Praise be to God, Lord of the worlds**, God says, "My servant has praised Me." When he says, **the Compassionate, the Merciful**, God says, "My servant has lauded Me." When he says, **Master of the Day of Judgment**, God says, "My servant has glorified Me and entrusted his affair to Me." When he says, **Thee we worship and from Thee we seek help**, God says, "This is between Me and My servant, and My servant shall have what he requests." When he says, **Guide us upon the straight path, the path of those whom Thou hast blessed, not of those who incur wrath, nor of those who are astray**, God says, "This is for My servant, and My servant shall have what he requests."'"[1]

---

1   Muslim, *Ṣaḥīḥ*, 603.

The nectar of witnessing is the secret of the acceptance of the prayer in which the Beloved Prophet led all of mankind during his Ascension; for he ﷺ is its reality and its essence. It is a magnetic beauty that annihilates all directions, spatiality, and sensoriality. The one who dwells in it with his heart is an imam even if he stands behind many rows, a preacher even if he is below the pulpits. It is the Path of Light. The Sultan of the Lovers says of it, may God sanctify his secret:

> *I jealously guard Her from my own love,*
> *But then I recall my standing, and renounce my jealousy.*

> *My spirit snatches repose in her presence,*
> *Though I do not absolve myself of the trace of ego.*

> *Though She is far from my eye, my ear sees Her*
> *In the specter of a critic as he rouses me.*

> *My eye envies my ear when She is mentioned;*
> *The part of me She annihilated envies what remains of me.*

> *I am the true leader of my imam;*
> *Mankind are behind me, and She is wherever I turn.*

> *My vision sees Her before me as I pray,*
> *While my heart sees me in front of every imam.*

Small wonder should the imam pray toward me,
For She resides in my heart, the Qibla of my Qibla.

All the six directions point toward me,
With every rite, pilgrimage, and visit.

My prayers in the Station of Abraham are offered to Her,
And in them I testify that She prays to me.

The two of us are one in prayer,
Each falling prostrate in unison before the other.

No one has ever prayed to me but I,
Nor have I bowed down before anyone but me.

Sidi Shu'ayb Abū Madyan
May God Sanctify His Secret

The Andalusian Sufi, Sidi Abū Madyan Shu'ayb al-Ghawth
(d. 1198) said, may God sanctify his secret:

Every land in which you alight is revived by you,
As though upon the land you are rain-showers.

Every eye yearns for a pleasant glance from you,
As though in the people's eyes you are flowers.

The nighttime traveler is guided by your Light,
As though you are moons shining through the dark.

May God not deprive any place of your visit,
O you who are remembered in the eye and the heart!

With the remembrance of the Folk of God, mercy descends.
To love them is to draw nearer to God; to believe in them is to
be among the spiritual elite. Their company is the antidote to
hearts poisoned by the darkness of sensoriality; for their spirits have settled over the water of transcendence, and when they
descend from the oceans of the invincible realm to the heart of

the disciple, they irrigate the dry earth of his heart with the water of life, so that the fruits of divine unity grow forth. Not just any water is suitable for performing ablutions that wash away the impurity of spatiality and the pollution of heedlessness, but only the water of the unseen; for it is non-delimited water, and non-delimited water is pure and purifying. The great Mālikī scholar Sidi Ibn ʿĀshir (d. 1631) says, "Purification is achieved by means of water that is free of adulteration. If it is adulterated by something impure, it must be thrown away; but if it is something pure that is usually found in its habitat, then it is suitable." Purification requires non-delimited water of the invincible realm (*jabarūt*) that has not entered the worlds of formal things, transcending image, space, direction, and limitation, retaining its origin without adulteration in its color, flavor, or odor. God says, **Behold, He covered you with sleepiness, security from Him, and sent down upon you water from the sky to purify you thereby, to remove the defilement of Satan from you, to fortify your hearts, and to make firm your steps thereby.**[1] This is that water, which purifies spirits from witnessing other-than-God, drives away the sly whispers and tricks of the Satan of spatiality, and binds the heart with the Lights of the Knower of the Unseen and the secrets of the gnostic sciences of witnessing.

It is a non-delimited water, unadulterated by the impurities of souls that enjoin love for the world and its pleasures, nor sub-

---

1   Q Anfāl 8:11.

stituted by the admixture of love for the hereafter and its delights. It is a holy and nonmanifest water that descends from the heaven of the gnostic's heart to the earth of the disciple.

The earth of the disciple is his human nature in the physical world, his body delimited by the levels and directions of spatiality. When he performs ablutions with this water, the pollution will leave him as the levels of spatiality come to naught, and his impure state of temporality will end as the directions of spatiality break down. This is one of the realities of the knowledge that the Prophet ﷺ referred to when he said, "The guidance and knowledge with which God has sent me is like rain that falls upon land. The fertile land absorbs the water and brings forth much grass and herbs. The solid land retains the water, and God benefits people with it so that they may drink, water their animals, and irrigate. The rest falls into an abyss, which neither retains the water nor produces plants. Such is the likeness of the one who understands the religion of God and benefits from that with which God has sent me, learning and teaching others. Then there is the one who neither raises his head to it, nor accepts God's guidance with which I have been sent."[1]

Ibn 'Aṭā' Illāh says in one of his aphorisms: "Your Shaykh is not the one from who you hear, but the one from whom you take. Your Shaykh is not the one whose verbal expressions reach you, but the one whose spiritual allusions flow within you. Your Shaykh is not the one who calls you to the door, but the one who

---

1   Muslim, *Ṣaḥīḥ*, 2282.

lifts the veil between you and Him. Your Shaykh is not the one whose words reach you, but the one whose state inspires you."

The word *shaykh* is made of the letters Shīn, Yā', and Khā', which stands for *shārib*, "to imbibe," *yaqīn*, "certainty," and *khamra*, "wine," the pre-eternal wine; the Shaykh is the one who imbibes the certainty of pre-eternal wine.

Anyone who denies the Mediator thereby lays claim to the station of Jesus ﷺ, who was created without a father and spoke in the cradle without instruction. Every person is accompanied by mediators from his first moment in the world of spatial existence. His first mediator is his mother, who teaches him how to gesture, eat, drink, and walk. Then he moves on to the mediator of the father, then the teacher, then the Shaykh. There can be no knowledge without a mediator. If it were not needed, then the Master of Existence ﷺ would have done without it.

If a person is fortunate enough to be led to a lordly Mediator, the first lesson he learns from him is the words of God, **Truly those who pledge allegiance unto thee pledge allegiance only unto God. The Hand of God is over their hands.**[1] The hand of the Shaykh is over the hand of the disciple, and the Hand of God is over both their hands. To each hand God has assigned a number, writing 18 on the right hand and 81 on the left, making a total of 99. Ninety-nine for the Shaykh, and ninety-nine for the disciple. These numbers may be broken down as follows:

---

1   Q Fatḥ 48:10.

99 = 9+9 = 18 for the Shaykh

99 = 9+9 = 18 for the disciple

This makes eighteen for the disciple, and the same for the Mediator, which may be further broken down as follows:

18 = 1+8 = 9 for the Shaykh

18 = 1+8 = 9 for the disciple

This makes nine for the Mediator, which are the levels of **transmission**, and nine for the disciple, which are the levels of **reception**. The sum of them is eighteen (18), and the Singular Alif that runs between them is one (1). That totals nineteen, which is the number of the Basmala; and as the hadith states, "anything that begins without the Name of God will be cut off and incomplete." All knowledge subsists through the secret of the Basmala, which is the index of openings and disclosures. God says, **Verily, it is from Solomon and verily it is, "In the Name of God, the All-Merciful, the Ever-Merciful."**[1] Our master Solomon ﷺ was the essence of "In the Name of God, the All-Merciful, the Ever-Merciful." It is related that our master ʿAlī, may God ennoble his countenance, the door to the city of the knowledge of God's Messenger ﷺ, said, "The secret of the Qurʾān is in the Fātiḥa, and the secret of the Fātiḥa is in the Basmala, and the secret of the Basmala is in the Bāʾ, and the secret of the Bāʾ is in the dot, and I am the dot." That dot is the disclosure-site of the Basmala, the balm of the impassioned, the wine of the lovers. Sidi Abū Madyan says of it, may God sanctify his secret:

1   Q Naml 27:30.

Arise, friend, and from the jug bring us
A wine that illuminates the spirit upon imbibing.

See how the eternal cupbearer serves it,
As though in the glass it were a lamp shining!

In the realm of eternity, it made Adam drunk,
Garbing him in robe and cloak.

Noah too was in the Ark enraptured,
Dazzled, as he moaned and shook.

After partaking, Abraham was smitten;
For God Himself fulfils its covenant.

When Moses was within earshot from it,
He threw down his staff and broke the tablets.

The Son of Mary too it enraptured,
And he wandered drunk and beguiled.

And from the outset, he was divinely elected to drink it,
For Muḥammad is the Pride of Heaven, the Noble Guide.

The *Basmala* in the spiritual world is the dot of the *Bā'*, which rose up and ascended to the *Nūn* of *al-Raḥmān*, then descended in a manner befitting it to the *Yā'* of *al-Raḥīm* and was divided into knowledge of the early generations and knowledge of the later ones. The *Basmala* has four outer dots, and three inner dots. They are the foundational edifice of the noble Ka'ba, which has four outer pillars and three inner ones if the building were completed up to the chamber of Ishmael, peace be upon himn. Four outer and three inner, totaling seven. Anyone who circumambulates seven times with seven recitations will truly be the vicegerent of the Lord of the Heavens.

Close your eyes and you shall see
Your secrets shining bright and clear.

Pass away from mankind,
And you will behold your own state.

When the mirror is polished,
Alterities disappear.

When the disciple pledges allegiance to the Light of the Path, which is the Shaykh of spiritual mentoring, the latter casts into his heart the dot of existence, which is God's words, **By the star when it sets.**[1] The star of inspiration descends to the lowest heaven in the heart of the disciple and shines upon his earth, and there grows the tree of the good word whose root is firmly planted in the disciple's heart, and whose branches are in the

1   Q Najm 53:1.

heaven of the innermost secret, providing its nourishing food of witnessing and unveiling at all times by the leave of its Lord. The disciple continues to water it with the water of non-delimitation by the invocation of the Supreme Name until it becomes firmly rooted in the innermost depths of his heart. When it becomes firm, it yields the fruits of divine unity and exclusive singularity. The spiritual realities of passion come to him from the ocean of divine invincibility bearing the breezes of the breath of All-Mercifulness, and in it flows the spirit of eternity with the Light of beginninglessness. The disciple's temporal attributes are then lifted, and the lamp of his witnessing shines upon the realm of his existence. He draws near to the holy presence and is clothed in the divine attributes. The barriers of contingency and spatiality are lifted for him that he may approach within two bows' length, and the realities of "God was, and there was nothing with Him" overwhelm him.

> *The sphere turns within you,*
> *Glittering and shining;*

> *The sun and the moon are in you,*
> *Setting there and rising;*

> *Look within yourself,*
> *And read that cosmic writing.*

When God grants someone the good fortune of keeping the company of a knower of God who lights the lamp of gnosis in the niche of his heart, He blesses him with a truly great gift. For gnosis begins with a Light that is disclosed from the heart of the Shaykh to the heart of the disciple, which he sees with the eye of his heart then the eyes of his head. His soul delights and the wine of eternity mixes in the cup of his senses; the more he drinks, the drunker he gets; the drunker he gets, the more his certainty grows, the more his certainty grows; the more his love grows; the more his love grows, the more his annihilation grows; the more his annihilation grows, the more his subsistence grows; the more his subsistence grows, the more sober he gets; the more sober he gets, the more his servanthood grows. When his servanthood becomes completely sound and perfected, he is lifted up through the heavens of his spirit, and beholds **the greatest signs of his Lord.**[1]

When you become connected,
You will behold on high

The Light that is there shining,
Made visible to the eye.

---

1   Q Najm 53:18.

Sidi Abū Ḥāmid al-Ghazālī,
May God Sanctify His Secret

The Persian Sufi scholar, Sidi Abū Ḥāmid al-Ghazālī (d. 1111), may God sanctify his secret, says:

Knowledge of the path is plain
To those who wish to find,

But I see that where the path is concerned,
Hearts have become blind.

I marvel when, though safety is near,
A man falls to ruination;

But I marvel too that anyone
Manages to find salvation.

The knowledge of the Path is plain and clear. Its night as bright as its day: Light upon Light; suns, moons, stars, and secrets; knowledge and presence; ascension and disclosure; annihilation and subsistence; differentiation and non-differentiation; unveiling and beholding with the eye; certainty unadmixed with doubt; reality unadulterated with illusion.

However, when the fog of other-than-God settles in the pupil of the heart's eye, the demonic tree of caprice and alterity grows there, and the inner vision is blotted out by the darkness of material vessels. The dark clouds of the veil appear in the sky of the heart, blocking the sun of realities and mysteries. The Lights of the meanings of existence are eclipsed because of the imprinting of their images upon the mirror of the heart. The disciple becomes veiled by the illusion of his own existence, and remains with the shell of the cosmos in the world of material bodies, a prisoner of spatiality and direction.

To this effect, Sidi Ibn 'Aṭā' Illāh says one of his aphorisms, "How can a heart be illuminated when the forms of creation are imprinted on its mirror? How can it travel to God when it is shackled by its desires? How can it wish to enter the Presence of God when it has not been cleansed from the impurity of heedlessness? How can it hope to understand the subtleties of mysteries when it has not repented of its follies?"

As for the one whom God honors with a luminous Mediator upon the Sunna of the Radiant Path, He takes him out of the worlds of illusion into the witnessing of the Lights of existence. The veils of worldly existence are pulled back for him and the cloak of protection is lifted for him. The turbidity of alterities and the gloom of sensoriality pass away, and the clouds of illusion dissipate from over the sun of meanings so that it shines forth in the heaven of his spirit, illuminating the hidden recesses of his existence.

Sidi Abū Ḥāmid says, may God sanctify his secret:

The Light of Your holy Face dazzles me;
I am bewildered by You, for You cannot be concealed.

You are closer than anything that can be seen,
Yet the farthest thing from ever being beheld.

The Light of His Face flows through everything in existence, manifest to anyone whose inner vision is opened by the secret of **Wheresoever you turn, there is the Face of God.**[1] The one who is bewildered by the Light of God sees the disclosures of his Lord in every atom; he sees the attribute of His power flowing through all things from root to branch, and beholds the passion that opposites feel towards each other despite their autonomous existence.

His Light transcends indwelling, partition, and division, for it is unlike the temporal entities that occupy space. It discloses itself in the mirrors of the saints, and lays down the curtains of majesty. The cosmos subsists only by the Light of His splendor, and remains stable only by the disclosures of His attributes. By the Light of His Face, all traces are erased in their subsistence and obliterated in their existence. One of the early Muslims said, "I went into a monastery when it was time to pray and said to one of the Christians, 'Show me to a clean place where I can pray.' He replied, 'Purify your heart from other than Him, and stand wherever you please.' I felt shame before him."

1 Q Baqara 2:115.

Jābir reportedly said, "The blessed Messenger of God ﷺ used to pray while riding his camel in whatever direction it was facing. When he wanted to perform an obligatory prayer, he would dismount and face the Qibla."[1]

God says, **How many a sign in the heavens and on the earth do they pass by and turn away from!**[2] That is, how **many a sign in the heavens** of the spirits and **the earths** of the bodies, pointing to the glory of God and His nearness, and the perfection of His power, yet they **pass by** without reflection or consideration because the eyes of their hearts are blinded and are heedless of the Lights of eternity that clothe the cosmos from the depths to the Throne.

Those who know God behold the disclosures in the mirrors of the cosmos by the Light of certainty, and ride upon the noble steeds of witnessing to the Throne of the All-Merciful, where they recognize Him through recognizing their own selves. He says regarding this, may God sanctify his secret:

You disclosed Yourself from me within me,
Until You manifested before me;

Yet not even thoughts could see You,
For You were hidden so completely.

1   Bukhārī, *Ṣaḥīḥ*, 388.
2   Q Yūsuf 12:105.

Every mountain crumbled to dust
Upon witnessing Your display.

You spoke to me secretly from within me,
And all besides You was swept away.

They emerged from the turbidity of human nature into the courtyard of true servanthood by breaking free from the chains of base desires, animalistic traits, and worldly carrion. They adorned themselves with the Name of Majesty in state, knowledge, and experiential taste, all the while serving upon the carpet of love and yearning. He disclosed Himself to them from them, and they realized that He is Manifest and Hidden, and that His hiddenness is His manifestation itself, and His manifestation is His hiddenness itself. They doffed the two sandals and became oblivious to the two worlds, and He disclosed Himself in His splendor in their hearts. The mountain of their existence crumbled to dust, and the Moses of their hearts fell down in a swoon. They understood the meaning and declared Him transcendent beyond all that does not befit Him, and so He annihilated their attributes in His, and their existence in His, and their names in His. They subsist through Him and for Him, realizing all the rights of lordship and the duties of servanthood—all this upon the carpet of Lights and witnessing.

Of this Abū Ḥāmid says, may God sanctify his secret:

The obfuscating distractions of the material world altogether left me,
And a flame like a lamp lit within my inner core.

I saw the divine Light shining through it,
Behind the subtle curtains that cover everything.

I realized that which before I had doubted,
And beheld what had been hidden inside,

And grasped the purpose for which I was made,
For which I was given life, then death, then revived.

Upon the two worlds from the mirror of the soul,
Every truth shone bright and distinct.

All of the doubts that people feel
About so many things, for me were extinct.

My soul threw down its staff, for it grasped
That my journey had uncovered my home, at last!

Doubts and suspicions are only put to rest by the Lights of the unseen, which dispel the darkness of uncertainty, annihilate the directions of spatiality, and crush the misgivings of duality. God says, **Say, "Truth has come, and falsehood has vanished.**

Truly falsehood is ever vanishing.[1] The Beloved Prophet ﷺ said, "O people! Beware of this idolatry, for it is harder to see than a creeping ant."[2] The basis of this comparison is that the creeping of an ant is subtle and obscure; it crawls in the night of the soul upon the rock of the heart hardened by distance from God, and so is all the more subtle and obscure. It is a blight that can only be cured by an expert who carries the elixir of Lights and has a connection to the olive-tree of secrets which erases the spatial delimitations of all things other-than-God.

When God blesses someone with the good fortune of keeping the company of one such expert and pledging allegiance to him, then that person has been divinely guided to the antidote of existence; whoever drinks this antidote will find the wick of his heart set aflame by the fire of yearning; the lamp of unity. The darkness of alterities will be dispelled from the glass of his heart, and his soul will be carried back to the spirit in the station of **truly we bear witness**, where it will grasp the purpose of its beginning and its resurrection. The heavens of his spirit will be rolled up like scrolls for writing, and he will return to the treasure of "God was, and there was nothing with Him." Then when wisdom returns him to the realm of spatiality, he will throw down the staff of his soul upon the Sinai of union, where the tree of the secret will say to him: **Truly I am God, there is no god but I.**[3]

---

1   Q Isrā' 17:81.
2   Aḥmad, *Musnad,* 19170.
3   Q Ṭā Hā 20:14.

Sidi Muṣṭafā ibn ʿAlīwa
May God Sanctify His Secret

May God sanctify the secret of the Algerian Sufi Shaykh, Sidi Muṣṭafā ibn ʿAlīwa (d. 1934), who says:

God's herald summoned us before we existed;
And when existence began, we heard his homily;

The dove of union cooed in the midst of separation,
And so by God's power, we set forth for unity.

We are the kings of the earth in nearness to Him;
For His love, we sacrificed both self and family.

We stand in sunlight while others are in shadow;
Wheresoever He discloses, keen is our sight.

Light upon Light from God have we been gifted,
For He guides whomever is worthy to the saint's Light.

Be not amazed, for to every community
He has sent guides to lead them aright.

The saints are God's bridegrooms. They are the dove of union in the presence of intimacy, the earth's trusted guardians, and the rope of connection. Sidi al-ʿAlawī calls them the dove of union by way of alluding to God's words, **And [for] every man We have fastened his omen** (*ṭāʾir*, literally "bird") **upon his neck, and We shall bring it forth for him on the Day of Resurrection as a book he will meet wide open.**[1] This is the bird of the innermost secret, that which people generally call the spirit. Every man's secret is upon his neck, which is why when God wishes to illustrate how near He is, though He transcends spatiality and physical distance, He says, **We are nearer to him than his jugular vein.**[2] And He says of His Beloved from the presence of supreme transcendence: **Had he ascribed any statements to Us, We would have taken him by the right hand, then We would have severed his life vein.**[3] These are all lordly allusions to that bird, which is called the bird of divine selfhood (*ṭāʾir al-huwiyya*).

God's folk are the doves of connection between temporality and eternity, between sensoriality and pure meaning. For that is what they always were in pre-eternity, transcendent letters preceding the word *Kun*, "Be!" They are the secret of union, may God be pleased with them, for they possess realization of the station of, **Truly those who pledge allegiance unto thee**

1   Q Isrāʾ 17:13.
2   Q Qāf 50:16.
3   Q Ḥāqqa 69:44-46.

pledge allegiance only unto God.[1] They offered their souls to God, and He in turn accepted and purified them. Then God annihilated His folk in His Essence so that they existed through Him and for Him. Then He formed their essences as brands kindled from His Lights, and their hearts as loci for His Name. They became kings upon the earth and kings in Heaven. Tradition relates that our master Gabriel said to the Beloved Prophet ﷺ when he saw Abū Dharr, "There goes Abū Dharr." The Beloved said, "Do you know him?" Gabriel عليه السلام replied, "Abū Dharr is better known in Heaven than he is on earth, because of how much he recites, **Say: 'He, God, is One.'**"

God has made for each thing a sign, a reality, and an elucidation; thus the Beloved ﷺ said to Ḥāritha, "Each thing has a reality." The reality of the saint is that he is a brand kindled from God's Light; his human nature is obliterated in both the sensory realm and the realm of pure meaning; he combines the levels of the cosmos, and the cosmos is rolled up in the blink of his eye, delimited from the ocean of the Cloud. His vision is piercing. The veil of spatiality has been lifted from him, so that for him there is no separation. His night is as bright as his day. He recognizes the truth in every word and meaning. His regard is of a higher order, for his being is rooted in All-Mercifulness, and so to be regarded by him is mercy, and to sit before him is forgiveness, and to pledge allegiance to him is victory and divine approval.

---

1   Q Fatḥ 48:10.

When God wishes to guide someone to His Light, He directs them to one of His saints, who will bring him into contact with the presence of nearness. "If not for the Mediator, as it is said, there would be no mediated."

Ibn ʿAṭāʾ says in an aphorism, "Glory be to Him who did not make the guide to His saints anything other than the guide to Him, and who does not let anyone reach them except those He wishes to reach Him!"

Sidi al-ʿAlawī describes the attributes of the Shaykh as follows:

If the master does not benefit the disciple with a mere glance,
Then he is confined by ignorance, surrounded by the ignorant.

The true Shaykh is he who is generous with his secret,
Putting the disciple's welfare above his own.

He will lift up the veils that cover his heart,
Preventing him from reaching the highest station.

He will enter God's presence, from which he was severed,
And see the Real manifest wheresoever he turns.

The glance of the Shaykh is like the primordial Cloud; there is no union above it, and no dispersion beneath it. It bears the disciple to his true origin, so that the reality of his station becomes manifest. The Shaykh sees the disciple as a heart, not as a mold. This heart then takes shape within the disciple's station, and manifests as a letter, name, attribute, or otherwise. The Shaykh thus knows what suits the disciple best and what does not, and he replenishes the disciple with the litanies and practices that are best for him, as per the dictates of divine wisdom. All of this, in no more than a glance.

Sidi al-'Alawī says, explaining the signs of the true Shaykh:

The true Shaykh is he who is generous with his secret,
Putting the disciple's welfare above his own.

The one who is not generous with his secret is not a Shaykh, for without the secret of Oneness God cannot be known, and in its absence the disciple will drown in the mires of distraction and immanence. Even if he supposes that he affirms God's transcendence and hallows Him, his gelid affirmation of transcendence is in fact nothing other than immanence and discourtesy before God. This is endemic in our time because of the prevalence of false Shaykhs; a disciple may boast of his Shaykh and call him the Pole, and the Supreme Aid from God, yet that same disciple is immersed in darkness and has no Light to erase spatiality for him, nor any secret to remove separation for him. If his Shaykh had truly attained, he would enable him to attain as well. The Shaykh is the one alluded to in the blessed ḥadīth about the perfume-seller as described by the Beloved ﷺ, who said according to Abū Mūsā, "The good companion and the bad companion are like the perfume-seller and the bellows-worker: the perfume-seller might gift you something, or you might buy something, or you might simply enjoy his pleasant fragrance. The bellows-worker will either burn your clothes or subject you to a foul odor."[1]

The true Shaykh shares his lordly perfume with you. He gifts you a cosmic fragrance blended from Oneness and Light. He takes you into the garden of gnosis and plants the seed of Singularity in your heart, then waters it with the water of transcendence. God says, **Say, "This is my way. I call unto God with clear insight—I, and those who follow me. Glory be to God! And I am not among those who ascribe partners unto Him."**[2]

Both Shaykh and disciple must be upon "clear insight." But in our times you may see a Shaykh surrounded by thousands of followers, all of them with blind hearts. They may speak much about dreams, or what they have read in Sufi books, but you do not sense ever a hint of Light or secret. All of them already know in advance, and it goes without saying, that the Shaykh will be succeeded by his eldest son. Therefore Sidi al-ʿAlawī says, may God sanctify his secret:

He will lift up the veils that cover his heart,
Preventing him from reaching the highest station.

He will enter God's presence, from which he was severed,
And see the Real manifest wheresoever he turns.

---

1   Muslim, *Ṣaḥīḥ*, 4768.
2   Q Yūsuf 12:108.

The Shaykh who has attained will lift the veils from your heart and give you the keys to the doors of self-knowledge. He will uncover for you the reality of your soul and expose it to you so that you may behold its levels plainly. He will wash the eye of your heart with the water of the unseen, removing from it the blindness of alterity. He will remove you from your rival and garb you in the robe of love, then bring you into the presence of the Almighty Judge. He will show you the beauty of the Real in every atom of His kingdom. He will show you how to read the stations of Oneness in the smallest thing. He will condense the cosmos for you upon the head of a pin, then make your soul pass through the eye of the needle, then take you on a stroll through the Holy Enclosure. Sidi al-'Alawī says, may God sanctify his secret:

Spirits wander the holy ground,
Like a lamp in the niche of sight and sound,
Kaleidoscopes of meaning, form-bound,
If you could but look behind the screen.
Praise be to God for what my eyes have seen!

The Shaykh transforms your heart into a lamp within the niche of your human substance. He causes pure meanings to take on a myriad of colorful forms, and erases your sensory realm with a flash of Light. He takes you on a journey through the spiritual world, and lifts the wool that was pulled over your eyes. He will draw you close to the presence of Beauty, and raise your foot above the lowly earth of the self so that you may doff the two sandals.

In the following lines, Sidi al-‘Alawī describes the state of the knower of God in the clearest possible terms:

Have you rolled up the cosmos with a single glance?
Have you witnessed the All-Merciful wherever He discloses?

Have you erased all mankind with a single blink?
Have you left behind all, the lofty and the lowly?

Have you circled the universe from every side,
And has the cosmos circled you, its Qibla, in turn?

Have the veils been lifted from before you in honor?
Has the screen been rent asunder, the cloak spurned?

Has the Summoner summoned you, and have you obeyed?
Has reverence surrounded you from every side?

Have you doffed the sandals and become a true traveler?
Did you lean into it when union arrived?

Have you kept the Lord's secret after it was revealed,
Guarding it faithfully, in His robe enclosed?

Such are the hallmarks of one who is near;
For there are secrets which must not be disclosed.

If all of this be true of you, then so be it;
If not, you are far from the presence of the Lord.

Avoid the Tribe's science, unworthy one!
Keep the orphan's property out of your reach.

God detests the one who replaces
Honest work with vainglorious speech.

Is there any use in praise won through boasting,
Any profit in counterfeit glory?

Can flattery cure an ailing patient?
Can any but loved ones console the lonely?

You may well learn to talk their talk,
But that's the hornet's wax, not the bee's honey.

To those who seek God's path: His path is Light. It is Light upon Light. Venture out into the sea of Lights and secrets upon the ship of a Shaykh who has attained, and it will transport you to the land of clear spiritual opening. You will taste the meaning of witnessing God with every breath. Sidi al-ʿAlawī says, may God sanctify his secret:

Plunge into the sea of Lights, meanings and secrets;
Obliterate the world, and your heart will find its delight.

Pass away in the Worshipped One, and taste the meaning of witnessing,
For all of this existence is from none other than God's Light.

Sidi al-Shushtarī
May God Sanctify His Secret

May God sanctify the secret of the Andalusian Sufi poet, Sidi
Abū al-Ḥasan al-Shushtarī (d. 1269), who says:

How sweet to imbibe the brew in our tavern;
Dear server, bring us another cup!

No crime do we commit by drinking this wine,
But we would be sinners to pass it up.

Its vintage was bottled before Adam lived;
Its origin is holy, its source sanctified.

Jurist, give me your verdict and tell me:
May it be imbibed upon Arafat's side?

May a pilgrim carry it around the Ka'ba?
Would his drunkenness render his rites in vain?

May a worshipper drink it as he prays,
Or recites the Qur'an, or invokes God's Name?

Said the jurist, "If it be wine made of grape
Which intoxicates and befuddles the mind,

To drink it is most certainly forbidden,
Like all other substances of its kind."

Ah dear jurist, if you could only taste it,
And hear what sweet music in our tavern plays,

You would abandon this world and your profession,
And live as a drunkard, till the end of your days!

Every word has a meaning and a significance which it bears, and every word has an identity which makes it distinct. The words "outward/exoteric" (*ẓāhir*) and "inward/esoteric" (*bāṭin*) are among those words which have been discussed at length, and for the sake of which much ink has been spilled among those who carry knowledge and so consider themselves knowledgeable, although often a person may convey knowledge to someone who understands it better than he does. Everyone speaks according to his own station, contriving sentences and arguments and then laying claim to possession of the Ark of Salvation. Some people deny inward knowledge altogether and cling to the threshold of the outward, as long as it suits his caprice; and when the outward meaning contradicts what seems suitable to his one-dimensional intellect, he struggles in vain to find interpretations and exceptions to get around it without any methodological consistency.

Yet there is a ḥadīth which plainly affirms inward knowledge: Abū Hurayra is reported to have said, "I received two bags from the Messenger of God ﷺ. One of them I have divulged; but if I were to divulge the other, you would have my head!"[1] The expression "two bags" means two kinds of knowledge: outward knowledge which is suitable to be divulged to all, and inward knowledge which is meant only for some.

Some try to take a middle position based on their personal reasoning, and say that every person must study some outward knowledge and some inward knowledge, as though inward knowledge can be learned from books. But they reject the name of Sufism, as though the masters were wrongly using that name for over ten centuries. What is more, they reject subtle truths and mysteries because they are unable to find sources for them in the primary texts of the Law, and because they lack the inner vision to behold the Lights of divine self-disclosure, which is purely a matter of firsthand experience and unveiling. Furthermore, they wish to alter the method of the great masters, and they claim that the current era is not suited to self-isolation, but only community engagement. They are heedless of the Creator's wisdom in His creation.

---

1   Bukhārī, *Ṣaḥīḥ*, 120.

When the early saint Abū al-Ḥusayn al-Nūrī ﷺ (d. 907) was being questioned during the inquisition of the Sufis during the time of Junayd of Baghdad (d. 910), the judge asked him, "What is the wisdom behind God's creation of humanity?" He replied, "In order for them to do exactly what they are doing." The judge said, "Do you mean that God wants them to disbelieve?" Abū al-Ḥasan retorted, "Could they disbelieve if He did not wish them to?"

To aspire to make all people the same is unrealistic. Diversity is one of the signs of God; and in His Book, He speaks of unbelievers, hypocrites, idolaters, Muslims, believers, the reverent, the righteous, those who seek forgiveness in the last third of the night, those who bow, and those who uphold justice. These are degrees in their Lord's sight, disclosures of His most beautiful names. If all of humanity became Muslim, where would the names of the All-Conquering and the All-Compelling be disclosed? If they all disbelieved, where would the All-Merciful, the Ever Merciful, and the Loving be disclosed? The multiplicity of stations is a disclosure of the multiplicity of divine names.

The Beloved Prophet ﷺ left us upon the Radiant Path. In the beginning, he ﷺ would keep solitary retreats in Ḥirā' Cave, until the dot of existence burst out from within his blessed interior and emanated upon his outer being, upon him be blessings and peace. If you do not make a solitary retreat into the cave of your heart; if you do not detach from your fellow creatures; if you do not read the meanings of your existence, then how will you serve God's calling? How can you call other people to meanings that you have not tasted yourself? How can you tell people about the presence of God when you have not entered it?

The first stage of rectification is to cleanse your inner being from the distractions of alterity, the delimitations of spatiality, the desires of the soul, and the hidden motives of base caprice. Once you have mastered your soul, you may then move on to those nearest to you, and the next nearest.

The Manifest and the Nonmanifest are two of the names of the Real, and so to deny either of them is to deny one of His names. Nonmanifestation precedes manifestation by the rule of the Hidden Treasure, and manifestation follows nonmanifestation by the rule of "I loved to be known." This is with respect to separation; as for union, there is neither nonmanifestation nor manifestation there.

We find the same in the life story of the Beloved, where in Mecca he preached only the Oneness of union, for there was no legislation in Mecca but only later in Medina. The call in Mecca was to the Essence, while the call in Medina was to the attributes; Mecca was for God's name the Nonmanifest, while Medina was for His name the Manifest. Mecca was the disclosure-site of "God was, and there was nothing with Him," while Medina was the disclosure-site of "He is now as He ever was."

Even when it comes to the distinctions between Meccan and Medinan suras, we find that all the suras that begin with the luminous letters are Meccan, except for the chapter of the Cow (al-Baqara) and the House of ʿImrān (Āl ʿImrān), the so-called

"Two Bright Ones" (*zahrāwān*). Every sura that speaks of divine Oneness and the Resurrection is Meccan. Every sura in which God addresses His servants as "O mankind" without differentiation is Meccan. Medinan suras, on the other hand, contain mention of legal sanctions, inheritance laws, rulings, and the acknowledgement of distinctions among mankind, so that God addresses His servants as "O you who believe." The Manifest and the Nonmanifest are thus foundational stages of the Prophetic mission and the Sunna of the Chosen One ﷺ.

As for God's Book, those who are dominated by spatiality read it as inscribed (*masṭūr*): **A Book inscribed on a parchment outspread.**[1] Others whose hearts God illuminates and whom He draws hear to Him when He discloses Himself with His Light recite the Qur'an as numbered symbols (*marqūm*): **A book [of] numbered [symbols], witnessed by those brought nigh.**[2] Then there are those whom He has elected for His Holy Presence. They come to naught in His Lights, and He purifies them from their own souls. They disappear from the star by virtue of its setting-place, and read the Qur'an as a Book concealed (*maknūn*): **Truly it is a Noble Qur'an, in a Book concealed. None touch it, save those made pure.**[3] To some He discloses Himself by His acts, to others by His attributes, and to others by His Essence.

Sidi al-Shushtarī says, may God sanctify his secret:

1   Q Ṭūr 52:2-3.
2   Q Muṭaffifīn 83:20-21.
3   Q Wāqi'a 56:77-79.

When in the sanctuary of contentment I found You,
They said I was astray, for I had lost my mind.

But I swear the lover is neither astray nor lost;
It was they who misjudged me, for they were blind.

Had they beheld Your beauty as I have,
With the eye of my heart, they would not deny my claim.

I threw off all shame in my love for You;
Sweet intimacy lies in choosing love over shame.

I tore the robes of dignity to pieces;
With Your love, how delightful was my pain!

Love brooks no complaint, though the heart be torn;
How could any lover of Yours complain?

God's folk are the folk or meaning, the folk of witnessing, the folk of Lights. Judgement falls to them due to the vast scope of their divine knowledge. They are aware of His intent in every word and every meaning; they perceive God's wisdom within the sphere of His power, and they bear witness to His power in the kernel of divine wisdom.

The story of Moses the Confidant and our master Khiḍr provide a sufficient answer to anyone who is able to understand and contemplate.

Al-Shushtarī also says, may God sanctify his secret:

Sober one, tell me: are these cups,
Or are they gleaming suns, shining bright?

Even suns bow down to this wine
When it appears with all its light.

A draught well-mixed, appearing to the drinker
As radiant as a bride decked in her finery,

A vintage whose juice was pressed
In the time before there was grape or vinery.

Named it was when time was young,
Before words had been set down on scrolls.

It is called wine, but in truth it is spirit,
For its every breath gives life to souls.

Its servers stand as they pass it around,
And its passionate lovers never sit down.

Al-Ghazālī, may God sanctify his secret, says in his commentary on the divine names, *al-Maqṣad al-asnā*:

These two attributes are also relative, in the sense that the Manifest is manifest to something and nonmanifest to something else; He cannot be both manifest and nonmanifest in the same aspect, but rather He is manifest relative to a given perceptive faculty, and nonmanifest relative to another. Manifestation and nonmanifestation are defined only by their relation to powers of perception. God Almighty is nonmanifest when sought through the perception of the senses or the imagination, but manifest when sought through the intellect by means of deductive reasoning.

You might say, "It is obvious how He is nonmanifest with respect to the perception of the senses, but what does it mean that He is manifest to the intellect? A manifest thing is something that is not doubted in the least, and something that all people perceive in the exact same way. Yet God is something that many people doubt greatly, so how can He be manifest?"

The answer to this is that He is only nonmanifest, despite His manifestation, precisely because of how manifest He is. His manifestation is the cause of His nonmanifestation, just as His Light is what veils His Light. "Everything that goes beyond its limit becomes its opposite." You might find this strange or far-fetched, in which case you must have an example to illustrate it. Suppose that you look at a single word which a scribe has written. From this word you will deduce that the scribe must be endowed with power, hearing, and sight, and you will be absolutely certain that he possesses these attributes. Indeed, upon seeing a written word you will be convinced that the scribe exists, and that this scribe possesses knowledge, power, hearing, sight, and life. A single word is enough for you to deduce the existence of the scribe as well as his attributes.

Now every atom in the heavens and earth; the stars, planets, sun, moon, animals, plants; every attribute and everything attributed by it—all of them bear witness in themselves to the need for a director who directs them, measures them, and assigns to them their attributes. Any person who examines one of his limbs or body parts, external or internal, or indeed any of his attributes or the states that pass over him involuntarily, will see them as eloquent witnesses to the existence of their Creator, their Compeller, their Director. The same applies to all the things that he perceives through his senses, whether in himself or outside himself. If things differed in their testimonial aptitude, such that only some of them bore witness while others did not, everyone would attain certitude. But because all things bear witness in agreement, people overlook their testimony: its very obviousness is what makes it unclear.

Another example: the most manifest of things are those perceived by the external senses, of which the most manifest are those perceived by the sense of sight. The most manifest thing that sight can perceive is the light of the sun, which shines upon physical bodies and by means of which all things are made manifest. If all things are manifested by means of something, then that thing must itself be manifest. Yet this is obscure for many people, to the extent that they say that colored things contain nothing except their colors, whether black or red, and do not realize that in addition to their color there is also a part played by light and reflected light. They are only aware of the role played by light in color because of the distinction they perceive between shadow and the places where light falls, or between night and day. Since it is possible to conceive of the sun being absent at night or obscured by dark objects during the day, when its influence upon colored objects is disconnected, the distinction is therefore perceived between objects that are illumined by it and dark objects that are veiled from it. Thus, the existence of light is known through the absence of light when the state of absence is contrasted with the state of presence. The distinction is perceived, though the colors persist in either situation. If the sun always shone upon all manifest bodies without ever setting, one would not perceive the distinction and one would not be able to recognize light as a thing that exists apart from color, despite the fact that light is the most manifest of all things, and the thing that makes all other things manifest.

If it were conceivable that God—transcendent though He is beyond any such notion—could be nonexistent or absent from certain things, the heavens and earth would cease to exist, as would everything else from which His Light was severed. The distinction between the two states would become apparent, and His existence would be known for certain. But since all things and all states equally attest to His existence, all of them in uniformity, this is the cause of His obscurity. Glory be to Him Who is veiled from creation by His Light, and hidden from them due to the intensity of His manifestation! He is the Manifest besides Whom there is none more manifest, and the Hidden besides Whom there is none more hidden.[1]

1   Ghazālī, *al-Maqṣad al-asnā*, pp. 106-107.

Chapter V
Luminous Vision in the Aphorisms of al-Iskandarī

Light is a Lordly Illumination
in the Mirror of the Pure Heart

How can a heart shine when the forms of created things are imprinted upon its mirror? How can it travel to God when it is shackled by its passions? How can it hope to enter the God's presence when it has not become purified of the dross of its heedlessness? How can it expect to understand subtle mysteries when it has not repented of its folly?[1]

The heart is a polished mirror with one face; no matter where you turn it, whatever it faces will be imprinted upon it. If it faces the forms of created things, the images of the senses, and the illusions of the imagination, then the dark shadow of sensorial things will fall over the heart's eye, veiling it from the suns of meaning. The longer it faces them, the darker it will grow until it becomes covered with rust. When this happens it will deny the Light of God entirely because of the extreme difficulty of weaning it from the darkness of sensoriality. Ḥudhayfa ﷺ related that he heard God's Messenger ﷺ say, "Temptations present themselves to the heart like a straw mat, reed

1   Ibn ʿAṭāʾ Illāh, Aphorism 13.

woven with reed. When a heart imbibes them, a black mark it made upon it. When a heart rejects them, a white mark is made upon it. This goes on until one heart becomes entirely white and clean, and no temptation can harm it as long as heaven and earth endure; and the other heart becomes ashen-black and twisted like a stalk, neither recognizing good nor condemning evil, but only its own base desire as it imbibes it."[1]

How then can the Lights of existence shine in a heart that is ashen-black, woven with heedlessness in layers of dark delusion, one atop the other? How can a heart journey to the presence of Lights when it is bound by the chains of desires and pleasures? God says, **Made to seem fair unto mankind is the love of passions, among them women, children, hoarded heaps of gold and silver, horses of mark, cattle, and tillage. Those are the enjoyment of the life of this world. And God, with Him is the beautiful return.**[2] The heart's attachment to things other than God prevents it from entering the presence. The resolve of the traveler who means to journey to the Holy presence is sapped because his application is attached to other than God, even if it is something permitted, let alone something unlawful. The presence of union will not brook duality or alterity. How could it accept the follies and attachments of delusion?

How could anyone enter the presence without first being cleansed of the impurity of heedlessness? To observe other-

---

1   Muslim, *Ṣaḥīḥ*, 211.
2   Q Āl ʿImrān 3:14.

than-God invalidates the ritual purity of union, and heedless-ness incurs major ritual impurity because the heart is wedded to the delusions of the imagination. Anyone with such attributes cannot enter the mosque of the presence before first performing the purificatory bath from the spring-water of life, that is, the Shaykh who has arrived and may lead others to arrive. His water is nondelimited: pure in itself, and purifying of other than itself. It is unchanged in color, form, or odor. It is of the realm of divine invincibility and has not entered the world of material form. If the disciple performs the ritual bath properly with the water of life, his impurity will be annulled. He will see nothing but the divine eternality wheresoever he turns. But in order to understand the subtle secrets, he must repent of the sins of nature and the subtleties of the soul; for "the good deeds of the pious are the sins of those brought near."

Ibn 'Ajība ﷺ says:

When God wishes to nurture His servant, He occupies his mind with the Lights of His spiritual realm and the secrets of His dominion, and does not let his heart become attached to any of the beings of darkness and the follies of delusion. The Lights of faith and excellence are imprinted in the mirror of his heart, and the moons of Oneness and the suns of gnosis shine there.

Al-Shushtarī alluded to this in one of his prose-poems when he said,

"Close your eyes and see,
and the truth will glimmer;
disappear to the world,
and your secrets will shimmer;
your blindness will fall away
when you polish the mirror."

Then he said,

"The sphere turns within you,
glittering and shining;
suns and moons inside you,
setting and rising."

That is, by polishing the mirror of your heart, your oblivi-ousness to God will be cured, and you will recognize Him in all things. Your heart will become the axis of the sphere of Lights, and in it will appear the moons of Oneness and suns of gnosis.

When God wishes to abandon His servant—in His justice and wisdom—He causes him to think of darkened beings and corporeal desires, which become imprinted upon the mirror of his heart. Their cosmic darkness and illusory forms veil him from the radiance of the suns of gnosis and Lights of faith. The more those images build up in it, the more its Light will be blotted out and its veil will thicken. It will see nothing but sensory things, and think only of sensory things. Some of them become so veiled that their Light is blotted out altogether, and they deny that the Light exists at all. This is the station of unbelief—we seek God's refuge! Others are less thickly veiled, so that they acknowledge the existence of the Light though they cannot see it. This is the station of the ordinary Muslims, though they differ in degrees therein, some nearer and some farther, some stronger in conviction and others weaker, each in the measure of his certitude and his lack of worldly attachments, passional impediments, and delusional ideas.

A hadith says, "Hearts become rusty just as iron does, and faith becomes worn just as a new robe does." Another reads, "When the servant commits a sin, a black mark is made upon his heart. If he stops and seeks forgiveness, it is erased. If he repeats it, the mark is added to until it covers his whole heart. That is the rust of which God says, **Nay! But that which they used to earn has covered their hearts with rust.**"[1] Or he ﷺ said words to that effect.

You understand, then, that the heart has only one direction; if Light faces it, it is illuminated, and if darkness faces it, it is dark. Darkness and Light can never come together.[2]

---

1   Q Muṭaffifīn 83:14.
2   *Īqāẓ al-himam,* 55-56.

The Corporeality of Bodies, and the Light of Spirits

Engendered existence is all darkness, and is only illuminated by the manifestation of the Real in it. Whoever sees the cosmos but does not see Him in it, or by it, or before it, or after it, is oblivious to the existence of Lights, and is veiled from the suns of gnosis by the clouds of ephemera.[1]

In the terminology of the Karkarī Order, engendered existence (*kawn*) is that which is brought to be by God's will and power, and includes every existential phenomenon located between the *Kāf* and the *Nūn* of the command *Kun*, Be!

Darkness of every kind is nonexistent, while Light is existential, and pertains to the station of "I loved to be known." God says, describing Himself: **God is the Light of the heavens and the earth. The likeness of His Light is a niche, wherein is a lamp. The lamp is in a glass. The glass is as a resplendent planet kindled from a blessed olive tree, neither of the East nor of the West. Its oil would well-nigh shine forth, even if no fire had touched it. Light upon light. God guides unto His Light whomsoever He will, and God sets forth parables for**

---

1   Aphorism 14.

mankind, and God is Knower of all things.[1] He then describes His Prophet ﷺ: **O Prophet! Truly We have sent thee as a witness, as a bearer of glad tidings, and as a warner, as one who calls unto God by His Leave, and as a luminous lamp.**[2] He also distinguishes between the living and the dead, and between the existent and the nonexistent, in the following verse, **Is he who was dead, and to whom We give life, making for him a light by which to walk among mankind, like unto one who is in darkness from which he does not emerge? Thus for the disbelievers, what they used to do was made to seem fair unto them.**[3]

I have said of this in a poem:

Dear seeker of knowledge, meaning, and virtue,
Here is the invoker's Door of Riḍwān.

Cling to the Prophet, may God ever bless him,
The Light of proof, the Gate of al-Raḥmān,

The greatest portal, pillar, and sanctuary,
Aḥmad, God bless him, the Light of Eternity!

Disciple, if you would seek your Lord,
Light is the way to the presence of His Majesty,

---

1   Q Nūr 24:35.
2   Q Aḥzāb 33:45–46.
3   Q Anʿām 6:122.

If you seek the secret of your Lord's love,
Light is the cure, and no other will do.

Cling to the guide, the Shaykh who knows God,
 If you are wise and your love is true.

He will turn your heart into a Ḥirā' to recite the names,
Lift you to the heavens and the Lote-Tree is his final goal.

Close yourself to the senses, and the suns will appear;
Become extinct to all but Him, annihilate this soul.

Swim with the supreme Name in the ocean of eternity,
See that all is naught, but the Glorious One.

Know the Real for real and exult in His glory,
Witness the stitching of what was undone.

Swim in the attributes, disappear in the Essence above;
Your time will be joyous, basking in His love.

If someone sees the cosmos but does not see God's Light before it, with it, or after it, this means that his inner vision is blocked, his heart darkened and rusted. The suns of pure meaning (*ma'ānī*) are veiled from him by the clouds of material vessels (*awānī*), and his sight is adrift in the directions of spatiality, and his perceptions are limited to those of the external senses.

As for those who walk upon the Radiant Path, they see engendered being by the Light of the Being-Giver, and so engendered things disappear from their inner vision. They are in constant witnessing, annihilated in His Lights, subsisting through His attributes, existing through His Essence. The illusions of material vessels do not veil them from the Lights of meanings.

Ibn ʿAjība says, may God be pleased with him:

The statement that "engendered existence is all darkness" is true only for those who are veiled due to the imprinting of external forms upon the mirrors of their hearts. As for those who recognize God, their inner vision penetrates through the realm of engendered being and they behold the Real, and so they see engendered existence as Light emanating from the ocean of divine invincibility, and so engendered existence for them is all Light. God says, **Say, "Observe that which is in the heavens and on the earth"**;[1] that is, of the Light of His spiritual realm and the secrets of His invincible realm, or from the secrets of meaning that subsist in the vessels.

The Messenger of God ﷺ said, "God is veiled from the people of heaven just as He is from the people of earth, and the people of the Supreme Assembly seek Him just as you seek Him. He does not indwell in anything, nor is He absent from anything."

---

1   Q Yūnus 10:101.

These meanings are solely a matter of taste; they cannot be apprehended by the intellect, nor transmitted upon the page, but can only be perceived by keeping the company of those who know through experiential taste. Defer to them, and do not criticize. If you have not seen the new moon for yourself, then defer to those who have seen it with their own eyes.

Beyond this, when it comes to beholding the Real people are divided into three groups: the masses, the elite, and the elite of the elite. Therefore the author says, "If someone sees engendered existence but does not see Him in it, or by it, or before it, or after it, then he is oblivious to the existence of Lights, and is veiled from the suns of gnosis by the clouds of ephemera." **Those who stand in the station of subsistence** behold the Real merely by their eyes falling upon engendered existence. They affirm the trace by reference to God, and do not behold anything but Him, except that in their perfection they affirm both the mediator and the Mediated. They witness God merely by witnessing the mediator, without giving priority of one over the other, and without regard for one being a container and the other being contained.

Spiritual travelers among the disciples behold engendered being and then behold the Being-Giver with it, or in its wake, whereupon engendered being is erased from their vision merely by their act of beholding the Being-Giver. This is the state of the "observers" who are raising up their gaze (*mustashrifūn*).

Those who pass away in God behold the Real before they behold creation, meaning that they do not see creation at all, for to them it may as well not exist since in their drunkenness they are entirely oblivious to the mediator, annihilated from wisdom, drowning in the sea of Lights, and blocked from seeing the traces. Concerning this station, one of them proclaimed, "I never saw anything without seeing God before it."

As for **those who are veiled from God** and rely on logical proofs and arguments, they only behold engendered being, and do not see the Being-Giver either before it or after it. The most they can do is to seek proof for His existence from engendered existence. These are the ordinary Muslims from among the folk of the right side, who are oblivious to the existence of the Lights, blocked from them, and veiled from the suns of gnosis by the clouds of ephemera, even after those suns have risen and their Light has shone forth.[1]

1   *Īqāẓ al-himam,* 63-64.

Light is the Ray of Inner Vision

The ray of inner vision shows you how close He is to you; the eye of inner vision shows you your nothingness before His existence; the truth of inner vision shows you His existence, not your nothingness or your existence.[1]

When the eye of a person's heart is opened at the hand of a gnostic who has arrived and can guide others to arrival, he witnesses, by the ray of the Light of presence, how near God is, as He says, **We did indeed create man, and We know what his soul whispers to him; and We are nearer to him than his jugular vein.**[2] He comes to know that the act subsists through the attribute, and the attribute subsists through the Essence; but in terms of union, He is He, and He transcends any comparability to temporal beings. There is neither distinction nor duality. The one who beholds the ray of subtleties, which shines from the suns of esoteric realities through the aperture of wisdom, will see the meanings of His nearness. When this nearness grows stronger and takes control of the heart, then its inner eye is purified from the blinding dust of "I" and sharpened by the

1 Aphorism 36.
2 Q Qāf 50:16.

metal of "He." His existence is noughted in the existence of his Beloved, and he separates from his "I" by his connection to the "He-ness" of the One he cherishes.

A man came to Abū Yazīd and, not recognizing him, asked him, "Where is Abū Yazīd?" Abū Yazīd replied, "He has died—may God not have mercy on him!" That is, "may God not send him back." When the servant gains mastery in witnessing, he seeks refuge from both nearness and farness, knowing that there is no direction, no spatiality, no distance, and no between. "God was, and there was nothing with Him; and He is now as He ever was." I have said of this in a poem:

My grave flows among graves,
But my spirit is my Lord's alone.

Your brilliant Light shines from my heart,
Your Name writ upon my gravestone.

In a daze, I ask refuge from what I fear:
Let me be neither far, nor near!

Ibn 'Ajība ﷺ says:
This is like someone who has heard of Mecca but never seen it. Such a person possesses "the knowledge of certainty." Then when he observes it for himself but does not go inside it, he has "the eye of certainty." Then when he enters the city and finds himself inside it, he has "the truth of certainty." The same

applies to the one who seeks God. While he remains behind the veil and annihilated in the acts, he possesses the knowledge of certainty. When he gets a glimpse of annihilation in the Essence but does not master it, he possesses the eye of certainty. When he masters it and becomes fully firm in it, he possesses the truth of certainty.

One could also say that the ray of inner vision is for those who know the physical realm, the eye of inner vision is for those who know the spiritual realm, and the truth of inner vision is for those who know in the realm of divine invincibility. Or one could say that the ray of inner vision is for those who experience annihilation in the acts, the eye of inner vision is for those who experience annihilation in the Essence, and the truth of inner vision is for those who experience annihilation in annihilation.

The ray of inner vision shows you how close God is to you; that is, it makes you witness the nearness of the Light of God to you, as He says, **We did indeed create man, and We know what his soul whispers to him; and We are nearer to him than his jugular vein;**[1] and He says, **He is with you wheresoever you are.**[2]

The eye of inner vision shows you your nothingness; that is, your erasure through the erasure of your delusion, before His existence; for it is impossible to witness Him while witnessing

1   Q Qāf 50:16.
2   Q Ḥadīd 57:4.

anything besides Him. When the delusion leaves you and you become annihilated from your own existence, you will witness your Lord through your Lord [...].

The truth of inner vision shows you the existence of the Real alone, not your own existence, because you are entirely absent. Moreover, it does not show you your nonexistence, for a thing cannot become nonexistent unless it existed to begin with, but nothing ever existed alongside God: "God was, and there was nothing with Him; and He is now as He ever was." Although the latter phrase is not part of the original ḥadīth, its meaning is correct and true, for it is not possible for God to change.

Muḥyī al-Dīn ibn al-'Arabī al-Ḥātimī ﷺ said, "The one who witnesses that created beings have no agency has succeeded; the one who witnesses that they have no life has advanced; and the one who witnesses that they are nonexistence itself has attained."[1]

---

1 *Īqāẓ al-himam,* 103-104.

Lights Are the Champions of Secrets

Lights are the riding-mounts of hearts and innermost secrets[1]

Light is a divine inrush that God casts into the hearts of His beloved servants at the hand of one of His friends, by which He brings them out of the darkness of heedlessness and the rebelliousness of their souls, and frees them from the bondage of alterities and the prison of base desires and selfish interests. This Light transports them upon the celestial steed of transcendent meanings and bears them to the realms of spirit and divine invincibility. The Light lifts them to the heavens of the spirit, where they taste the pleasure of nearness and annihilation. The doves of their spirits thus ascends to the Throne of the All-Merciful, where they may roam in the gardens of nearness, the meadows of gnosis, and the courtyards of love and affection.

Whoever is in such a state is the true martyr who dies in the cause of the Majestic Name, *Allāh*. The Messenger of God ﷺ said, "When your brethren fell at Uḥud, God placed their spirits into the breasts of green birds, which visit the rivers of Paradise, eat its fruits, and nest in golden lamps hanging in the

1   Aphorism 55.

shade of the Throne. In the midst of their food, drink, and shelter, they said, 'Who will tell our brothers that we are alive and well in Paradise, so that they do not neglect the struggle or shrink from battle?' God Almighty said, 'I will tell them for you.' Then He revealed, **And deem not those slain in the way of God to be dead. Rather, they are alive with their Lord, provided for.**"[1]

Ibn ʿAjība ☙ says:

The word *maṭāyā* (riding-mounts) is the plural of *maṭiyya*, which means a camel used for riding. The heart (*qalb*) is the receiver (*qābila*) of understanding, and the innermost secret (*sirr*) is the receiver of divine self-disclosures. The innermost secret is subtler and purer than the heart, but both are different names for the spirit (*rūḥ*). As long as the spirit is darkened by acts of disobedience, sins, and base desires, it is called the lower self (*nafs*). When it desists and becomes tied down (*inʿaqal*) like an animal, it is called an intellect that shackles (*ʿaql*). When it wavers (*tataqallab*) between heedlessness and presence, it is called a heart (*qalb*). When it becomes tranquil and peaceful and finds spiritual repose (*istarāḥat*) from the toil of lower human nature, it is called the spirit (*rūḥ*). When it is purified from the dross of sensoriality, it is called the innermost secret (*sirr*) because it has become one of God's secrets by returning to its origin, which is the secret of divine invincibility. When God wishes to connect His servant to His holy inti-

---

1   Q Āl ʿImrān 3:169; Abū Dāwūd, *Sunan*, 2520.

mate presence, He replenishes him with luminous inrushes like riding-mounts. These inrushes transport him in the carriage of protection, cooled by the breeze of guidance, surrounded by divine succor and nurture. The spirit journeys from the human realms to the spiritual realms, until it becomes one of God's secrets.[1]

1   *Īqāẓ al-himam,* p. 129.

The Armies of Light are the Antidote
for the Darkness of Alterity

Light is the army of the heart, just as darkness is the army of the lower self. When God wishes to aid His servant, He reinforces him with armies of light, and cuts off from him the reinforcements of darkness and alterity.[1]

The lower self, heart, spirit, and innermost secret are names and levels designating one single reality, whose names differ according to the state and station of the servant. When the latter is aided and supported by the Lights of guidance, he is referred to as a heart (*qalb*), for the heart is that which fluctuates (*taqallub*) between the stations of the lower self and the spirit. When the servant disappears into the Lights of existence and plunges into the subtle meanings wherein he finds tranquility, he becomes a spirit.

But when someone is destined to commit acts of disobedience or to stumble in a manner that causes separation, the forces of darkness dominate, and they return to the level of the lower self. In contrast, when a person is destined for guidance, fate directs them to someone who has deep knowledge of the

---

1   Aphorism 56.

divine presence, and the breezes of divine proximity blow upon him, bringing with them the clouds of guidance that shower rains of transcendence upon the earth of their heart. In the core of their heart, the tree of divine Oneness grows, bearing the fruits of God's exclusive singularity. Then the clouds of ephemera clear away, and the evil armies of lower self and ego are defeated, and the obstacles of caprice melt away, allowing them to walk the path of divine grace, strengthened and protected by God's help.

Ibn 'Ajība 🙶 says:

Darkness is a blot caused by caprice. It stains the soul due to the impulses of delusion, and blinds it to God, thereby allowing falsehood to overpower truth. So said Shaykh Zarrūq. We saw earlier that lower self, intellect, heart, spirit, and innermost secret are all names for the same thing, which is the lordly luminous subtlety that is deposited in this dark corporeal human shell; the names of this lordly luminous subtlety differ only according to its differing states and transforming stages. It is like rain that falls upon the roots of a tree, then rises through its branches and emerges as leaves, then bright blossoms, then produces fruit, then grows until it is complete. It is all the same water, but its names differ according to its stages. Al-Sāḥilī (d. 1353) said as much in his treatise, "The Aspiration of the Wayfarer" (*Bughyat al-Sālik*) [...].

Thus the heart is engaged in a back-and-forth war with the lower self. For the spirit finds difficulty in passing from the darkness of the lower self to the abode of Light which is the heart and what lies beyond it. The heart wars with it to transfer it to its origin, while it makes itself a deadweight and falls to the earth of humanity and its base desires. The heart thus possesses luminous inrushes that bring it nearer and support it so that it is able to ascend to the presence which is its origin and homestead. The Lights are like its army, strengthening it and helping it gain victory against the darkness of the lower self [...].

When God wishes to protect and help His servant, He reinforces his heart with the armies of Light and cuts it off from the flow of alterities from the side of the soul, so that Light conquers darkness and the lower self is defeated. When God wishes to bring down His servant, He feeds his lower self with alterities and cuts off the rays of Light from his heart. Thus the one He helps is restored to how he ought to be, in contrast to the one He brings down.[1]

---

1   *Īqāẓ al-himam,* p. 130.

<h2 style="text-align:center">Light is the Door to Unveiling</h2>

Light unveils, inner vision discerns, and the heart draws near or turns away.[1]

Light is that which is manifest in itself, and makes other things manifest. The realities of things are unveiled by it. It is the differentiator and the isthmus between the real and the unreal, beauty and ugliness. By means of its opposition, things become distinguished. If the Light of the attributes is not disclosed to someone, they will not understand the ugliness of darkness, because to know something one must know its opposite. This is why idolatry is likened to a black ant crawling upon a smooth rock in the dead of night.

Darknesses, one above the other;[2] darkness in perceiving the ruling property, the act, and the attribute. These darknesses can only be dispelled by the divine Light. When the realities of things are uncovered, beauty becomes distinguished from ugliness. The one who stands in the station of separation can discern ugly things as being ugly, and beautiful things as being

---

1 Aphorism 56.
2 Q Nūr 24:40.

beauty, through inner vision. The heart then draws toward what leads to its wellbeing and turns away from what leads to its ruin and corruption.

Sidi Ibn ʿAjība says:

You could say that this means the Light of submission, faith, and spiritual excellence (*islām, īmān, iḥsān*). The Light of submission unveils the darkness of unbelief and sin and reveals the Light of surrender and resignation. The inner vision discerns between the ugliness of unbelief and sin and the beauty of the Light of submission and resignation, and the heart draws toward obedience to its Lord and turns away from anything that distances it from its Lord.

The Light of faith unveils the darkness of hidden idolatry and reveals the splendor of sincerity and faithfulness. The inner vision discerns between the ugliness and harmfulness of idolatry and the beauty and goodness of sincerity, and the heart draws toward its Lord's Oneness and turns away from idolatry and its evil.

The Light of spiritual excellence unveils the darkness of other-than-God and reveals the Light of the existence of the Lord. The inner vision discerns between the ugliness of the darkness of ephemera and the beauty of the Light of the One who produces the ephemera, and the heart draws toward the recognition of its Lord and becomes entirely oblivious to all other than Him.

Or you could say that it is the Light of the outer law, the spiritual path, and the inner reality (*sharīʿa, ṭarīqa, ḥaqīqa*).

The Light of the outer law unveils the darkness of negligence and sloth and reveals the Light of effort and solemnity. The inner vision discerns between the ugliness of sloth and the beauty of effort, and the heart draws toward bodily struggle in obedience to God and retreats from the pursuit of selfish interests and caprice.

The Light of the spiritual path uncovers the darkness of ugly deeds and defective traits and reveals the splendor of purity and the fruits of unseen knowledge. The inner vision discerns between the ugliness of defective traits and the beauty of purity and unseen knowledge, and the heart draws toward the means of purification and retreats from anything that prevents self-effacement and adornment.

The Light of inner reality, for its part, uncovers the darkness of the veil and reveals the beauty of the beloved ones; or one could say that the Light of inner reality uncovers the darkness of engendered beings and reveals the Light of direct witnessing and firsthand vision. The heart draws toward witnessing loved ones inside the veil, and turns away from anything that severs it from good comportment with the loved ones. May God allow us to be with them always, in this life and in the Abode of Peace, amen![1]

---

1   *Īqāz al-himam,* p. 132.

The Lights of the Inmost Heart are Unending

He has illuminated outward appearances with the Lights of His ephemeral traces, and illuminated inmost hearts with the Lights of His attributes. This is why the Lights of outward appearances can set, but the lights of hearts and their inmost realities never set. Thus it is said:

The day's sun sets by night,
But the heart's sun shines ever bright.[1]

External appearances (*ẓawāhir*) are the images of engendered beings that appear before the eye. God illuminates them with the Lights of power sent down into the vessels of divine wisdom. God says, **Truly We have adorned the lowest heaven with lamps and made them missiles against the satans; and We have prepared for them the punishment of the Blaze.**[2] And He says, **Truly We adorned the lowest heaven with an ornament, the stars.**[3] He adorned the heaven with the planets, stars,

1   Aphorism 103.
2   Q Mulk 67:5.
3   Q Ṣāffāt 37:6.

and suns, which are mere distractions to those who stop at external appearances, but admonitions for those who understand transcendent meanings.

He illuminates the pure hearts of His loved ones with His Lights. Some of them He annihilates in the Light of the act, so that they see only His omnipotence. Others He annihilates in the Light of the attribute, so that they see only His self-disclosures. Others He annihilates in the Light of the Essence, so that they are entirely bewildered and incapacitated.

There is a vast difference between the Lights of outward appearances and the Lights of inmost hearts (*sarā'ir*). The Lights of outward appearances set and vanish, for they draw from a created being governed by the laws of wisdom. The Lights of inmost hearts, however, are enduring and unending; they are a Radiant Path whose night is as bright as its day, never setting or disappearing, for they are from the Creator of the heavens and the earth.

Ibn 'Ajība says:

For this reason, the Lights of outward appearances set while the Lights of inmost hearts do not. This is because the Lights of outward appearances are merely the Lights of the ephemeral trace, and it is the nature of the ephemeral trace to undergo influence and change through rising and setting. The setting of the Lights of outward appearances takes the form of either conventional setting [as the sun sets], or by absolute obliteration. But the Lights of hearts, which are the Lights of submission and faith, and the Lights of inmost hearts, which are the Lights of spiritual excellence, never set. The Lights of submission and faith are the Lights of turning one's attentiveness to God (*tawajjuh*), while the Lights of spiritual excellence are the Lights of face-to-face encounter (*muwājaha*). Light is an expression of the certainty that results in the heart and produces the fruit of sweetness in action. When this certainty becomes stronger, the Light becomes stronger and the sweetness increases until it reaches the sweetness of witnessing, which envelops the sweetness of action. This is why the knower of God performs fewer actions with his body, since the sweetness of witnessing replaces everything else; and "to be informed is not like firsthand vision" [...].

Shaykh Zarrūq ﷺ said, "The sun of the heart never sets, but is perpetual and uninterrupted, enduring and unwavering. This is because its replenishing source is also everlasting, namely the meanings of lordly attributes and their constant loci, the spiritual horizons. The one who attaches himself to these everlasting sources is attached to a reality that never wavers. This is why the Sufi camp is only needful of God, not material means, and is only attached to Him and no other."[1]

1   *Īqāẓ al-himam,* pp. 214-215.

The Purity of the Inmost Heart is Measured by Light

Replenishment comes in accordance with preparedness, and Lights shine forth in accordance with the purity of the inmost heart.[1]

Replenishment is a lordly water that rains down from the heavens of the unseen and falls upon the earth of the worthy disciple's heart, so that the earth of his existence is watered with the benevolent rains of "Indeed, we bear witness!." The Master of Existence ﷺ said, "The guidance and knowledge with which God has sent me is like rain that falls upon land. The fertile land absorbs the water and brings forth much grass and herbs. The solid land retains the water, and God benefits people with it so that they may drink, water their animals, and irrigate. The rest falls into an abyss, which neither retains the water nor produces plants. Such is the likeness of the one who understands God's religion and benefits from that with which God has sent me, learning and teaching others. Then there is the one who neither raises his head to it, nor accepts God's guidance with which I have been sent."[2]

1   Aphorisms 112 & 113.
2   Muslim, *Ṣaḥīḥ*, 2282.

Guidance to the Radiant Path is thus a spiritual rain, watering the lands of hearts that thirst for knowledge of their Maker, purifying them from the pollutants of sensoriality and spatiality and cleansing them of the intrusive parasites of alterity and separative existence. This occurs in accordance with how prepared the earth of the heart is to be cleansed, ploughed, and planted, and the quality of its soil.

The rain of transcendence continues to fall, sinking into the earth of immanence until the tree of Oneness grows, its root firm in the earth of immanence and its branch in the heaven of transcendence, providing its fruit in every experience of witnessing and unveiling, according to the purity of the heaven of the inmost heart of the disciple's spirit, and according to the solar radiance of the realities in the heaven of his spirit. Adornment is commensurate with purification, witnessing with effort, replenishment with preparedness, and radiance with purity. Sidi Ibn ʿAjība says:

The Shaykh of our Shaykh Moulay al-ʿArabī al-Darqāwī ﷺ said in one of his letters, "You ask when will it be that you become like mountains that one bethinks to be still when in fact they move as the clouds move. Our answer: When you become completely detached from the world and give up any hope of ever returning to it, and then believe in your Shaykhs that they are perfect and that they are walking in the footsteps of the Prophets, upon them be peace, and that they are the heirs of the Prophet ﷺ. When you achieve this, then by God, replenishment will descend upon you day and night, month by month, year by year, in every moment and instant. Your hearts will be filled with knowledge of God, and your hearts will be made tranquil by remembrance of Him, and you will become like firm mountains."

That is the gist of what he said; and what he said is the exact truth, because the one who renounces the world empties his heart [...] and readies himself for the Lights. When replenishment descends, it finds the heart expansive and purified, and fills it with its Lights and adorns it with its secrets [...]. The degree of its purification and erasure determines the extent of the radiance of its Light. When the clouds of ephemera disperse from the heaven of the heart, and the fog of alterities clears, the Light of annihilation shines forth. The heart and the spirit become oblivious to external forms, and nothing remains but the Living and All-Sustaining. Then when the mist of Lights disperses from the inmost heart, the Light of subsistence shines there. That which has no existence passes away, and that which ever was remains. Al-Jīlī ﷺ says of this in his *'Ayniyya*:

In it I extinguished, and there was no more "I,"
For the identity of Laylā severed my own identity.

I was as though I was not, and He was He,
As He always was, all-embracing Singularity.

My moon ascended in the east of lordliness,
My sun rose upon the horizon of divinity,

And I noughted them both, as though they never were,
As though they had always been illusory.[1]

---

1   *Īqāẓ al-himam*, pp. 229-230.

The Ritual Prayer for the Righteous
is a Luminous Connection with God

In the ritual prayer, intimate discourse and spiritual purification are found, secrets expand, and the Lights shine forth. He knew that you would be weak, so He reduced its numbers; and He knew that you would be in need of His grace, so He multiplied its replenishment.[1]

Prayer (*ṣalāt*) is a flood of witnessing that cannot be qualified. It is expressed by the unseen half circle of lordship that hovers above the *bā'* of servanthood. This form of prayer transcends number, time, and all levels of corporeal existence, to the extent that all atoms vanish in the process of performing it and the All comes into manifestation. What remains is the nearness of Him Who has no likeness, beyond the circle of lordship and servanthood, where only the rule of One remains. This prayer takes place beyond the furthest Lote-Tree that is messengerhood, at the beginning of the Lote-Tree that is sainthood, and within the reality of "Peace be upon us, and upon God's righteous servants." Prayer is the locus of intimate discourse. The Master of the Two Worlds ﷺ said, "Purity is half of faith; 'praise

1   Aphorism 120.

be to God' fills the scale; 'glory be to God and praise be to God' fills everything between the heavens and the earth; prayer is Light; charity is proof; patience is illumination; the Qur'ān is an argument for you or against you. All people rise in the morning and sell themselves, free themselves, or ruin themselves."[1]

And because prayer is Light, the Beloved Prophet ﷺ used to say on his way to the mosque, "Dear God, place Light in my heart, and Light in my sight, and Light in my hearing, and Light to my right, and Light to my left, and Light above me, and Light below me, and Light before me, and Light behind me, and make for me Light."[2]

Prayer is the disclosure-site for the secret between the one named servant and the One called Lord. The vast fields of this secret are contained within it. Therefore God says in the Sacred Ḥadīth: "'I have divided prayer into two halves between Me and My servant, and My servant shall have what he requests.' When the servant says, **Praise be to God, Lord of the worlds**, God says, 'My servant has praised Me.' When he says, **the All-Merciful, the Ever-Merciful**, God says, 'My servant has lauded Me.' When he says, **Master of the Day of Judgment**, God says, 'My servant has glorified Me and entrusted his affair to Me.' When he says, **Thee we worship and from Thee we seek help**, God says, 'This is between Me and My servant, and My servant shall have what he requests.' When he says, **Guide us**

---

1   Muslim, *Ṣaḥīḥ*, 333.
2   Bukhārī, *Ṣaḥīḥ*, 5868.

upon the straight path, the path of those whom Thou hast blessed, not of those who incur wrath, nor of those who are astray, God says, 'This is for My servant, and My servant shall have what he requests.'"[1]

Prayer is the manifestation-site of all the levels of annihilation: standing, bowing, and prostrating are annihilations in act, attribute, and Essence. And since prostration is the highest level, God says, **Nay! Obey him not! But prostrate and draw nigh.**[2] Although the prayers are few in number outwardly, they contain manifold replenishments inwardly. Sidi Ibn 'Ajība says:

A tradition states that when the servant stands in prayer, God lifts the veil between Him and him, and faces him directly. When purification is completed and love is strong, and when the servant's thirst is true and his dazzlement manifest, the spirit deserves to have the veil lifted and the door opened, that it may enter into the presence of the loved ones and have the barrier removed between it and them. It emerges from of the confinement of matter into the vast expanse of the realm of spirits, or from the confinement of the physical world into the vastness of the spiritual world. This is what the author means when he says, "the fields of secrets expand," which is the fifth consequence. The word *maydān* (field) means a field where horses are kept; here it symbolizes the vastness of the spiritual world. When the spirit roams freely in that world and journeys

1 Muslim, *Ṣaḥīḥ*, 603.
2 Q 'Alaq 96:19.

through its vast Lights by means of contemplation, the Lights of the glory of the world of divine invincibility shine upon it. This is what he means by "the gleams of Lights shine forth," which is the sixth consequence.

By "secrets" he means the secrets of the Essence, which are for the people of annihilation; and by "Lights" he means the Lights of the attributes, which are for the people of subsistence. God knows best. He is speaking of the prayer that moves one from state to state, station to station, the prayer of those who travel the path at the hands of Sufi Shaykhs, not the prayer of the heedless, nor the prayer of the diligent worshippers and ascetics, for they do not participate in this journey. God knows best.

Abū Ṭālib al-Makkī said, "We have been told that when the believer performs ablutions for the ritual prayer, the devils flee from him to the farthest regions of the earths, fearing him because he is preparing for an audience with the King. When he enters into the prayer by uttering the first *takbīr*, Iblīs is veiled from him and barriers are set up to keep him from looking upon him. The Almighty faces him directly. When he says, 'God is Greatest,' an angel looks into his heart, and if there is truly nothing held greater than God therein, he says, 'You have spoken the truth.' Light shines forth from his heart and reaches as far as the regions of the Throne. The dominions of heaven and earth are unveiled by it, and good deeds are written for him as far as that Light reaches.

"But when the heedless ignorant person goes to perform ablutions, devils surround him like flies on honey. When he says, 'God is Greatest,' the angel looks into his heart and sees that everything is held greater than God therein. The angel says, 'You have lied! That is not how you truly hold God in your heart.' Smoke bellows from his heart up to the reaches of heaven, veiling his heart from those dominions; and that veil sends back his prayer. Devils crowd his heart and go on blowing into it and whispering temptations and distractions until he is entirely diverted from his prayer and has no idea what he is saying."

The author then explains the wisdom of the prayers being confined to a specific number, namely five, saying: "He knew that you would be weak, so He reduced its numbers." The prayer was reduced to five after it had been fifty. In His kindness to humanity, he reduced its number despite the great amount of time available, and asked you to pray at the start of the day to give thanks to Him for the dazzling Light He manifests to you, and so that you head directly toward Him when you first rise, to make up for your obliviousness while you were asleep. He then ordained a prayer for you in the middle of the day in order to put out the flames you have lit during that time; and another before the day ends, so that it might attest to your obedience before the Forgiving King, and that the angels of the All-Merciful might bear witness before Him that you prayed [...].[1]

---

1   *Īqāẓ al-himam fī sharḥ al-ḥikam*, p. 242.

Light is an Instantaneous Folding
of this Word and the Next

If the Light of certitude were to shine upon you, you would see the hereafter so close to you that you would not need to journey to it, and you would see the splendors of this world eclipsed with the shadow of annihilation.[1]

When the Lord loves someone, He directs them to a lordly Shaykh, the elixir of existence. Upon the Shaykh's hands, He provides them with a portion of Light that makes the realities of things manifest to them. The veil is pulled back from the delights of this world, and they find them to be false illusions and vain distractions. God says, **Know that the life of this world is but play, diversion, ornament, mutual boasting among you, and vying for increase in property and children—the likeness of a rain whose vegetation impresses the farmers; then it withers such that you see it turn yellow; then it becomes chaff. And in the Hereafter there shall be severe punishment, forgiveness from God, and contentment, and the life of this world is naught but the enjoyment of delusion.**[2] They

1   Aphorism 136.
2   Q Ḥadīd 57:20.

realize that it is an illusory dream, and its splendors are eclipsed. They are woken from the sleep of heedlessness by the inrush of presence, and within them stirs the urge to turn away from the abode of delusion. When He adds to them Light upon Light, their vision becomes sharpened, and concepts and entities are turned upon their heads, and everything is switched around and changed. The spiritual world becomes the physical world, the unseen becomes visible, the future becomes present, and far becomes near. We have said of this in a poem:

> *My resurrection appeared then,*
> *As the Prophets in scripture foretold;*
>
> *The cosmos and its contents burned away,*
> *All things vanished, became dark and cold.*
>
> *Then Light shone so that I could see,*
> *And all things became for me the same;*
>
> *By Your Light what was dead came to life,*
> *Like earth revived by falling rain.*
>
> *A secret flowing through attribute and name,*
> *Harbored by the hearts of those who love;*
>
> *Light upon Light, to which God guides*
> *All who dwell on earth and in heaven above.*

The earth of their existence quakes in awe of His disclosure, and yields up the burdens hidden within it, and conveys the chronicle of its secrets. Their Resurrection takes place, and their balance is set up, and their register is published. They see the hereafter so close they do not need to journey to it, as Ḥāritha ﷺ did. Anas related that the Prophet ﷺ ran into a man named Ḥāritha on one of the streets of Medina, and said to him, "How are you this morning, Ḥāritha?" He replied, "This morning I am a true believer." He said, "Every faith has its reality. What is the reality of your faith?" He replied, "I have withdrawn myself from the world, and gone thirsty by day and sleepless by night. It is as though I can see the Throne of my Lord before me, and as though I can see the denizens of Paradise in their bliss, and the denizens of Hell in their torment." The Prophet ﷺ said, "You have hit the mark, so persevere! Here is a believer whose heart God has illumined."[1]

Another narration states that as the Messenger of God ﷺ was out walking one day, he was approached by a youth among the Helpers. He said, "How are you this morning, Ḥāritha?" He replied, "This morning I am a true believer in God." The Messenger of God ﷺ said, "Watch what you say, for every claim has its reality." He said, "Messenger of God, I have withdrawn myself from the world, and gone without sleep by night and without drink by day. It is as though I can see the Throne of my Lord before me, and as though I can see the denizens of Para-

---

1   Bazzār, *Musnad*, 2451.

dise visiting one another therein, and as though I can see the denizens of Hell warring with one another therein." The Prophet ﷺ said, "You have seen, so persevere. Here is a servant in whose heart God has illuminated faith." Ḥāritha said, "Messenger of God, pray to God to grant me martyrdom." The Messenger of God ﷺ did so.

One day a call went up to battle, and Ḥāritha was first in the saddle, and first to be martyred. When his mother heard of this, she went to the Prophet ﷺ and said, "Messenger of God, if he is in Paradise, I will not weep or grieve. If he is in Hell, I will weep as long as I live in this world." The Prophet ﷺ said to her, "Umm Ḥāritha, there is not only one Garden, but many. Ḥāritha is in the Highest Paradise." She went away laughing and saying, "Ah Ḥāritha, rejoice!"[1]

Anas ibn Mālik also related that Muʿādh ibn Jabal ﷺ once visited the Prophet ﷺ, who said, "How are you this morning, Muʿādh?" He replied, "This morning I am a believer in God." He said, "Every claim has its proof, and every truth has its reality. What is the proof of your claim?" He replied, "Prophet of God, every time I reach the morning I expect that I will not see the afternoon; and every time I reach the afternoon I expect that I will not see the next morning; and every time I take a step I do not expect to take another. It is as though I can see every community standing and calling to its book, with its Prophet and whatever idols it worshipped alongside God. It is as though

1   Bayhaqī, *Shuʿab al-Īmān*, 9884.

I can see the denizens of Hell being punished and the denizens of Paradise being rewarded." He said, "You have come to know, so persevere."[1]

When lordly Light enters a heart, the breast of the intellect expands with it, and the eye of the unseen opens. Such a person sees what no eye has seen, and hears what no ear has heard, and knows what no human heart has imagined. When such a person comes to know, he is affirmed; and when he is affirmed, he is required to have courtesy and keep his secret, so that his words will not confuse the people of sensoriality and alterity.

Ibn ʿAjība ﷺ says:

Certitude (*yaqīn*) is knowledge unshaken by suspicion, unadulterated by doubt, unmarred by agitation. It comes from the verb *yaqina*, which means "to be still" in the sense of water, i.e., not to flow. This is how knowledge is when it is accompanied by tranquility, so that it causes no motion or disturbance in the heart.

The shining of His Light means the manifestation of His trace upon the limbs, which manifests in detachment from the herebelow and desire for the hereafter, and gives rise to total devotion to God, yearning for the presence of His Beauty, stillness and submission before the all-conquering power of His Majesty, eagerness to please Him and to win His love, engagement of the tongue in His remembrance, occupation of the heart in contemplation of His glory, the bewilderment of the

---

1   *Ḥilyat al-awliyāʾ*, 850.

spirit in the presence of His nearness, its intoxication on the wine of His love, and its immersion in the beholding of His nearness. These are the signs that the Light of certitude shines in the heart. Another of its signs is that future becomes present, far becomes near, and unseen becomes visible.[1]

1   *Īqāẓ al-himam*, p. 268.

The Heart is the Locus of Light

The horizons of Lights are hearts and innermost secrets.[1]

The word *maṭāliʿ* (horizons) is the plural of *maṭlaʿ* (literally "rising-place"), which is a noun that incorporates the meaning of time as well as place. The horizons of Lights are the loci in which the meanings of divinity shine bright in the heaven of the human substance. The Lights of the attributes dawn upon the hearts of the names and the inmost heart of the Essence. The time for the rising of the eye's sun is when the darkness of spatiality is shed, and night of separation fades. The heart is the isthmus between the soul and the spirit, and the spirit is the isthmus between the heart and the innermost secret, and the innermost secret is the isthmus between the spirit and "that which is more hidden still" (*al-akhfā*), or the secret of the secret, as in God's words: **And if thou speakest aloud, verily He knows what is secret and what is more hidden still;**[2] that is, more hidden than the secret, which is the secret of the secret. It is the most hidden thing in existence, the most difficult to perceive. Recognition of the *akhfā* is ignorance, and it may only be

1   Aphorism 151.
2   Q Ṭā-Hā 20:7.

spoken of in allusion and signs. Knowledge of it is not something other than it; it is the reality of knowledge and the known. By the Light of its moon all those who affirm God's Oneness are illuminated, and by the rays of its sun all those who know have knowledge. It is the upholder of justice, the witness and the witnessed. Ibn ʿAjība says:

Many Sufis hold that the lower self, the intellect, the heart, the spirit, and the innermost secret are all the same thing, and that they are all different stages through which the spirit passes depending on its degree of purification and ascent. As long as it is engrossed in its selfish interests and base desires, it is a lower self, and its Light is eclipsed. When it desists and becomes restrained by the Law, although still inclining to sin, sometimes sinning and repenting, other times crying out to God, it is called the intellect, and its Light is dim because it is still confined in the prison of cosmic beings, hobbled by rational proofs and arguments. When it abates from sin but still wavers between heedlessness and wakefulness, between desire for obedience and sin, it is called the heart. This is the first horizon of Lights, and the Lights of "turning toward God" (*tawajjuh*) shine upon it. It is constantly visited by inrushes—which are the Lights of turning toward God—until it finds peace with God and finds tranquility in His remembrance. It is then that it is called the spirit, which is the first of the Lights of face-to-face encounter (*muwājaha*). With these Lights the veil is lifted and the door opened for entry into the presence of the loved ones. When it is purified from the dross of sensoriality and the pollution of alterity, it is called the innermost secret, which is the first horizon of the Lights of eye-witnessing (*mu'āyana*) and converse (*mukālama*), whereafter there is neither state nor station: **There is no stand for you; so turn back.**[1] As for ascension in knowledge and gnosis, it is never-ending.[2]

1   Q Aḥzāb 33:13.
2   *Īqāẓ al-himam*, p. 296.

The Light of Primordial Nature
and the Light of the Pledge of Allegiance

There is a Light stored in hearts that is replenished from the Light that rushes in from the treasuries of the unseen.[1]

The Light stored in the hearts is the primordial nature that God instilled into mankind when He created them. God says: **The primordial nature from God upon which He originated mankind—there is no altering the creation of God; that is the upright religion, but most of mankind know not.**[2] God made His servants to be innately disposed to none other than His Light when He disclosed Himself to them in the realm of the seed and asked them, **"Am I not your Lord?"** The Messenger of God ﷺ said, "When God created Adam, He patted his back, and from it fell all the people He would create from his progeny until the Day of Resurrection. Between the eyes of each of them, He placed a mark of Light."[3] The mark of Light refers to the primordial nature and preparedness that God created in His servants to know Him. It is the reverence that God granted to souls:

---

1   Aphorism 152.
2   Q Rūm 30:30.
3   Tirmidhī, *Jāmiʿ*, 3021.

He inspired it as to what makes it iniquitous or reverent.[1] Its iniquity is its darkness, and its reverence is its Light. When fate leads the seeker to a lordly treasury of Light, that is, to a Shaykh who knows how the path is traversed and how to interpret signs, the Shaykh gives him luminous replenishment from the treasury of his heart, returning the seeker to the realms of **"Yes, we bear witness!"** The covenant with lordship is renewed, and he breathes in the majesty of divinity.

Sidi Ibn 'Ajība ﷺ says:

The Light that is stored in hearts is the Light of certitude. At first it is weak like the stars; this is the Light of submission. Then it grows stronger, drawing replenishment from the Light that inrushes from the treasuries of the unseen, until it is like the moon; this is the Light of faith. Then it continues to grow through obedience, invocation, and companionship until it becomes like the Light of the sun; this is the Light of spiritual excellence.

The treasuries of the unseen are the Lights of the attributes and the secrets of the Essence. The Lights of submission and faith draw replenishment from them until the Lights of excellence shine forth, covering over the existence of cosmic beings [...].

Know also that the reason why the Sufis commonly rank submission first, then faith, then spiritual excellence is that as long as the servant is engaged in outward sensory worship, this

---

1   Q Shams 91:8

station is called the station of submission. When the activity moves to the heart and he busies himself with refining, purifying, and adorning it, and with realizing sincerity, it is called the station of faith. When the activity moves to the spirit and the innermost secret through contemplation and meditation, it is called the station of spiritual excellence [...].

One of the truth-realizers said that the physical realm, which is the visible realm, contains outward Lights, while the spiritual realm, which is the realm of the unseen, contains inward Lights. The most well-known Lights in the physical world are three: the sun, the moon, and the stars. In the spiritual world their counterparts are gnosis, understanding, and knowledge. When the star of knowledge rises in the night of ignorance, the Hereafter and matters of the unseen come into view. When the moon of understanding rises above the skyline of Oneness, the nearness of God is beheld. When the sun of gnosis rises above the horizon of Singularity, certitude strengthens and witnessing begins.

The first Light that enters the breast is the Light of submission. When the heart expands, the Light of faith is cast into it. When it strengthens within it, it begins to witness [...]. By means of this Light, the heart becomes vast enough to accommodate gnosis of God. It is to this that the Sacred Ḥadīth alludes, "My earth and My heaven cannot contain Me, but the heart of My faithful servant can." Consider the heart that could contain the Lord, and how tremendously vast and glorious it would have to be. Dear brother, seek the company of those who have such hearts that can contain the Knower of the Unseen, that they may bring you to the knowledge of the unseen that they themselves have attained. All success is from God.[1]

1   *Īqāẓ al-himam*, p. 297-8.

Light is the Disclosure-Site of the Acts and Attributes

There is a Light by which He unveils to you His traces, and a Light by which He unveils to you His attributes.[1]

Light is the unseen meaning that annihilates the shadows of sensoriality and the distances of separation. As al-Ghazālī ﷺ defined it, it is "that whish is itself manifest, and which makes other things manifest." There is a Light by which God unveils His traces to the disciple; traces are the reflections of the Tracer upon the earth of existence, lordly allusions which God unveils to the wayfaring disciple so that his human acts are annihilated in God's acts, and he comes to know that all is from Him from beginning to end, and that every motion and stillness is by His leave.

Then there is a Light by which He unveils His attributes, of which He says, **Light upon Light!** You come to know His attributes in your attributes: His strength in your weakness, His knowledge in your ignorance, His independence in your dependence, His power in your powerlessness, His existence in your nonexistence.

---

1 Aphorism 153.

Ibn ʿAjība ❀ says:

Inward supra-sensory Light is divided into three categories relative to its strength and weakness. There is the Light of submission which is like the stars, by which God unveils to you the existence of His traces, through which you deduce the existence of their Maker. Then there is the Light of faith which is like the moon, by which He unveils to you the affirmation of His attributes, such that whenever anything moves or is still, you see that it is by God's power, will, knowledge, life, and other attributes. Then there is the Light of spiritual excellence, by which He unveils to you the reality of His Essence, so that whatever you see, you see its Maker in it through the medium of His self-disclosures. **God is the Light of the heavens and the earth**. The unveiling of the first Light ends with annihilation in the acts, the second with annihilation in the attributes, and the third with stability in annihilation in the Essence. Shaykh Ibn ʿAṭā Illāh did not mention the third Light because it is enough to mention the second; annihilation in the attributes is close to annihilation in the Essence, because the attributes cannot be separated from That to which they are attributed. The one who hears through God, sees through God, and moves through God, will see that his existence is through God too. Conversely, this is why some of them speak of annihilation in the Essence and let that stand for annihilation in the attributes too, due to how closely related they are. When one is achieved, the other is as well. God knows best […].

It could also be that by "a Light by which He unveils to you His traces," Ibn ʿAṭāʾ Illāh means the sensory Light by which outward sight perceives things. The Light of sensory vision cannot independently perceive the Tracer in the traces unless it is replenished by inner intellectual Lights. The inner Lights are pivotal, while sensory Light is perceived by all, even by animals, and so it does not have this special status.[1]

1   *Īqāẓ al-himam,* p. 298.

The Veil of Lights

Sometimes hearts may halt at the Lights, just as souls may be veiled by the density of alterities.[1]

Know that you are veiled by whatever you halt at. You are the slave of whatever you love. The one who halts at the experiences of witnessing is a slave of witnessing; the one who halts at saintly miracles is a slave of saintly miracles. So it is that Lights may veil the one who tastes their sweetness and is so comforted by them that he comes to rely upon them, and finds it difficult to be weaned from them. As a result, the disciple becomes cut off after having drawn near. He feels as though he has had his fill of them, but to have one's fill of God is itself a deprivation: **Say, "My Lord! Increase me in knowledge!"**[2] The wayfarer must always seek to ascend further into the presence without halting. No matter how many cosmic beings appear and reveal their beauty, their secrets, and their treasures, you must always realize that they are only temptations, and that what you seek lies beyond them.

1   Aphorism 154.
2   Q Ṭā-Hā 20:114.

The disciple might halt at the secret of the Oneness of acts, imagining that he has arrived to the end of his journey. Yet in fact he is only a beginner. The cause of this is either weak aspiration, or the lack of a perfect guide. The perfect Shaykh is the one who annihilates you and then annihilates you again in the midst of your annihilation, and then again annihilates you to that. Your incapacity becomes manifest to you, and you realize that there is no "attainment," and that you will only attain what you have been destined to attain. When this incapacity overcomes you, it becomes the ship upon which you sail across the ocean of the Essence amidst the mighty waves of the attributes. The breezes of God's oneness propel those who are chosen and selected for all eternity, bearing the ship of their incapacity to the shores that are nowhere.

Ibn 'Ajība says, may God sanctify his secret:

Some hearts might halt with the Lights of the stations without reaching the goals, and thereby become veiled from arrival, just as souls are veiled by the density of alterities and sensory things, and so do not perceive the subtlety of meanings and understandings. This may be due to the lack of a mentoring Shaykh, or to the disciple's weak aspiration for ascent. A heart might receive an unveiling of the secret of the Oneness of the acts, and therefore become annihilated in the act, tasting its sweetness; but then it halts here, while the heralds of reality keep of calling to it, "What you seek is yet ahead of you!" Or it might receive an unveiling of the secret of the Oneness of the attributes, such that the Lights of stations flash before it: the realization of detachment and piety; the fulfilment of reliance, contentment, and resignation; the sweetness of love and yearning, and so on. But the heart imagines that this is all there is, and so halts there, when in fact the goal is to uncover the secret of the Oneness of the Essence and the Lights of the attributes: **The ultimate end is unto thy Lord.**[1]

---

1   Q Najm 53:42; *Īqāẓ al-himam,* p. 299.

The Lights are Concealed
by the Wisdom of the Almighty

He has concealed the inmost hearts with the densities of outward appearances in order to preserve their dignity, lest they be cheapened by exposure and bandied about on the common tongue.[1]

The Lights of the inmost heart are the disclosure-sites of God's power, while the densities of outward appearances are the mirrors of His wisdom. These densities conform to the wisdom of the Muḥammadan laws in order to facilitate the stages of servanthood, while the Lights of inmost hearts conform to the decree of Aḥmadan wisdom, thereby manifesting the stations of lordship. **It befits not the sun** of lordly realities **to overtake the moon** of ritual laws, **nor** does it befit **the night** of exquisite unveilings to **outstrip the day** of legal rulings; and **each glides in** the **orbit** of the Essence.[2]

Ibn ʿAjība ☙ says:

The wisdom of the existence of these sensory Lights and dark alterities is to cover and veil the Lights of the inmost heart [...]. The Lights of the inmost heart are God-given teachings

---

1   Aphorism 155.
2   Q Yā-Sīn 36:40.

and lordly sciences, collectively described as the knowledge of lordship, which must be concealed from those who are unworthy of it. Those who divulge it forfeit their lives, and it was because of this that al-Ḥallāj was killed. The densities of outward appearances are manifestations of human nature. Or one could say that the Lights of the inmost heart are inward freedom, while the densities of outward appearances are outward servanthood. Or one could say that the Lights of the inmost heart are the knowledge of God's hidden power, while the densities of outward appearances are the knowledge of His outward wisdom. The Lights of the inmost heart are subtle and refined meanings which God covers in outward densities. That is why those who affirm them have and will always be censured by others; thus the unbelievers said, **"What ails this Messenger, who eats food and walks in the markets?"**[1] And they said, **"This is but a human being like you."**[2] It is an ancient and ongoing custom for people to censure the saints. The wisdom of this is to preserve the dignity and grandeur of inward realities lest they be cheapened by being exposed and bandied about on the common tongue, whereupon they would remain neither secret nor precious. This is why the saints are required to be obscure and to employ deception [...].

In sum, all things subsist between essence and attribute, sensory and supra-sensory, power and wisdom. God covers the

1   Q Furqān 25:7.
2   Q Mu'minūn 23:33.

secrets of the Subtle Essence with the manifestation of dense essences, and covers supra-sensory meaning with dense sensoriality, and covers power with wisdom; and all of it is from God and to God, for nothing exists but Him. These outward densities are the cloaks in which subtle meanings are clothed; or one could say that they are the protective cloak that was spread over the cosmos. If the cloak were pulled away or ripped, the suprasensory meaning would remain in its flawless state. Miraculous displays of divine power do no more than tug at the cloaks and coverings, and have no effect upon the suprasensory meanings or the Light. God is far above being overcome by that which overcomes His servants. Delve no further into this; for the incapacity to perceive is an attribute that is inherent to servants.

The subtle meanings that lie hidden in dense bodies have also been likened to dry seeds in moist branches. The seeds are ensconced and hidden within, but when rain falls the trees yield them up and the fruit that was ensconced within them comes forth.[1]

1   *Īqāẓ al-himam*, 300-301.

The Secrets of Verbal Expressions
are the Lights of Self-Disclosures

The Lights of the wise precede their words; wherever the illumination goes, the verbal expression follows.[1]

The wise are those who put the proper thing in its proper place. By my life! The wise are none other than the Knowers of God, for they know the reality of the names and their requirements, which makes them the crossbeam of the balance of existence. They possess the Light of the star and the secret of the setting-place. The pinnacle of wisdom is the fear of God, and such fear is manifested only in those who know Him: **Only those among His servants who know fear God.**[2] They are His saints and His loved ones. The Lights of the wise, the Shaykhs and the gnostics, precede their words; when they wish to speak, the station discloses itself to them and the suprasensory meaning spreads out from their hearts, so that their Lights precede their words. The one who hears them experiences the bliss of their station before even hearing their words; and so wherever the illumination goes, the expression arrives. Therefore our master

1 Aphorism 180.
2 Q Fāṭir 35:28.

'Alī said, may God ennoble his countenance, "When the knower of God speaks, we recognize him in an instant; and if he does not speak, we recognize him within a day." Another saying goes, "When speech comes from the heart, it lands in the heart; and when it comes from the tongue, it goes no further than the ear."

Ibn 'Ajība ﷺ said:

The wise are the gnostics who speak by God, are silent by God, and are absent from themselves. They witness that what comes from God returns to God. When they wish to express the knowledge and gnostic sciences that their Lord has gifted them, the Light that they witness first touches the hearts of their listeners, and flows into them according to the measure of their sincerity. For some the Light reaches all the way to the center of the heart; for others it stops at the surface of the heart; and for others still it penetrates only one side of the heart. When the gnostic gives expression to stations and states, the expression goes only as far as the Light flows. If the Light reaches the very center of a person's heart, he immediately rises toward his Lord. If the Light reaches only the surface of his heart, he becomes fearful and reverent and resolves to be righteous. If the Light reaches one side of the heart, he recognizes the truth and believes. Wherever the illumination goes, the verbal expression follows [...].

One of the gnostics said that if a person's heart is on the level of the spirit, his speech is suprasensory, and it descends into the vastest spaces of peoples' hearts. However, if a person's heart is on the level of the lower self, his speech is sensory and he only speaks of and ponders sensory things. Likewise, if the ears of the heart are covered by the veils of this world, such a heart will neither hear nor be heard. Some people have knowledge upon their tongues, but their hearts are ignorant; the sign of this is that they prefer to speak of the herebelow rather than the hereafter, or of the sensory rather than the suprasensory. Beware such people, for their hearts are dead and their words are carrion.[1]

1   *Īqāẓ al-himam*, pp. 339-341.

Luminous Beginnings and Luminous Ends

There are lights which are permitted to arrive, and lights which are permitted to enter.[1]

قلب = ق + لب

Qalb = [the letter] *Qāf* + [the word] *Lubb*

God has made for the heart (*qalb*, Q-L-B) an outward dimension and an inward dimension; the *Qāf* is its outward dimension, and the Lubb (core) is its inward dimension. The *Qāf* is for the people of faith, and the Lubb is for the people of spiritual excellence. As such, the "Lights which are permitted to arrive" are those that touch the surface of the heart and illuminate its secret inscriptions, so that the pure meaning of faith becomes apparent and the Light of the unseen is reflected upon the heart's mirror. The people of faith thus heed God's cue, which is represented as it were by the "Q" of the letter *Qāf*. For their inner vision is opened and divine omnipotence is disclosed to their hearts, so that they see His mercy when the Lights arrive.

---

1   Aphorism 201.

The "Lights which are permitted to enter" are those that penetrate to the deepest recesses of the heart and illuminate the heavens of the unseen, so that the concealed knowledge of spiritual excellence becomes apparent and they melt in the Lām of the Mediator. When the Lights enter, the dot of the Bā' is unveiled to them and they are allowed to access the secret pages of the Qur'ān. They are the people of spiritual excellence, gazing upon the face of the All-Merciful in the mirrors of the realm of possibility.

Ibn 'Ajība ﷺ says:

The "Lights which are permitted to arrive" are the Lights of faith, which are meant for the people of rational proofs and argumentation. For their hearts have yet to become detached from separative entities and the traces of ephemeral forms have yet to become erased therefrom. When the Lights arrive, they find the heart to be filled with the ephemeral forms, and thus halt at the heart's surface. The "Lights which are permitted to enter" are the Lights of spiritual excellence which come from witnessing and firsthand vision. When their hearts detach from other-than-God, the Lights enter them and find that their interiors are vast enough to accommodate them in their innermost cores.

The sign of Light that has arrived and entered is that when Light has only arrived to the outward dimension of a person's heart, you sometimes see him engaged with the herebelow and other times with the hereafter; sometimes with his selfish interest and other times with the rights of his Lord; sometimes with heedlessness and other times with wakefulness. Conversely, when Light enters the innermost core of a person's heart, you see that he is always with his Lord and never distracted by the selfish interests of the herebelow or the hereafter, oblivious to himself and present with his Lord [...].

The Messenger of God ﷺ said regarding this, "When Light enters the heart, it expands and opens." Someone asked, "Is there a sign of this, Messenger of God?" He replied, "Yes: aversion to the abode of delusion, turning to the abode of eternity, preparing to dwell in the grave, and dread of the Day of Resurrection."

The suprasensory Lights often visit you to break you free of the prison of material vessels, but they find that your heart is filled with them and so they leave you in their midst, veiled by them. Or one could say that the Lights of the spiritual world often visit you, but find your heart filled with the darkness of the material world and so they leave you in the darkness of cosmic existence. Or one could say that the Lights of the world of divine invincibility visit you, but find your heart filled with the Lights of the spiritual world, rejoicing in them and content with their radiance, and so they leave you halting with them, crying to you, "To have one's fill of God is to be deprived! What you seek is yet ahead of you." If knowledge had a fixed end, God would not have said to the greatest of all gnostics: **Say, "My Lord! Increase me in knowledge!"**[1] The Prophet ﷺ said, "If a day were to go by in which I did not increase in knowledge, may

---

1   Q Ṭā-Hā 20:114.

I not be blessed by that day's sunrise." Or he said words to that effect. What prevents the Lights from entering the heart is the present of separative entities therein.[1]

1   *Īqāẓ al-himam*, pp. 372-3.

Lights Reflect Off a Surface that is Filled with Alterities

Sometimes the Lights visit you but find your heart filled with ephemeral forms, and so they return whence they came.[1]

Those who do not empty their hearts of alterities are veiled from seeing the Lights and beholding the Almighty. For the presence is too exalted to be revealed to any heart that retains even an atom's weight of distraction. The adorning of the soul is commensurate with its degree of purification. When you draw a hand's span nearer to God, God draws an arm's length nearer to you; when you go to God walking, God comes to you running. When the ephemeral traces of the material world are imprinted upon the heart's tablet, they form a black mark upon its mirror. This mark impedes the heart from witnessing the mysteries of the worlds and the intangible realities of the spheres. When these ephemeral traces are multiplied and the heart imbibes their pleasures and becomes immersed in seeking the sweetness of their forms, it grows dark and blackens to the point that it becomes **darknesses, one above the other,**[2] veiled by itself from itself, veiled by its darkness from its Light,

1   Aphorism 202.
2   Q Nūr 24:40.

veiled by what it sees from the unseen. When the gentle breezes of union blow through the cosmic levels upon the pages of the heart and find it filled with the images of alterities, the marks of ephemeral traces, and the darkness of other-than-God, they reflect off the outer shell of the heart and return to the heavens of the spirit. The Prophet ﷺ said, "Temptations will be displayed before the heart just as reed mats are plaited, strip by strip. Whichever heart imbibes them will be marked by a black dot, and whichever heart rejects them will be marked by white dot. Thus, there will be two hearts: one white as a white stone, unharmed by temptations as long as the heavens and the earth remain; and another black and dust-colored like a turbid vessel, neither recognizing good nor rejecting evil, consumed only by its passions."[1]

Ibn ʿAjība ﷺ says:

Disciple, empty your heart of alterities—from anything besides God—so that it is not attached to anything in the cosmos, whether it be high or low, worldly or otherworldly, sensory or supra-sensory such as love for distinction or other selfish interests. When your heart journeys entirely out of this world and retains nothing but love for its Lord, it will be filled with gnostic sciences. The veil of illusion will be lifted from you, and the darkness of sensoriality removed. You will witness all things as Lights of the spiritual world, and this witnessing will be experiential and stable. Your heart will also be filled with the

---

1   Muslim, *Ṣaḥīḥ*, K. al-Īmān, #211.

secrets of the realm of invincibility. In union you will become oblivious to separation, and in witnessing the realm of invincibility you will become oblivious to the spiritual realm. The secrets of divine omnipotent will be unveiled to you, and the cool breeze of contentment and surrender will blow upon you in the royal presence of endless bliss.

From this perspective, secrets (*asrār*) are more far-reaching than gnostic mysteries (*ma'ārif*), for mysteries are the Lights of the spiritual world while secrets are the Lights of the world of invincibility. The Light of the spiritual world might be unveiled to a wayfarer so that he witnesses the entire cosmos as Light, but he still needs those Lights in order to ascend to stability in witnessing the Essence, just as the reader needs to look at the words written upon the page. But when the reader takes the meaning to heart and becomes stable in it, he can erase the writing, for he no longer needs it. Likewise, the wayfarer is first shown the Light of the spiritual world so that he witnesses the entire cosmos as Light, and in the Light he becomes oblivious to the darkness of sensoriality. Then he continues to advance until he grasps the meaning and becomes stable in it, whereupon he no longer needs witnessing, and the Light of divine invincibility frees him from need for the Light of the spiritual realm [...]. As such, other-than-God becomes erased from the eye of his heart entirely, and he becomes oblivious to himself and his senses through witnessing God's exclusive unity.[1]

---

1   *Īqāẓ al-himam*, p. 374.

Knowledge is Light, Not Lines on a Page

Beneficial knowledge is that which shines in the breast and lifts the veil from the heart.[1]

The nobility of any branch of knowledge is defined by the nobility of its subject. This makes the knowledge of divine Oneness the noblest and most important branch of knowledge, for it is knowledge of God Himself, which was the reason why the world was created and made manifest. And since manifestation is Light that was disclosed from the Hidden Treasure upon the tablet of "I loved to be known," the true nature of knowledge is Light that shines in the breast of the intellect. This Light makes one conscious of just how ugly the darkness of heedlessness actually is, and causes the flaws of the soul to rise to the surface. When the soul is purified from the follies of its desires, it ascends to the presence and the veils of base desires, heedlessness, and created beings are lifted. The heart is then free to engage with love of the presence and to draw close to the courtyard of contentment and the fields of divine proximity. This it does by adhering to the divine command and heeding the divine prohibition, outwardly and inwardly, until the tree of

1   Aphorism 227.

fearful piety grows in the heart. Vainglorious hope is abandoned, the fog of the herebelow clears, and the mirage of the hereafter dissipates. Forms are erased, and names dissolve into that which they name, and the fragrance of divine knowledge begins to emanate. That is beneficial knowledge.

Ibn ʿAjība says in his commentary on Ibn ʿAṭāʾ Illāh's aphorisms:

Beneficial knowledge is knowledge of the heart, which in essence means purifying the heart from vices and adorning it with virtues; or one could say that it is divestment (*takhliya*) and adornment (*taḥliya*) [...]. When the heart is purified from all of them, it becomes adorned with the attributes of perfection such as faith, certitude, tranquility, vigilance, and witnessing. It is also adorned with forbearance, compassion, generosity, nobility, altruism, and all other beautiful character traits. The ray of knowledge that shines in the breast is the snow of certitude, the coolness of contentment and resignation, the sweetness of faith, and the ecstasies of gnosis. This gives rise to fear and awe of God, shame before Him, peacefulness and tranquility, and other beautiful character traits mentioned above.

The veil that is lifted from the heart is heedlessness, which is caused by self-satisfaction, which is caused by love for the herebelow, which is the root of all error. Love for the herebelow gives rise to envy, pride, spite, anger, stinginess, meanness, lust for power, cruelty, coarseness, anxiousness, and other flaws. When these things are lifted from the heart, knowledge shines within it, meaning the snow of certitude, the coolness of contentment, and so on as above. This is because knowledge of God is a Light in the heart from which emanates rays that shine in the breast, inspiring it to become detached from the herebelow. The one who detached from the herebelow will find that his breast expands with certitude, contentment, resignation, and the other beautiful traits [...].

Shaykh Abū al-Ḥasan al-Shādhilī said, "Knowledge is like money: if God wills He will benefit you with it, and if He wills He will harm you with it." [Ibn ʿAṭāʾ Illāh] says in his *Subtle Graces* (*Laṭāʾif al-minan*), "The sign of the kind of knowledge that God desires from His servants is godfearing, and the sign of godfearing is obedience to His command. As for knowledge marred by desire for the herebelow, obsequiousness to its lords, aspirations of amassing treasures, pride, arrogance, overconfidence in one's future security, and forgetfulness of the hereafter—the person who possesses such knowledge is as far as can possibly be from the heirs of the Prophets, upon them be peace. Can an heirloom pass to an heir without retaining the qualities it had when it was in the possession of its original owner? Such a learned man is like a candle, providing illumination to others even as it burns itself. God will cite his knowledge as an argument against him and a justification for punishing him."

Shaykh Zarrūq said, "This implies that if a learned man is not godfearing, he is not an heir. But this subject is open to debate, for if an heirloom is corrupted and used poorly, this does not mean that the heir is no longer an heir, but only that he is a poor heir. Dishonoring one's parents does not sever the bond of parentage with them, after all. God affirms that even those who do not fear Him can possess knowledge, and does not negate this possibility."

One might argue that what is inherited from the Prophets is the purpose and fruit of knowledge, namely godfearing and gnosis, not merely formal learning. But God knows best.[1]

1   *Īqāẓ al-himam*, pp. 408-410.

Conclusion

God has made the path to Him clear and plain. The Master of Creation called it the Radiant Path, whose night is as bright as its day; for the sun of reality sits at the zenith of its sky, never setting or falling, unaffected by the vicissitudes of history, a single glimmer of its Light containing the entire expanse of time. Those who cling to its Light will find clarity, guidance, and illumination from their Lord. Their worship will be real, their remembrance real, and their existence real; for it will be from the Real, to the Real, and through the Real. Those who deny it and turn their backs to it in darkness, choosing the murk of separation and the confines of spatial dimensions, will be blind in the herebelow to the vision of reality, and blind in the hereafter to the Paradise of subtlety.

Hold to the Light of the Path and cling to its people, may God have mercy upon you. Stand at the door of those whom God has graced with the task of serving it. They are the masters of the herebelow, the kings of the hereafter. To look upon them is mercy, and to hear them is to draw near, and to learn from them is to be chosen by God.

Bibliography of works cited

1. The Holy Qur'ān, the narration of Warsh from Nāfi' through al-Azraq. [English translation consulted: Nasr, Seyyed Hossein; Dagli, Caner K.; Dakake, Maria Massi; Lumbard, Joseph E.B.; Rustom, Mohammed. *The Study Quran.* Harper One, 2015.]

2. Ibn Kathīr, Abū al-Fidā' Ismā'īl, al-Dimashqī, *Tafsīr al-Qur'ān al-'Aẓīm*, Dār Ṭayba, 1st edition, ed. Sāmī al-Salāma.

3. Qurṭubī, Abū 'Abd Allāh Muḥammad al-, *Tafsīr al-Jāmi' li-Aḥkām al-Qur'ān*, Mu'assasa al-Risāla, 1st edition, ed. Dr 'Abd Allāh al-Turkī.

4. Ibn 'Ajība, Abū al-'Abbās Aḥmad al-Ḥasanī, *Tafsīr al-Baḥr al-Madīd*, Dār al-Kutub al-'Ilmiyya, 2nd edition, ed. Aḥmad al-Rāwī, 'Umar al-Rāwī.

5. Baqlī, Abū Muḥammad Ṣadr al-Dīn Rūzbihān al-, *Tafsīr 'Arā'is al-Bayān*, Dār al-Kutub al-'Ilmiyya, 1st edition, ed. Shaykh Aḥmad Farīd al-Mazīdī.

6. Bayḍāwī, Abū Sa'īd Nāṣir al-Dīn al-, *Tafsīr Anwār al-Tanzīl wa-Asrār al-Ta'wīl*, Dār al-Rashīd, 1st edition, ed. Muḥammad Ṣubḥī Ḥallāq, Dr Maḥmūd al-Aṭrash.

7. Rāzī, Najm al-Dīn Aḥmad al-, *al-Ta'wīlāt al-Najmiyya fī al-Tafsīr al-Ishārī al-Ṣūfī*, Dār al-Kutub al-'Ilmiyya, ed. Aḥmad Farīd al-Mazīdī.

8. Ḥaqqī, Abū al-Fidā' Ismā'īl, *Tafsīr Rūḥ al-Bayān*, Dār al-Fikr, Beirut.

9. Wāḥidī, Abū al-Ḥasan 'Alī al-, *Asbāb Nuzūl al-Qur'ān*, Dār al-Kutub al-'Ilmiyya, 1st edition, ed. Kamāl Zaghlūl.

10. Bukhārī, Abū 'Abd Allāh Muḥammad al-, *Ṣaḥīḥ*, Dār Ṭawq al-Najāt, 1st edition.

11. Muslim, Abū Ḥusayn al-Qushayrī, *Ṣaḥīḥ*, Dār Ṭayba, 1st edition.

12. Tirmidhī, Abū 'Īsā al-, *al-Jāmi' al-Ṣaḥīḥ*, Muṣṭafā al-Ḥalabī, 2nd edition, ed. Aḥmad Muḥammad Shākir.

13. Ibn Mājah, Abū 'Abd Allāh Muḥammad, *Sunan*, Dār al-Ṣidq, ed. 'Iṣām Mūsā al-Hādī.

14. Ibn Ḥanbal, Aḥmad ibn Muḥammad, *Musnad*, Dār al-Ḥadīth, Cairo, ed. Aḥmad Muḥammad Shākir.

15. Bayhaqī, Aḥmad ibn al-Ḥusayn al-, *Shu'ab al-Īmān*, Maktabat al-Rushd, 1st edition, ed. Mukhtār Aḥmad al-Nadwī, 'Abd al-'Alī 'Abd al-Ḥamīd Ḥāmid.

16. Ḥākim, Abū 'Abd Allāh Muḥammad al-, *al-Mustadrak 'alā al-Ṣaḥīḥayn*, Dār al-Kutub al-'Ilmiyya, 2nd edition, ed. Muṣṭafā 'Abd al-Qādir 'Aṭā.

17. Ṭabarānī, Abū al-Qāsim Sulaymān al-, *al-Mu'jam al-Kabīr*, Maktabat Ibn Taymiyya, 2nd edition, ed. Ḥamdī 'Abd al-Majīd al-Salafī.

18. Ṭabarānī, Abū al-Qāsim Sulaymān al-, *al-Mu'jam al-Awsaṭ*, Dār al-Ḥaramayn, 1st edition, ed. Ṭāriq ibn 'Iwaḍ Allāh, Muḥsin al-Ḥusaynī.

19. Bazzār, Abū Bakr Aḥmad al-, *Musnad*, Maktabat al-ʿUlūm wal-Ḥikam, Medina, 1st edition, ed. Dr Maḥfūẓ al-Raḥmān Zayn Allāh.

20. Bukhārī, Abū ʿAbd Allāh Muḥammad al-, *al-Tārīkh al-Kabīr*, Dāʾirat al-Maʿārif al-ʿUthmāniyya, ed. Hāshim al-Nadwī et al.

21. Ṭabarānī, Abū al-Qāsim Sulaymān al-, *al-Duʿāʾ*, Dār al-Bashāʾir, Beirut, 1st edition, ed. Muḥammad Saʿīd ibn Muḥammad Ḥasan al-Bukhārī.

22. Aṣfahānī, Abu Nuʿaym Aḥmad al-, *Ḥilyat al-Awliyāʾ*, Dār al-Fikr, Cairo, ed. Abū Hājar Muḥammad Saʿīd Basyūnī Zaghlūl.

23. Haythamī, Nūr al-Dīn ʿAlī al-, *Majmaʿ al-Zawāʾid*, Dār al-Kutub al-ʿIlmiyya, 1st edition, ed. Muḥammad ʿAbd al-Qādir Aḥmad ʿAṭā.

24. Ibn ʿAjība, Abū al-ʿAbbās Aḥmad al-Ḥasanī, *Īqāẓ al-Himam fī Sharḥ al-Ḥikam*, Dār al-Kutub al-ʿIlmiyya, 1st edition, ed. Shaykh ʿĀṣim Ibrāhīm al-Kayālī.

25. Ghazālī, Abū Ḥāmid al-, *Mishkāt al-Anwār*, ʿĀlam al-Kutub, 1st edition, ed. Shaykh ʿAbd al-ʿAzīz al-Sayrawān.

26. Ghazālī, Abū Ḥāmid al-, *al-Maqṣad al-Asnā fī Sharḥ Asmāʾ Allāh al-Ḥusnā*, Dār al-Kutub al-ʿIlmiyya, 1st edition, ed. Shaykh Aḥmad Qabbānī.

27. Ibn ʿAlīwa, Aḥmad ibn Muṣṭafā al-Mustaghānamī, *al-Minaḥ al-Qudūsiyya*, Dār Ibn Zaydūn, 1st edition, ed. Suʿūd al-Qawwāṣ.

Index of Names

A

Abū al-Dardā' 53, 90.

Abū Bakr 49, 52, 259, 260.

Abū Dharr 45, 46, 47, 341.

Abū Hurayra 32, 39, 45, 203, 236, 317, 351.

Abū Lahab 236, 237, 239, 269.

Abū Madyan, Shu'ayb 123, 321, 325.

Abū Mūsā 49, 50, 90, 291, 343.

Abū Yazīd 76, 376.

Abū Zubayr 34.

Abū 'Uthmān 249.

Adam 32, 33, 39, 65, 115, 145, 148, 149, 150, 151, 152, 153, 157, 213, 218, 237, 282, 306, 307, 308, 326, 349, 415.

'Alawī, Aḥmad, al- (Muṣṭafā Ibn 'Alīwa) 152, 165, 180, 193, 195, 218, 220, 261, 340, 342, 343, 344, 345, 346, 348.

'Alī (Father of Ḥasan) 52, 86, 237, 269, 325, 432.

'Aqīlī, Abū Razīn, al- 87.

Ash'arī, Abū Mālik, al- 44, 48.

B

Baqlī, Rūzbihān (al-War-tajībī) 77, 96, 152, 156, 208, 214, 226, 238, 244, 249, 257, 263, 271, 276, 277, 281, 449.

Bayḍāwī, al- 211, 262, 449.

Bayhaqī, al- 41, 59, 60, 118, 149, 408, 450.

Bukhārī, al- 33, 34, 44, 50, 90, 161, 194, 209, 218, 229, 230, 234, 248, 334, 351, 400, 450, 451.

Būṣīrī, al- 297, 298, 304.

Būzīdī, al- 92.

C

Christ (Jesus) 20, 36.

D

Darqāwī, al-'Arabī, al-396.

Dhū Sharā 241.

G

Gabriel 31, 42, 45, 46, 49, 68, 95, 159, 194, 256, 341.

Ghazālī, Abū Ḥāmid, al- 63, 83, 108, 112, 119, 331, 356, 360, 419, 451.

H

Ḥākim 48, 49, 52, 450.

Ḥallāj, Abū Manṣūr, al-19, 128, 313, 428.

Ḥamza 223, 224, 269.

Ḥāritha ibn al-Nu'mān (Ḥāritha) 40, 41, 280, 341, 407, 408.

Ḥarrāq, al- 126.

Ḥasan, al- 19.

Ḥudhayfa 42, 52, 363.

Ḥusayn, al- 19, 274.

I

Ibn 'Abbād 74.

Ibn 'Abbās, 'Abd Allāh 40, 43, 44, 74, 207, 212, 223.

Ibn 'Ajība 69, 97, 123, 128, 129, 141, 155, 160, 166, 186, 195, 199, 225, 230, 253, 260, 266, 276, 292, 365, 372, 376, 380, 384, 388, 392, 396, 401, 409, 412, 416, 420, 424, 427, 432, 436, 440, 444, 449, 451.

Ibn al-'Arabī, Muḥyī al-Dīn 72, 378.

Ibn al-'Āṣ, Ibn 'Amr 229.

Ibn al-Fāriḍ 182, 311, 312, 314.

Ibn al-Khaṭṭāb, 'Umar 51, 101, 206, 233.

Ibn 'Amr, 'Abd Allāh 18, 39, 61, 227.

Ibn Anas, Rabī' 74.

Ibn 'Āshir 73, 322.

Ibn Ḥibbān 18, 32, 46, 87, 188, 227, 239.

Ibn Isḥāq 239.

BY THE SAME PUBLISHER

At the Service of Destiny

*A Biography of the Living Moroccan Sufi Master
Shaykh Mohamed Faouzi al-Karkari*

....

In the Footsteps of Moses

*A Contemporary Sufi Commentary on the Story
of God's Confidant (kalīm Allāh) in the Qur'ān*

....

Sufism Revived

*A Contemporary Treatise on Divine Light,
Prophecy and Sainthood*

....

The Foundations
of the Karkariya Order

....

Introduction
to Islamic Metaphysics

*A Contemporary Sufi Treatise
on the Secrets of the Divine Name*

Printed and bound
in the United States of America

www.ingramcontent.com/pod-product-compliance
Lightning Source LLC
LaVergne TN
LVHW031244190726
843493LV00011B/3004